WOODWORKING SOLUTIONS

HANDYMAN
CLUB OF AMERICA

MINNETONKA, MINNESOTA

WOODWORKING SOLUTIONS

Printed in 2004.

ABOUT THE AUTHOR

Robert J. Settich writes extensively on woodworking and home improvement topics. His writing, photographs, and designs have appeared in leading magazines and on television. This is his second book. He lives in Gladstone, Missouri, with his wife, Barbara.

Special thanks to Carl Voss, Barbara Settich, Gary Webster, Klingspor Woodworking Shop, Paxton Beautiful Woods Store, Keller Fire and Safety, and Touch-Up Depot.

TOM CARPENTER
Creative Director

HEATHER KOSHIOL
Managing Editor

JENNIFER GUINEA
Senior Book Development
Coordinator

JULIE CISLER
Book Design

LAURA HOLLE
Assistant Book Development
Coordinator

CARL VOSS
Editor

MARK MACEMON
Commissioned Photography

BILL NELSON
Illustrations

SPECIAL THANKS TO: Mike Billstein, Dan Cary, Terry Casey, Janice Cauley, Mark Johanson, Chris Marshall and Greg Wallace.

2 3 4 5 6 7 8 / 09 08 07 06 05 04
ISBN 1-58159-214-0
© 2004 Handyman Club of America

HANDYMAN CLUB OF AMERICA
12301 Whitewater Drive
Minnetonka, MN 55343
www.handymanclub.com

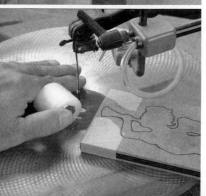

TABLE OF CONTENTS

INTRODUCTION

The subject of woodworking is like the Mississippi River — it covers a tremendous amount of territory. That river and its tributaries span from the western rise of the Appalachians to the eastern slope of the Rocky Mountains, and from the northern wilds of Minnesota to the southern stretches of Louisiana. The river is ancient tradition and constantly new — at the same time. It can be treacherous enough to take your life or so tranquil that it fills your soul. You can spend your life trying to understand it, and be constantly humbled by the amount of area that remains to be explored.

So it is with woodworking, a topic that is both wide and deep.

As a woodworker, you could begin a project with carefully planned chainsaw cuts that unlock the beauty hidden within rough logs. Months later, you may polish that same wood to a mirror finish. In between those two days, you'll face hundreds of challenges in more than a dozen skill areas. Those disciplines, which form the chapters of this book, include project design, machine setup, stock preparation, cutting joints, jigs and fixtures, gluing and clamping, sanding, shop organizers, and several other essential areas.

As you explore each chapter, you'll discover practical, shop-proven tips that will save you time and money. You'll benefit from the experience of others who scouted the territory before you, and are willing to share the secrets that take the hard work out of woodworking. You'll find hundreds of ways to improve accuracy and get great results faster, easier — and with more certainty — than ever before.

The question-and-answer format of this book gives you quick access to exactly the advice and solutions you need. It's plain talk in honest language that gets right to the point. Hundreds of photos work with the words to make each concept and all its details absolutely clear. And when a drawing would carry the information better, that's precisely what you'll see. This hardworking combination of words and images makes this book easy to pick up, quick to understand, and difficult to put down.

Despite all of the effort that went into this book, I'll confess that writing it was an extremely satisfying experience. Even though many of the subjects were already familiar territory, I was pleased to discover — and pass on to you — new paths and fresh information. After all, the exploration of woodworking is a learning experience that never ends. There is always one more traditional skill that needs to be tried, a brand-new idea that needs to be tested, and, if the budget allows, another "must have" tool to add to your collection.

Serving as your guide is a pleasure, but joining you in a journey of discovery is even better.

Robert J. Settich

1
DESIGNING
PROJECTS

HERE'S THE LINE ON TECHNICAL DRAWINGS

When I look at a set of plans for a project, the variety of the lines confuses me: some are different thicknesses, some are dashed, some have a long-short dash pattern, and so on. What's with all of that confusion?

Visible outline

Hidden outline

¾ IN, HOLE

¾ IN,

1½ IN,

Centerline and its symbol

Extension lines

Dimension line

It may look like a maze at first glance, but the lines in a drawing follow a system that's really an international language. Drafters, in fact, refer to the alphabet of lines. Take a look at the sample drawing, and you'll understand what's happening.

The lines that are full width (drawn with a 0.5 mm mechanical pencil lead, for example) show the physical characteristics of a piece: whether that's the edges and ends, the perimeter of a hole, or the outline of a joint. Light lines (0.3 mm wide) show layout information, such as centerlines, extension lines, dimension lines, and so on.

- The full unbroken line indicates the visible outline of the part. You can follow it completely around the perimeter.

- The full dashed line that consists of dashes of equal length indicates a hidden outline. In this case, it's showing the location of a rabbet along the edge of a board.

- A light line with alternating long and short segments is a centerline. You'll see that a hole's location is defined by the intersection of its vertical and horizontal centerlines. The centerline of a part is sometimes identified with a symbol consisting of an overlapped C and L.

- A light extension line is close to, but does not touch, the line it is referencing. One use of extension lines is to move the dimensions a convenient distance from the outline of the part. It's considered good technique to keep as many dimensions as possible off the surface of the piece.

- A light dimension line indicates where the referenced measurement begins and ends. The tips of the dimension lines may have arrowheads.

A GOOD DRAWING FROM EVERY DIRECTION

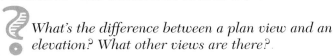

What's the difference between a plan view and an elevation? What other views are there?

The orthographic system is a method of representing a three-dimensional object by utilizing one or more two-dimensional views. Imagine an object suspended inside an imaginary glass box, and you'll understand the system. The way that you would trace the appearance of the object on each pane of glass represents that view.

Because there are six sides to the box, there are six possible views of each object, as shown in the drawing. The top view is often called the plan view, while the front view sometimes goes by the name of elevation.

By the way, the unfolded version of the cube shows how these views would be placed next to each other on a single sheet of paper. It is extremely rare, however, to show all six views of an item because some add no useful information.

In the table shown here, for example, the top view isn't very informative — the size of the top can be indicated on the elevation and a side view — so it can be eliminated. The rear view is a duplicate of the front view, so the rear is deleted. The left and right side views repeat each other, so one goes. The bottom view could be useful for showing the method of attaching the aprons to the top, so it may remain. Or the drafter could choose to show that information in a detail or verbally with a note.

THE IMAGINARY GLASS BOX

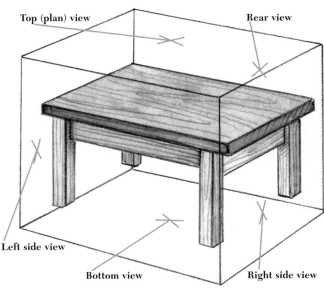

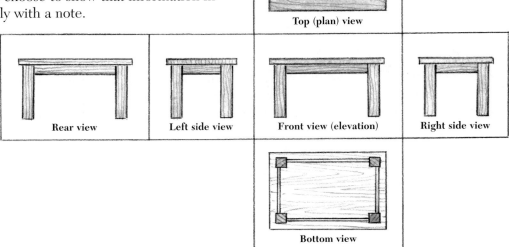

HOW DRAFTERS SAVE SPACE ON DRAWINGS

 Why do drawings have lines that indicate breaks? How do I draw or read them?

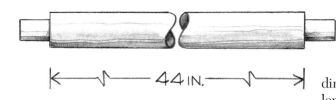

The main purpose of a break line is to conserve space on a drawing. For example, the break in the drawing of the rod indicates that you should make it as a solid piece without showing its full outline. The break in the dimension line shows that it's referring to a longer length than is actually shown on paper.

SLICE UP YOUR PROJECTS FOR BETTER INFORMATION

 Every so often, the woodworking magazines will include a section view of a project. What is a section, and how do I read this drawing?

The section view represents what you would see if you sliced downward along the line through the construction, then looked in the direction indicated by the arrows on the section line.

A long line segment interrupted by two short segments, as shown in the drawing, indicates the section line. This line may also be shown as a cutting plane, indicated by a series of equal-length dashes.

Letters at the ends of the line identify the section. In this case, it's Section A-A. This view is sometimes also called a cross section.

The section view is valuable for explaining how parts go together or for evaluating whether the interior of an object will be the correct size.

If you imagine a section view as a wafer-thin slice of your project, you'll understand how the shading is employed. Everything that's a part of the slice is shown with shading (a diagonal pattern in this case). Information that's relevant to understanding the drawing, such as the top and bottom of the box, is shown with solid lines but there's no shading.

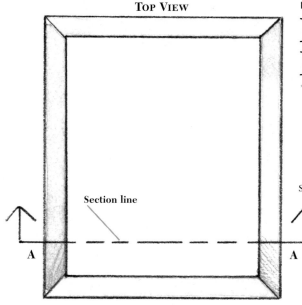

TOP VIEW

Section line

A   A

SECTION A-A

No Matter How You Measure It, the Information Is Good

 I've seen several different ways of expressing dimensions on a drawing. Which one is correct?

It all depends who is doing the drawing. An engineer, for example, will typically indicate inch measurements with whole numbers plus decimals. For example: 30.25 in. An architect may use feet, inches, plus fraction, for example: 2' 6¼" or simply 2-6¼. A cabinetmaker/builder may use inches plus fraction, for example: 30¼ in. All three of these examples are merely different ways of expressing the same dimension.

Whatever system you choose must be used consistently throughout the drawing. If you select the inch-fraction method, an item is 24 in. long, not 2 ft. By the way, some drafters don't repeat the scale designation with every occurrence, simply indicating 3 instead of always adding the abbreviation in. or the " symbol after each number.

Edges and Ends

 I was reading the directions for a woodworking project, and the writer sometimes referred to edges and other times to ends. Aren't these the same thing?

In technical how-to writing, there is a real distinction between an edge and an end — whether it's an individual component or a completed assembly, like a door.

The end of a board shows the end grain — the growth rings of the tree. The edge of a board is composed of long grain, parallel to the tree's vertical growth. When a door is assembled and held in an upright position, the upper and lower horizontal surfaces are the ends; the vertical outer surfaces are the edges.

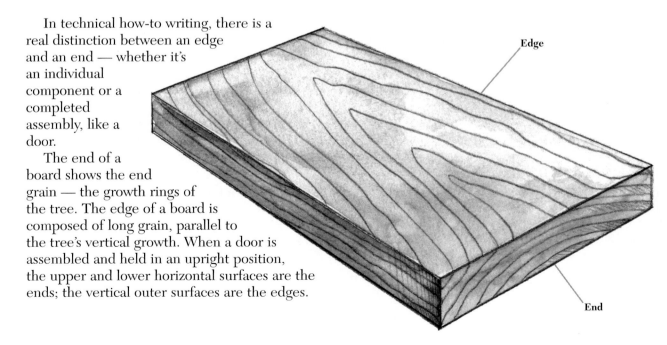

Edge

End

GOING WITH THE GRAIN ON DIMENSIONS

What's the correct sequence of writing dimensions?

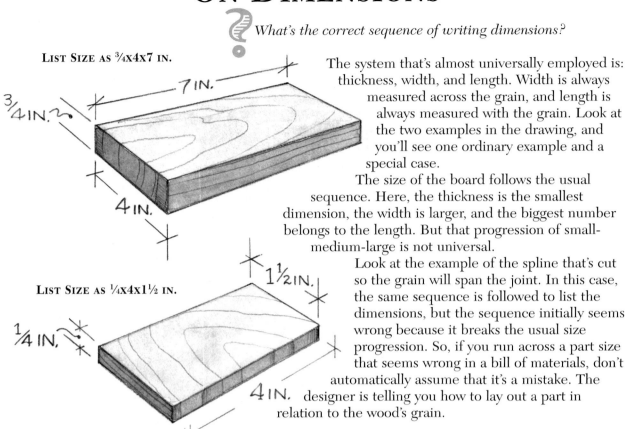

LIST SIZE AS ¾x4x7 IN.

7 IN.

¾ IN.

4 IN.

LIST SIZE AS ¼x4x1½ IN.

1½ IN.

¼ IN.

4 IN.

The system that's almost universally employed is: thickness, width, and length. Width is always measured across the grain, and length is always measured with the grain. Look at the two examples in the drawing, and you'll see one ordinary example and a special case.

The size of the board follows the usual sequence. Here, the thickness is the smallest dimension, the width is larger, and the biggest number belongs to the length. But that progression of small-medium-large is not universal.

Look at the example of the spline that's cut so the grain will span the joint. In this case, the same sequence is followed to list the dimensions, but the sequence initially seems wrong because it breaks the usual size progression. So, if you run across a part size that seems wrong in a bill of materials, don't automatically assume that it's a mistake. The designer is telling you how to lay out a part in relation to the wood's grain.

DRAWING FROM THE BUILDER'S PERSPECTIVE

When I'm doing a drawing, I sometimes get confused about the best way to indicate dimensions. What's the rule of thumb?

The designer should dimension with the builder's needs in mind. That's why you should always dimension a location on a drawing by using the same reference points you'll measure from when laying it out on the actual part.

For example, you as designer may decide on the location of a series of shelf-pin holes by reference to the vertical centerline of a cabinet's side. But you as a builder will want to know how far the centerpoint of the hole is from the edge of the cabinet. A builder wants to follow the simplest route to determining the shelf pin holes, so mark their locations in relation to the to cabinet edge.

MITERED DOOR VS RAILS AND STILES

 I'm designing a small mantel clock, and I'm wondering whether I should I choose a mitered door or one with rails and stiles?

The mitered door offers one machining convenience — you can run the rabbet for the glass in a continuous piece of stock, then cut and assemble the frame. With a rail-and-stile door, you'll need to rout the rabbet after assembly, then chisel the corners square.

But the mitered door has a serious drawback. If it's too wide or tall for its opening, fitting is extremely difficult. As you can see in the drawing, changing one side of a mitered door affects the three other sides. If you change the frame's height, you'll also need to alter its width to maintain matched corners. To achieve a perfect fit, consider making the door first, then building the carcase around its dimensions.

A rail-and-stile door is considerably easier to fit. You can shave or sand a bit of wood from any end or edge without affecting the other parts.

MITERED DOOR

RAIL AND STILE DOOR

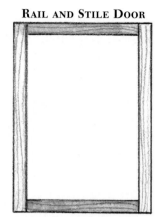

You can trim an end or edge without affecting the other parts.

ENLARGED DETAIL

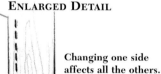

Changing one side affects all the others.

COMPUTER DRAWINGS NOT FOR THE TIMID

 What about using a computer program for designing projects? Wouldn't that be faster and easier?

If you understand the principles of manual drafting, you'll be able to produce fine drawings after you figure out the computer software. But if you don't know the basic concepts, you'll be trying to learn visualization and the software at the same time.

For woodworking designers, one of the limitations imposed by computer-aided drafting (CAD) is not the software itself but the limited capabilities of most printers. Unless you have access to a large plotter, you'll have to settle for outputting your drawings onto 8½ x 11-in. paper. That may be fine for developing an overall concept, but refining the design often requires that you look at full-size drawings of certain details. To do this, you may have to revert to manual drafting.

YOUR FIRST PROJECT DRAWING

I'd like to try my hand at designing a project, but I frankly don't know where to begin. What's a logical starting point?

Keep your first few project designs relatively simple — a kitchen table, for example, is easier to design and build than an entertainment center. The table will have fewer parts, hardware and critical tolerances to take into consideration. Review as many published table designs as you can, carefully noting what you do and don't like, and what refinements might make the project better looking or more functional for your family's needs. For example, adding a drawer to a kitchen table could make it work better as an area for doing homework or paying bills.

When you're ready to put pencil to paper, consider whether you need to design the project from the inside out or from the outside to the inside. For example, if you want to build a box that holds 3 x 5-in. index cards, you can easily see how the design process moves from the inside of the container to its exterior. But if you're designing a cabinet to fit between the fireplace and a wall, the exterior dimensions dominate the process.

DISTINGUISHING DADOES AND GROOVES

Dado

Groove

What's the difference between a dado and groove? They look like the same cut to me.

The shape of the cut is the same, but its direction in relation to the wood's grain determines what it's called. A dado cut goes across the grain of the wood; a groove follows the grain. One easy way to remember the association is that grain and groove both begin with the letter g.

THE BASIC LINE ON DRAWINGS

 What kind of pencils and lead should I use for drawing plans? The mechanical pencils I have tend to dig into the paper as I push them along the straightedge.

Mechanical pencils are a good choice because the hardness and diameter of the lead produces a line of constant width. With ordinary graphite-and-wood pencils, achieving a consistent line width requires some real finesse and a light touch. Every drafter has a favorite grade of lead — some prefer a hard lead to produce faint preliminary layout lines, while other people like a softer lead because it makes a bold dark line with very little pressure applied. If you don't already have a lead preference, try a medium hardness grade like HB. A little experience will direct you to either harder or softer leads.

A pair of pencils should handle most of your needs. Get a 0.5 mm size for drawing visible and hidden lines, and a 0.3 mm pencil for scribing extension lines, dimension lines, and other lightweight features.

When a pencil digs in, it's usually because you're pushing it, not pulling it. As you can see in the photo, correct technique inclines the pencil in the direction of the stroke. You pull, or draw, the pencil along a straightedge. That's why the task is called drawing, not pushing.

Also check that your drawing surface is smooth and flat. A smooth plastic laminate tabletop is far better than sheathing plywood. But topping the laminate with a

layer of heavy brown wrapping paper will cushion the paper for even smoother results. The ideal drafting table cover is a special mat with a specific amount of resiliency engineered into it, but it's a pricey luxury if you draw only occasionally.

BUILD PROTOTYPES TO AVOID ERRORS

 I've heard that some designers build a prototype before launching into construction of the actual project. I'd like to try that, but how can I accomplish it without spending a lot of money?

One method is by knocking together a scale model from illustration board. Or you can purchase foam-core board in various thicknesses from most art-supply stores. Cut either type of board with a band saw, scroll saw, or table saw to any size or shape you want. You don't have to make every detail — use a pen to draw in doors or drawers. Hold it together with hot-melt glue or clear tape.

To make a full-size prototype that's both quick and on the cheap, use wood scraps joined with a finish nailer. If you use a hodgepodge of different scrap materials, give the assembly a quick coat of white primer to make all the parts look like they are made of the same material. Doing this will help minimize distractions when studying the project's design.

Corrugated cardboard is another low-cost prototype medium. If you need large pieces of this material, check at a local appliance store. The heavy box stock that protects refrigerators and stoves is ideal for making mock-ups.

If you're designing a table, assembling one corner should provide all of the information you need to evaluate the proportions.

UNDERSTANDING CHAMFERS

 When woodworking plans call for a ¼-in. chamfer, how is that dimension figured—along the face of the chamfer or vertically?

Measure the size of a chamfer vertically, as shown in the drawing. Technically, the designer should also specify the angle of the chamfer because chamfers aren't limited to 45 degree angles. For completeness,

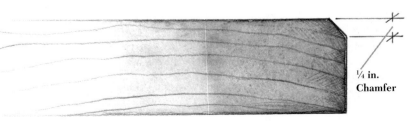

you'd specify both the angle and size; for example: a 45 degree x ¼-in. chamfer. When a chamfer's angle isn't stated, you can usually assume that it's 45 degrees.

¼ in.
Chamfer

EUROPEAN THINKING FOR HINGE PLACEMENT

 I always thought that you described the location of a hole by specifying its vertical and horizontal centerlines. Then I noticed that European hinges show the location of the cup hole based on the distance from the rim of the hole to the edge of the door. How do I convert that information to mark a centerpoint?

Simply add the offset to one half the cup hole's diameter and you'll have the centerpoint. For example, if the offset is 5 mm and the cup diameter is 35 mm, the centerpoint is 5 + 17.5 = 22.5 mm from the edge.

Many drilling jigs that are used with European hinges have a built-in adjustment feature, such as a rotating cam, that makes it easy to change this offset distance. The cam is calibrated with a variety of offset positions, so it eliminates the need for calculations.

SLEEP ON YOUR PROJECT PLANS

 After I've finished drawing a project design, is there anything else to do before I begin building it?

Try not to be in too big a hurry to start cutting up lumber. If you're building a project that will last a generation or two, thinking about the design for a few more days may improve it. As a comparison, if you smash grapes and drink them right away, all you'll have is grape juice. But if you wait a while, you'll enjoy wine.

Tape the drawing to a wall or set your model in a location where you'll see it several times during the course of a day. Even during times that you're not aware of it, your brain will analyze the design. You might even process your design while you sleep. If you think of a change, alter your drawing and study it over the next few days to discover whether it's a genuine improvement or merely an alteration.

While you're pondering your design, another task you can take care of is ordering hardware for the project. Make a careful list of every piece of hardware you'll need, and buy it all at once. That way, you won't be caught shorthanded if the supplier suddenly discontinues the hardware you still need.

GOLDEN RECTANGLE: THE KEY TO DESIGN

I've heard that the Golden Rectangle is a good proportion to use when designing a piece of furniture. Exactly what is this proportion?

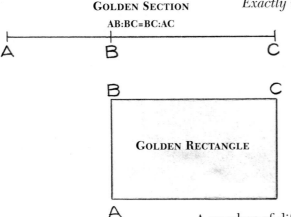

GOLDEN SECTION

AB:BC=BC:AC

A   B   C

B   C

GOLDEN RECTANGLE

A

A brief guide for the construction of a Golden Rectangle is this: the length of the longer side is 1.618 times the length of the shorter side. An even easier approximation to remember is that the sides have the ratio of about 5:8.

The precise definition is that the ratio of the short side to the long side is the same as the ratio of the long side to the total of the two sides. Look at the drawing, and you'll see this relationship. When a line is divided into two parts according to this principle, it is called the Golden Section.

A number of different cultures have admired these proportions since ancient times. The Greeks designed the famous Parthenon according to its principles, and you'll also see Golden Rectangles utilized in the composition of classical paintings.

PERFECT HEXAGONS AND OCTAGONS

DRAW A HEXAGON INSIDE A CIRCLE

3   4

A   B

5   6

I'm working on a design for an end table, and I'd like to make the top a hexagon or an octagon. The only problem is that I don't know an easy way to draw either one of these shapes. What's the method?

After you know the system, the actual drawing of either shape is quite easy. Refer to the drawing, and you'll see that you begin making a hexagon (a regular six-sided figure) by drawing a circle. With a straightedge and pencil, draw line AB through the center of the circle. Set your compass at point A, and swing an arc that touches the centerpoint and the perimeter of the circle at points 3 and 5. Repeat the process at point B to set point 4 and 6. Connect the points with a straightedge, and your hexagon is complete.

To make an octagon (a regular eight-sided figure), draw a square, and connect the corners with diagonal lines to locate the center. Place your compass at any corner, and adjust it so that its writing point touches the center. Swing an arc to the perimeter of the square. Repeat at the other three corners. Connect the dots, and you're finished.

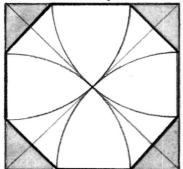

INSCRIBE AN OCTAGON INSIDE A SQUARE

THE KNOW-HOW BEHIND KITCHEN DESIGN

 Our kitchen is outdated, and I was thinking about whipping up a new design and then building the cabinets. What do I need to know in order to tackle this design project?

Kitchen design is a specialized craft that requires extensive product knowledge, design experience, and an ability to accommodate the needs of the owners into a room that works well and looks great. Not to dampen your enthusiasm, but you'd be undertaking an enormous challenge. Subcontracting the design phase would allow you to focus your energy on the actual construction.

When you're looking for a kitchen designer, seek a person accredited by the National Kitchen and Bath Institute (please see Resources, page 314). There are three levels of accreditation that reflect increased levels of formal training plus hands-on design experience:

- **AKBD:** Associate Kitchen and Bath Designer

- **CKD or CBD:** Certified Kitchen Designer or Certified Bath Designer (some individuals hold both designations)

- **CMKBD:** Certified Master Kitchen and Bath Designer

If you simply can't resist the temptation to sketch out some designs, the drawing gives you some basic dimensions for base and wall cabinets. Here are a few more design guidelines: a cabinet door should never be wider than it is high; an individual door shouldn't be narrower than 6½ in. or wider than 27½ in. Full-height cabinets (in a room with 8-ft. ceilings) would be 42 in. tall. A table-height counter would range from 28 to 32 in. high; standard counter height is 36 in; and bar height is 42 to 45 in.

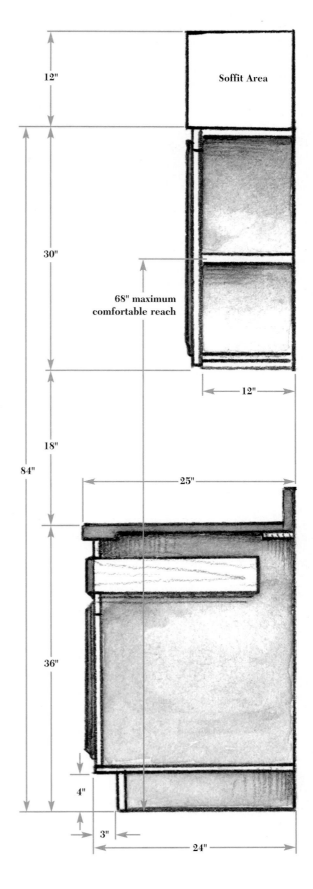

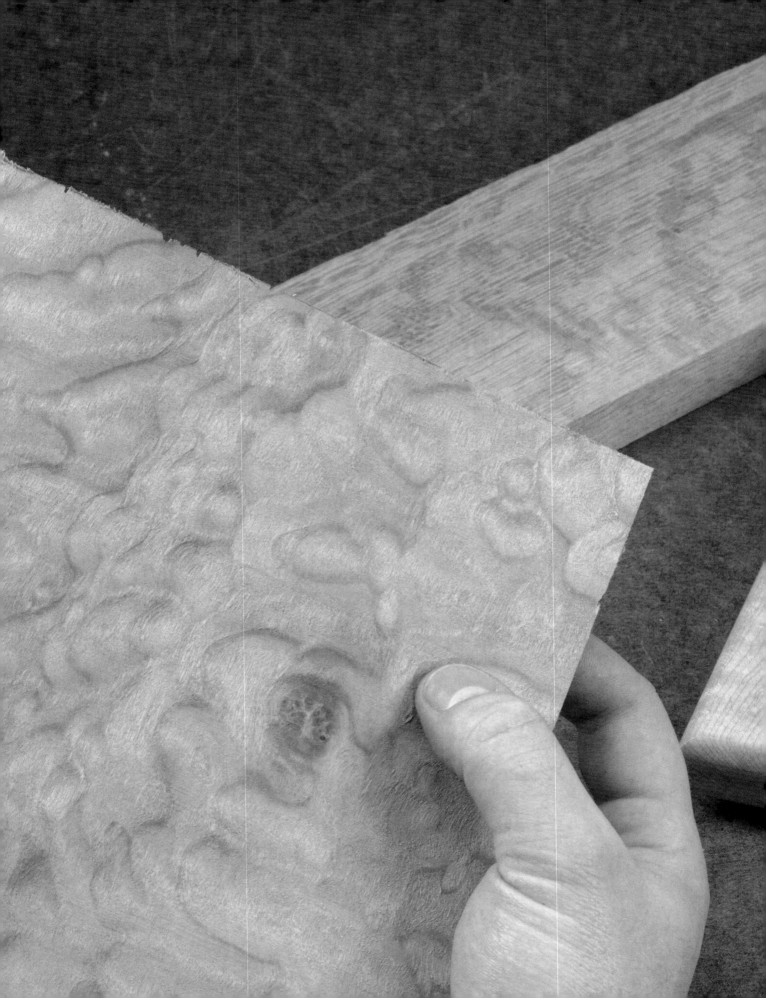

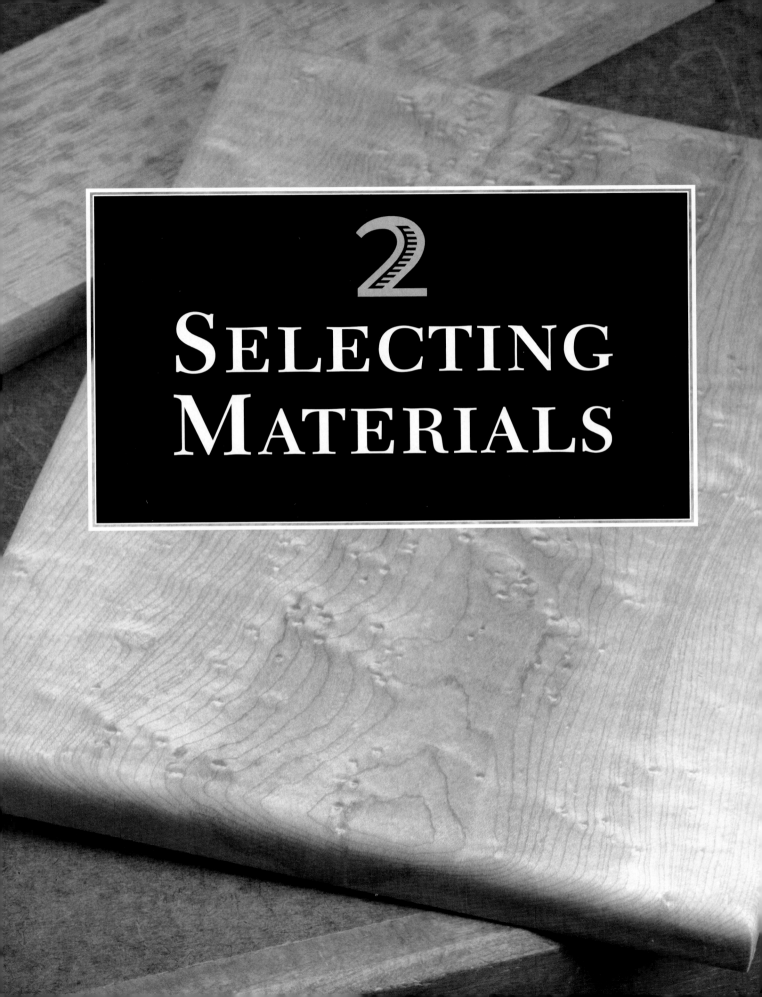

2
SELECTING
MATERIALS

BOARD FEET: A BASIC MEASUREMENT

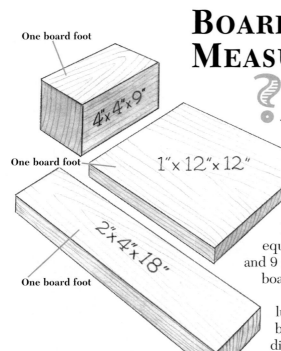

One board foot

4"x 4"x 9"

One board foot

1"x 12"x 12"

2"x 4"x 18"

One board foot

I know that hardwood lumber is sold by the board foot, but I don't understand precisely what that means. What's a good working definition of a board foot?

A board foot is a measure of the wood volume, not a linear measurement. One board foot contains 144 cubic inches of wood. For example, a piece of lumber that is 1 in. thick, 12 in. wide, and 12 in. long equals one board foot. A block that is 4 in. thick, 4 in. wide, and 9 in. long also contains 144 cubic inches, so it also is one board foot.

To determine the number of board feet in a piece of lumber, measure the thickness, width, and length of the board in inches, multiply these three figures together and divide the answer by 144.

HARDWOOD VS. SOFTWOOD DIMENSIONS

How come hardwood lumber is usually sold in random lengths and widths instead of standard sizes like most softwood lumber?

There are several compelling reasons:

- Softwood lumber generally ends up in construction applications where standard widths and lengths speed production.

- Hardwood lumber, which is used more often for millwork or cabinet and furniture construction, gets cut into so many different widths and lengths that standardizing sizes for custom applications would be a futile task.

- Hardwood lumber is a scarcer product than softwood. Producing standard sized hardwood lumber would increase waste, further depleting the supply and increasing costs.

THE SKINNY ON MINIMUM WIDTHS AND LENGTHS

 How do I know if my shipment of lumber will contain reasonable widths and lengths?

Ask your lumber dealer if you can specify minimum widths and lengths; otherwise, the lumber grade or the company's standard guidelines will be in effect. Be aware that specifying what you need may result in a surcharge tacked onto your bill.

Policies on the minimum width of stock in the shipment will vary among dealers, and even a single dealer may have guidelines that change for various grades of wood. For example, if you order Selects and Better, the minimum width may be 3 in., but that could increase to 4 in. for Firsts and Seconds. If you have any doubts, be sure to ask.

Your dealer should know the average lengths in a standard shipment. For example, one dealer supplied this information on Selects and Better: the minimum width of any board is 3 in., but 85 percent of the lumber in the order will range from 4 in. to 6 in. wide. Lengths range from 3 to 9 feet; 85 percent of the boards will be 5 to 8 feet long.

Many lumber dealers charge a premium for wide stock, so that's another area where you should understand the seller's policies before you buy.

GRADING POLICIES FOR LUMBER

 When does lumber grading take place?

Various suppliers have different policies: some grade the lumber before it's kiln-dried, others inspect it after lumber emerges from the kiln, and still others grade it after it's surfaced. As lumber moves through the various drying and surfacing processes, it can suffer a loss of grade rating but it won't step up from a lower to a higher grade.

It pays to know your supplier's timing so that you'll pay for lumber that's graded in the condition that you receive it, not as it once existed.

LUMBER THICKNESS: STORY OF QUARTERS

 What's all this business of expressing lumber thickness in quarters? Why can't I just say that I want wood that measures ¾ in. thick?

Measuring in quarters is a traditional system, and it can refer to either rough or surfaced lumber. For example, if you purchase rough 4/4 lumber, it will measure about 1 in. thick. But if you buy 4/4 lumber that's surfaced two sides (S2S), it will measure slightly more than ¾ in. thick.

Measurements expressed in quarters may refer to either rough or surfaced lumber, but actual dimensions always refer to stock that's been surfaced.

By the way, when you speak about lumber in the quarter system, you say "four quarter" or "eight quarter."

The following chart will serve as a handy reference. You'll note that some thicknesses of rift and quartersawn woods are slightly different from other hardwood cuts.

Rough Thickness (in.)	Quarters	Hardwoods S2S (in.)	Rift & Quartered Hardwoods S2S (in.)	Softwoods S2S
⁵/₈		⁷/₁₆	⁷/₁₆	¹/₂
³/₄	3/4	⁹/₁₆	⁹/₁₆	⁵/₈
1	4/4	¹³/₁₆ or ²⁵/₃₂	³/₄	²⁵/₃₂
1¹/₄	5/4	¹¹/₁₆	¹¹/₃₂	¹⁵/₃₂
1¹/₂	6/4	¹⁵/₁₆	¹⁹/₃₂	1¹³/₃₂
1³/₄	7/4	1¹/₂	—	1¹⁹/₃₂
2	8/4	1³/₄	1¹¹/₁₆	1¹³/₁₆
2¹/₂	10/4	2¹/₄	2¹/₄	2³/₈
3	12/4	2³/₄	2³/₄	2³/₄

QUARTERSAWN BY ANOTHER NAME

 What is vertical grain wood?

That's another name for quartersawn lumber. It gets its name from the fact that the annual rings on the end of a quartersawn board are nearly vertical.

NOT ALL 4/4 LUMBER IS SURFACED THE SAME

 I bought 4/4 red oak from one hardwood dealer, and he surfaced it to $^{13}/_{16}$ in. Later, I bought some oak from another dealer, and it was slightly thinner, measuring $^{25}/_{32}$ in. I know it's only a small difference, but why the variance in thickness among dealers?

Some lumber dealers feel that the rough lumber cleans up better by removing an additional $^1/_{64}$ in. from each side, so the board ends up $^1/_{32}$ thinner. Other dealers leave more clean-up work for you to do. You'll need to decide which surfacing approach you like better.

Switching back and forth between dealers with differing policies can create additional work for you, requiring surfacing in your shop to bring your lumber inventory to a consistent thickness.

LEAVES SEPARATE HARDWOODS AND SOFTWOODS

 I'm confused by what characteristics separate hardwoods from softwoods. How can we have hardwoods that are actually soft?

The distinction is based on the foliage of the living trees. Hardwood lumber comes from deciduous trees, the type that shed their leaves each year. Softwood lumber comes from coniferous (sometimes called evergreen) species that retain their needles or foliage year-round.

As you note, this can produce some confusion if a person thinks of soft and hard as referring to the lumber's density. Balsa, one of the least dense woods, is correctly classified as a hardwood. Douglas fir, a softwood, has impressive strength in architectural applications. Walnut, a hardwood, machines nearly as easily as cedar or redwood, which are both softwoods.

TWO STANDARDS FOR GRADING LUMBER

 Are there different grading systems for hardwood and softwood lumber?

Not only are there different rules, the grading mindset is considerably different. The grade of a softwood board usually refers to the entire piece. By contrast, a hardwood board is judged by its net usable content after allowing for cuts that remove defects such as knots, splits, and wane (bark along an edge). So you can have a piece of hardwood lumber with some truly ugly defects that nevertheless rates remarkably high.

The difference in approach makes sense when you consider the ways that the two kinds of lumber are used. Softwood lumber, such as joints or studs, is typically used even with minor defects, provided the defects don't impair strength.

Appearance is generally more important with hardwood lumber, so defects include not only structural faults but also visually undesirable flaws. Hardwood boards are usually cut into smaller pieces of various sizes to make parts for cabinets or furniture, so the approach of usable yield is more appropriate.

YES, WOODY, THERE ARE LUMBER STANDARDS

 Does every hardwood lumber dealer make up his own rules, or is there a nationwide standard in the United States?

The National Hardwood Lumber Association (NHLA) formulates and publishes rules for the measurement and inspection of hardwood lumber. You can download a copy from the association's Web site (www.natlhardwood.org), or call for your copy in print 901-377-1818.

This nonprofit trade association was organized in 1898 to develop a uniform system of grading rules for measuring and inspecting hardwood lumber. It continues that function today. The NHLA has a network of 1,800 members that include individuals and firms that produce, sell, and utilize hardwood lumber.

MAKING THE GRADE WITH HARDWOOD LUMBER

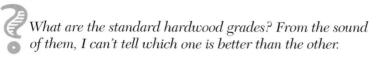

What are the standard hardwood grades? From the sound of them, I can't tell which one is better than the other.

Here's a quick rundown, from the best to the least desirable:

- **Clear Face Cuttings:** the highest grade

- **FAS (Firsts and Seconds):** usually the highest grade carried in quantity by lumber retailers.

- **FAS one face (FIF):** a useful grade for portions of your project that are seen from only one side.

- **Selects:** some lumber dealers will lump all the higher-grade categories into one grouping called "selects and better."

- **No. 1 Common**

- **No. 2A Common:** Grades 2A and 2B may be combined into a single classification: No. 2 Common

- **No. 3A Common:** Grades 3A and 3B may be combined into a single classification: No. 3 Common

- **Sound Cuttings**

- **No. 2B Common**

- **No. 3B Common**

- **Sound Wormy**

THE X FACTOR IN PLYWOOD

What does the abbreviation X at the end of a plywood description mean? One example is C-D-X.

In this case, X doesn't mark the spot, but it does signify that the adhesive used in the construction of the panel is rated to withstand exposure to the elements for exterior applications. Of course, that doesn't mean that you can skip applying a finish. You'll still need a good quality finish to protect the panel from the ravages of water, weather, and the sun's ultraviolet rays.

ESTIMATING HARDWOOD DEFECTS

If the grading rules are based on net usable lumber, it seems I would save money by purchasing a lower grade and then simply trimming away the defects.

The grading rules also deal with the size of the pieces the lumber yields after cutting away the defects, and the number of pieces you can cut from the board to make the grade. Both of these factors affect yield.

For example, the FAS grade states a minimum piece size of 4 in. wide by 5 ft. long, or 3 in. wide by 7 ft. long. Yield for the board must be at least 83.5%. The No. 3B common grade allows clear pieces as small as 1½ in. wide by 2 ft. long. Acceptable yield per board may be as small as 25%.

If you are able to use all the clear pieces that the boards will theoretically produce, buying FAS grade may produce a waste factor of 16.5% while No. 3B can generate up to 75% waste. At that lower grade, you're throwing away three-fourths of what you buy — not a good feeling.

Another limiting factor is that hardwood lumber dealers who supply woodworking amateurs usually don't deal in the lower grades of lumber.

IT'S OUT THERE: MICROSCOPIC-THIN PLYWOOD

I'd like to make a jewelry box with a curved panel in the lid. What's the thinnest plywood that's available?

The lightweight champion of plywoods is an astonishing ¹⁄₆₄ in. thick. It's called aircraft plywood because it's specially made to meet the exacting requirements of people who build flying model aircraft. It's also made in heavier versions that are ¹⁄₃₂ in. and ¹⁄₁₆ in. thick. The next step in thickness brings you into the realm of ordinary plywood at ⅛ in. thick.

Aircraft plywood, available at some hobby stores, is very difficult to make, and its high-flying price reflects that fact.

CALCULATING WASTE COULD PREVENT A RETURN TRIP TO LUMBERYARD

 When I buy lumber for a project, how much of a waste factor should I add to the actual requirement?

If you buy FAS or better lumber, you may be able to limit your waste factor to as little as 15%; allowing for 25% waste is more realistic. It gives you some breathing room so you'll be sure to have enough lumber on hand and select the best cuts for visually important parts of the project.

If you're picking out individual boards, you can take a parts list and tape measure with you to the lumber dealer. As you visualize the clear cuts in each board, you can then do a cutting layout that minimizes waste and yields the parts you need. Even for a relatively small project, doing this can be an exercise in mental gymnastics that can be quite difficult. And if you make a mistake when cutting or run into a hidden defect, you're sunk. It's always safer to buy some extra lumber — this way you'll have surplus stock to apply to your next project.

THE BEAUTY OF MEDULLARY RAYS

 What are medullary rays?

The medullary rays are a system of tissues inside a tree. They extend across the tree's annual rings and function to distribute sap and nutrients throughout the living tree. When the tree is converted to lumber, the rays become part of the wood's figure.

Although all trees have these structures, the rays are subtle in many species. However, some species, such as sycamore and oak, show prominent ray figure when the wood is quartersawn.

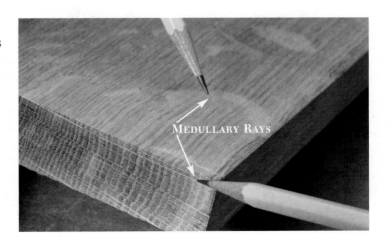

MEDULLARY RAYS

OLD WOOD NOT
NECESSARILY DRY WOOD

A guy at work said that his grandpa's barn has a bunch of oak and walnut lumber that's been stacked in it for probably 25 years. So it's surely plenty dry by now, and ready to make into furniture, right?

Not so fast. Unless that barn is out in the middle of the desert, the moisture content of the wood is probably still too high for cabinet making. That's because air-drying is not a one-way process of simply losing moisture. Although the wood has had plenty of time to lose moisture, it's probably also had an equal amount of time to gain moisture.

Wood that's being air-dried goes through cycles in an attempt to come to a state of balance with the surrounding atmosphere. Initially, the wood has much more moisture than the air, so it releases its water relatively rapidly. But when the humidity of the air is higher than the moisture content of the wood, the lumber absorbs moisture.

For example, the wood may reach a relatively dry state (let's say 20% moisture content) during the winter, when humidity is low because free water vapor is quickly trapped into ice and snow. But in the spring, when the relative humidity rises above 20%, the wood is not going to continue losing moisture — it will start to gain. It's like hanging up a damp towel inside a steam room — it can't get any drier than the surrounding air, no matter how long you leave it hanging.

If you attempt to make furniture with this lumber, you're inviting problems when you bring it into a heated house with a humidity level that's less than the wood's moisture content. You'll see shrinkage, possible cracking, and other defects.

The safest bet is to find a mill with a kiln that can complete the drying process for your wood. Even after kiln-drying, wood still absorbs and releases moisture, but at a much slower rate. Keep your lumber dry and stored in a location where the humidity level can be controlled.

BOARDS IN A TENSE SITUATION

 I bought some lumber from a new retailer in my area, including a nice wide board. But when I ripped the board to the width I needed, the kerf closed up as soon as it exited the table-saw's blade. Then the pieces warped almost instantly. What in the world happened?

It sounds like a reaction wood situation. When you cut the wood, you released energy that was trapped inside the lumber.

Boards store energy based on where they were in relation to the tree as well as the growing conditions and location of the tree. For example, if a tree grows on a slope or leans for any reason, the tree will grow larger annual rings on the downhill side than on the half that is up the slope, as shown in the drawing. The uphill side is in tension, and the downhill side is in compression. (The next time you look at the cross section of a tree limb, you'll see the large difference in ring sizes.)

When a leaning tree is felled, it no longer needs to combat gravity, so it will start fighting itself. Your rip cut was the opening shot of the battle, and the reactions of both sides were swift.

Two other possibilities: the tree may have grown with a twist to its trunk. You'll sometimes notice this by "reading the bark" of living trees. The story inside may show spectacular swirling grain with perhaps a subplot of tension. One other potential source of the reaction you experienced is called case-hardening (See page 32).

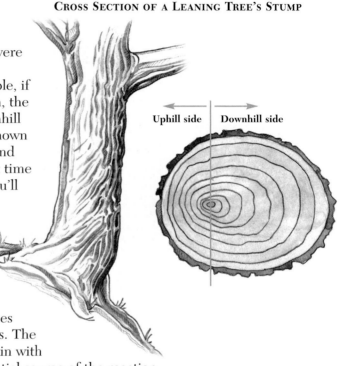

CROSS SECTION OF A LEANING TREE'S STUMP

Uphill side   Downhill side

IT'S ALL IN A NAME AND IT'S ALL ONLINE

 So if I know only the common name of a tree, how do I find its botanical name so I can make sure of what I'm buying?

You can consult the index of a field guide to trees, or search the Internet using your computer. One excellent Web site (up and running as of this printing) that covers North American trees is www.treeguide.com. You can enter either a common or botanical name and get the other, a map showing the tree's distribution, plus other helpful information.

TALES TOLD OF SLOPPY KILN-DRYING

 I've heard a little about case-hardened lumber, and none of it was good. Exactly what is case-hardening, and how do I avoid it?

Case-hardening is a lumber defect that occurs when the outer shell of a board (literally, its case) dries more rapidly than its core. The resulting imbalance in the lumber can cause problems in cutting and machining the wood, as well as potential problems later when the core finally dries. The difference in moisture content between the inner and outer portions of the board can lead to deep checks (cracks) and other serious defects.

A kiln operator who tries to take shortcuts with the drying process often causes this problem. A too-rapid heat rise early in the drying cycle pulls out moisture from the case, setting up the problem. It can also occur late in the process, when the moisture level of the kiln should be slowly raised to condition the wood. But if the kiln operator overcompensates the conditioning, he can create the opposite problem, called reverse case-hardening.

Rip board in half, cut out core

Core   Case

Lumber OK   Case-hardened   Reverse case-hardened

Case-hardening isn't usually obvious on a board's surface. Fortunately, you can make a couple of simple test cuts that will reveal the situation almost immediately.

Referring to the drawing, rip a suspect piece of lumber down the middle, then cut out the core. With a sample 12 inches or longer, you can remove the core with a dado blade in your table saw. With a short sample, you can scroll-saw the core.

If the board is properly conditioned, the edges of the sample will remain parallel. The edges of a casehardened piece will curl inward, while reverse case-hardening will cause them to splay outward. There is nothing you can do in your shop to fix case-hardening, but it can be reversed by a special trip through the kiln. There is no known cure for reverse case-hardening.

WOOD GRAIN AND FIGURE — THERE IS A DIFFERENCE

 Is there actually a difference between a wood's grain and its figure?

Grain deals with the alignment of the wood's cells, and figure describes the pattern that the grain produces. Specifically, the term grain describes how the cells line up in relation to the axis of the tree.

Visualize each stack of cells as a soda straw, and a tree trunk as a bundle of those straws. If each straw stands vertically, then you'd say that wood is straight grained. But the bundles of straws can also be wavy, irregular, spiral, or diagonal.

A great number of factors influence the tree's grain, including the species, whether it grew on a slope, sustained damage suffered through periods of drought or flood, and so on. Ultimately, the tree and its environment determine what kind of grain it has.

Figure is the appearance of grain (and other features of the wood) on the surface of a board. Considering the soda straw example again, you can begin to image how various ways of slicing down the different stacks of straws would reveal distinct patterns.

Poet Joyce Kilmer observed that only God can make a tree, and taking that one step further, the grain it contains. But the guy operating the sawmill has a lot of control over the figure in the wood.

THE STRAIGHT STORY ON SELECTING LUMBER

Sorting through the hardwood lumber stack at a local supplier, I couldn't find a single board that was straight for its entire 8-ft. length. So I went home without the lumber for the medicine cabinet I want to build.

Unless you're building a medicine cabinet that's 8 ft. long, you don't really need lumber that's perfectly straight for this entire length. By the time you crosscut the lumber into the actual lengths you need, you'd probably discover that the pieces are straight enough for your project. To further straighten them, you can flatten the stock on a jointer. Provided the lumber is thicker than you need it to be, most reasonably flat lumber can be made dead flat and straight with just a few passes over the jointer.

FIGURING OUT WOOD'S FIGURE

A hardwood lumber dealer I recently visited labeled not only the wood species but also the type of cut made to create the boards. Several examples were plain-sawn, quartersawn, and rift-sawn. How are these produced?

PLAIN (FLAT)-SAWN

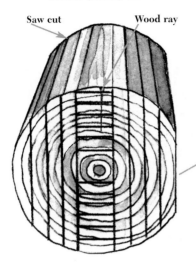

Saw cut   Wood ray

The position of the tree's annual rings relative to the saw blade define the various methods of cutting lumber and also have a profound influence on the figure revealed on the surface of the board.

You may not think that philosophy has much to do with running a sawmill, but the business approach of the mill can determine the appearance of the lumber it produces. For example, if the sawmill wants to get the maximum number of wide boards and minimal waste, it will probably adopt a **plain-sawn** approach as shown in the first drawing. This method is also called flat sawing. The figure produced is the familiar cathedral figure, named for the way that the lines of grain resemble a church spire.

QUARTERSAWN

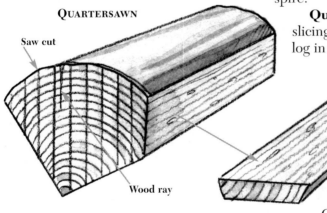

Saw cut

Wood ray

Quartersawing, as the name implies, begins by slicing the log into four parts. With the point of the log in a V position as shown in the drawing, succeeding cuts produce boards that reveal a different aspect of figure. In woods such as the oaks with dominant medullary rays, quartersawing produces a dramatic figure that's called flake or ray. (Quartersawn oak was used almost exclusively in Gustav Stickley's Arts and Crafts furniture.)

Compared to plain sawing, quartersawing yields relatively narrow boards and more wasted lumber.

RIFT-SAWN

Saw cut

Wood ray

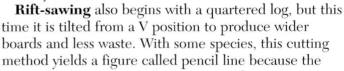

Rift-sawing also begins with a quartered log, but this time it is tilted from a V position to produce wider boards and less waste. With some species, this cutting method yields a figure called pencil line because the tree's annual rings appear at an angle that makes them look like a system of finely drawn lines.

DECIPHERING LUMBERMAN'S LINGO

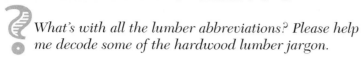

What's with all the lumber abbreviations? Please help me decode some of the hardwood lumber jargon.

- **KD** = kiln dried, usually to a moisture content of 8 percent or less.

- **LF** = lineal foot, also called running foot. This is a pricing system often employed for moldings and similar items that are sold in random lengths.

- **RL&W** = random lengths and widths, which is the usual method of selling hardwoods.

- **S2S** = surfaced two sides, meaning that the lumber has been machined smooth on both faces. Unless otherwise stated, edges are rough.

- **S4S** = surfaced four sides, meaning both the faces and edges are smooth and the edges are parallel. S4S lumber sells at a premium compared to S2S because of the extra machining and additional waste that occurs.

- **SLR and SLR1E** = straight line ripped and straight line ripped one edge. Although some lumber sellers describe this as an edge-gluing surface, you'll get better results by machining a fresh edge. This designation is sometimes combined with S2S to indicate lumber that has two smooth faces and one true edge.

- **SM** = surface measure, the same as square footage.

- **VG** = vertical grain (quartersawn) lumber.

BRUSH UP ON YOUR LATIN

 Why do some people refer to woods by their botanical names? Are they simply showing off a little bit of knowledge about Latin?

Using botanical names promotes accuracy, while common names can cause miscommunication and confusion.

The first part of the botanical name is the genus, or the broad category, of the plant. The second part zeroes in on a particular species. When more than one species is included in the grouping, the abbreviation spp. indicates that fact.

A single wood may have dozens of common names, and those monikers can vary by region, or refer to woods in several genera (the plural of genus), or allude to characteristics of the tree or wood that are familiar to one person but unknown to the next. An interesting example goes by a number of names: Osage orange (for the tribe that introduced the wood to European settlers plus the color of the fresh-cut wood; bois d'arc, (French for wood of the bow), a reference to one use of the wood by Native Americans; bodark, a corruption of the French name; hedge-apple, a reference to the practice of boundary planting plus the jumbo fruit of the female tree. Despite all of those common names, there is only one botanical name: *Maclura pomifera*.

NO LIE: DEFECTS ALLOWED

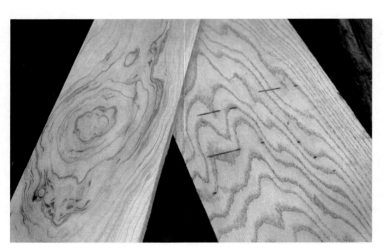

 Since when is a defect not defective? Signs near some woods at my lumber dealer announce "sticker stain not a defect" and "pitch no defect."

Lumber grading rules permit certain defects in some species but not others. An example that's no surprise is pecky cypress. For that wood, marks resembling those caused by bird pecks are not considered defects. (The holes are actually the result of a burrowing fungus.) Maple is susceptible to localized staining from stickers, the small pieces of wood that separate boards in a stack during drying. And cherry often shows a pitch pocket, which is an accumulation of resin between the growth rings. These are not defects for these wood species either.

The fact that the lumber grading rules permit a defect doesn't prevent your dealer from adopting tighter standards. Shopping at several dealers may enable you to find a significant upgrade in quality.

VENEER TELLS A-PEELING STORY

 What are the different ways that veneer is arranged on the face of plywood? I've seen several different styles. But I don't know their names or why I should choose one instead of another.

The drawing illustrates the three principal ways that veneer is laid: rotary, book-matched, and slip-matched.

The rotary method describes the way that the mill produces the veneer. A log spins against a stationary knife that slices the lumber into a continuous sheet, like unfurling a gigantic roll of paper towels. The method economizes both time and materials because there's no tedious joining of individual pieces, and waste is minimal. Most mills produce most softwood plywood this way. About the only drawback is that the rotary method produces undulating figure patterns, but that's fine in softwoods because it's usually painted or covered with siding, shingles, or carpet.

Some mills make an economy grade of hardwood plywood using rotary-cut veneer, and many people find its looks so unnatural and objectionable that they avoid it entirely. If you don't share that aesthetic objection, you can save some money by choosing this plywood instead of book-matched or slip-matched varieties.

Both book-matched and slip-matched veneers are the result of a completely different veneer slicing method. In this case, giant arms slam the log against the stationary knife, chopping thin sheets of veneer away. The paper-thin slice of veneer is called a flitch. All the flitches are stacked in the order that they were cut from the log.

To lay veneer in a book-matched pattern, a worker turns every other flitch face down, as if turning the pages of a book. The alternating sides of the wood create an attractive mirror-image pattern. Book-matching is the most common method of making quality hardwood plywood. On the negative side, the two facing book-matched flitches reflect light differently, making one appear darker. Staining the wood often accentuates this effect.

Slip-matched veneer results when the worker puts the flitches down in sequence, laying them down side by side like dealing cards face down from the deck. Slip-matching overcomes the light-dark problem of book-matching, but this method creates a striped look. Slip-matched veneer plywood is harder to find than book-matched plywood.

ROTARY

BOOK-MATCHED

SLIP-MATCHED

STEAMING MAY REDUCE COLOR DIFFERENCES

 What's this I hear about steamed walnut? I thought the whole idea was to remove moisture from freshly cut wood, not add more.

Steaming is a process that helps diminish the contrast between the heartwood and sapwood of certain wood species such as walnut and cherry. For example, walnut straight from the sawyer's blade shows sapwood that's nearly white, a sharp difference from the dark heartwood that's characteristic of walnut. Sawing off all of the sapwood could result in a significant loss of material, so steaming helps to minimize the waste.

In the process, the freshly cut walnut is placed into a steaming vessel and covered with its sawdust and other mill refuse. The injection of steam then helps equalize the coloration of the heartwood and sapwood. After the treatment is complete, the drying process begins.

The contrast doesn't completely disappear, but a finisher with some skill can blend the two tones seamlessly, conserving valuable lumber.

OH, NO! MORE TERMS TO ABSORB

 What's the difference between a clear face cutting and a sound cutting?

Clear has more to do with appearance, and sound deals with structural integrity.

As the name implies, a clear face cutting is a lumber surface free of defects. The reverse side must be a sound cutting, which means that it cannot have rot, pith (the tree's soft central core), wane (a bark edge), or shake (a lengthwise separation that results from violent storms or damage inflicted by improper felling). However, a sound cutting can include solid knots, streaks, wormholes, and shot holes.

MDF A FIT FOR SOME APPLICATIONS

 What's the big appeal of medium-density fiberboard? The weight alone is enough to make it unattractive to me.

As long as you're mentioning negatives, you forgot to mention that sawing or sanding it also produces clouds of fine dust. It also has minimal spanning capability because it's an amalgamation of wood fibers and resin, not a sandwich of plies.

On the positive side, medium-density fiberboard (MDF) has a lot going for it. Cutting or routing MDF produces smooth edges that hold a nice profile, and there are no internal voids to fill on the edges or to show through a painted finish. MDF also is an excellent substrate for plastic laminates because it's dimensionally stable. For outdoor applications or when used as a substrate for a countertop that includes a sink, specify Medex, a medium-density fiberboard made with exterior grade adhesive.

One other advantage of MDF is that it's usually made in an oversized panel — 49 x 97 in. — instead of 48 x 96 in., the standard dimension for most sheet goods. The extra inch of length and width sometimes enable you to get more cuttings from the sheet or at least provide some extra material to remove dings and dents that happen during shipment.

CORE DETAILS ON HARDWOOD PLYWOOD CORES

When I went to the lumber dealer and asked for hardwood plywood, he asked what kind of core I wanted. I didn't even know that I had a choice. What are the options and their characteristics?

Not every dealer will stock every one of the cores shown in the drawings because of the tremendous inventory expense involved. However, you may find that in certain thicknesses of particular veneered plywoods, the dealer may stock more than one type of core to meet the demands of clients.

The dealer may be willing to special-order a particular core if you agree to purchase a certain number of sheets, but this figure may represent a lifetime supply if you're an amateur woodworker. Your other option is to seek a dealer who routinely carries the type of panel you want.

A **flakeboard** or **particleboard core** offers a smooth surface for the face veneers, so there will be no internal voids that can telegraph their shape through the panel's surface. Flakeboard and particleboard are manufactured by mixing wood pieces with synthetic resins, spreading the mash between metal platens, and applying heat and pressure. This type of core is economical but it doesn't always cut cleanly, provide a high quality glue surface, or receive mechanical fasteners securely.

The manufacture of a **fiberboard** or **MDF core** is similar to the process used for particleboard; the chief difference is the much finer size of wood fibers. Its higher density creates the liability of increased weight per panel but also the asset of improved machining properties. Compared to particleboard, you gain glue strength, but you still must select mechanical fasteners carefully to prevent splitting.

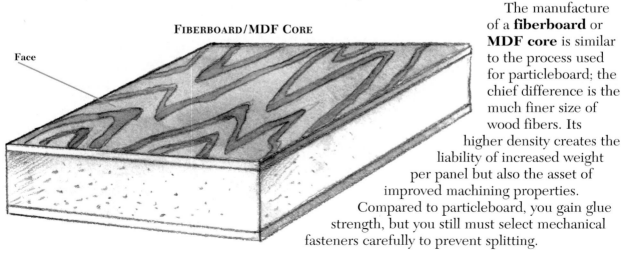

FLAKEBOARD/PARTICLEBOARD CORE

Face

FIBERBOARD/MDF CORE

Face

Veneer core is probably the most prevalent type. Sheets of veneer-core plywood that are manufactured with strict quality control have fewer and smaller internal voids that can show through the face. The edges and ends are both good gluing surfaces, and the core holds mechanical fasteners solidly.

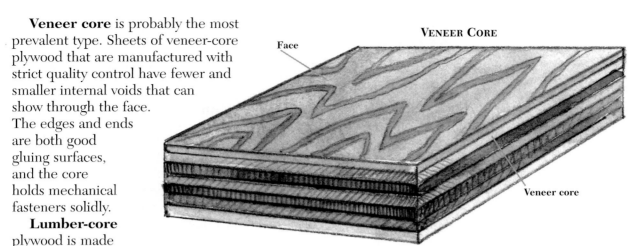

VENEER CORE

Face

Veneer core

Lumber-core plywood is made of edge-glued strips of solid wood. The strips are generally 2½ in. wide or narrower to minimize the potential for warping. A crossbanded veneer layer on both sides of the lumber further stabilizes the assembly. As its name implies, the crossband grain direction is at right angles to the core and the faces. The edges of lumber-core form excellent long-grain gluing surfaces, but the end grain offers very poor adhesive compatibility. Mechanical fasteners hold well.

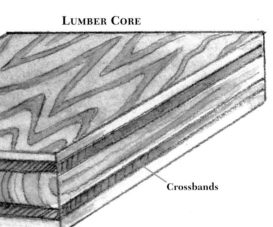

LUMBER CORE

Face

Crossbands

Composite core plywood has a heart of veneer sandwiched between crossbands of particleboard that are a smooth substrate for the face veneers. (In this case the crossbands don't have a distinct grain.) Some people consider this type of construction more environmentally friendly than veneer-core because the particleboard layers make use of lumber byproducts instead of virgin raw materials directly from the tree. The central portion of this construction has the gluing and fastener-holding strengths of veneer core.

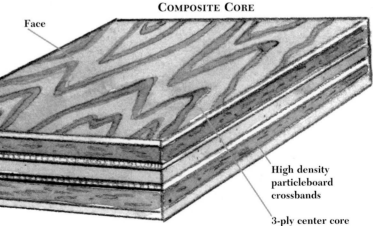

COMPOSITE CORE

Face

High density particleboard crossbands

3-ply center core

HARDWOOD AND SOFTWOOD HAVE SEPARATE PLYWOOD STANDARDS

 I'm vaguely familiar with the grading system for softwood plywood. Does hardwood plywood employ the same system?

The materials are different, so it's no surprise that there's a contrast between the grading systems. Softwood plywoods are typically made from pine, fir, larch, hemlock, and spruce. They may be made with adhesives rated for interior or exterior applications. Many hardwood panels have a core of plies made from aspen, a hardwood. Virtually all hardwood plywood is designed for interior use only.

HARDWOOD PLYWOOD GRADING SYSTEM

In hardwood plywood grading, the prime side is rated A through D according to the terms described in the chart. A number from 1 to 4 designates the back grade.

Face Grade	Quality of Veneer	Allowable Defects
A	Sliced veneer is book-matched or slip-matched, with tight edge joints. Alternatively, the face may be one piece that's rotary cut.	Pin knots and burls must be small and scarce. Tiny patches allowed.
B	Sliced veneer need not be matched, but there must not be great contrasts in figure or color.	Burls and slight color streaks permitted. Pin knots must be small and scarce. Tiny patches allowed.
C	Face must be sound, with no open defects and only small areas of rough grain.	Variations of color, color streaks, and spots are unlimited.
D	Face must be sound, with no open defects. Allowable area of rough grain depends on the species.	Variations of color, color streaks, and spots are unlimited.

Back Grade	Quality of Veneer	Allowable Defects
1	No open defects; color and grain match not required.	Sound knots, smooth patches, and discoloration permitted.
2	All defects must be repaired.	Knots must be sound and tight.
3	Some open defects permitted; sound surface.	Knotholes permitted, splits may be repaired.
4	Reject material.	Knotholes up to 4 in. permitted, major discoloration allowed.

For softwood plywood, the scale ranges from A through D. Only A and B are considered suitable for appearance after painting. A is the top painting grade, a sound surface without pitch pockets or knots. Numerous neat patches are allowed. B is called a solid grade, with no large open defects. This designation permits small tight knots, discoloration, streaks from pitch, patches, and synthetic plugs. Both C and D grades are considered material that's suitable only for panel backing or for sheathing plywood. It's sometimes called "reject" material, meaning that it couldn't meet the minimum requirements for the B grade. The pair of letters describing softwood plywood designate the grades of the two faces. Here are the most common combinations:

TYPICAL SOFTWOOD PLYWOOD DESIGNATIONS

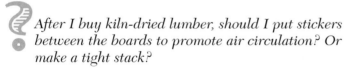

A-A	The best panel, manufactured with your choice of interior or exterior glue.
A-B	Sound one side, solid back, interior or exterior glue.
A-D	Sound one side, reject back, interior glue.
B-B	Solid both sides, interior or exterior glue.
Shop	This catchall designation may include panels from grades A-A through B-D that didn't make it past final inspection.
C-D	Unsanded sheathing grade that permits open defects. You may also find this grade with a plugged face that's touch-sanded.

HOW LUMBER SHOULD STACK UP AT HOME

After I buy kiln-dried lumber, should I put stickers between the boards to promote air circulation? Or make a tight stack?

Build a tight stack to minimize the surface area of the lumber in contact with the air. This discourages moisture absorption from the atmosphere. This practice is also called dead stacking.

There are several other storage considerations. Elevate the pile so that it doesn't absorb moisture from a concrete floor or permit an easy path for insect or fungal infestation. Concrete blocks are an economical method to create a firm foundation. Add a sheet of plywood, and you're ready to stack your lumber.

Make sure that the foundation is flat and level. If your base is twisted, all of your lumber can take on that same set. Cap the stack with another piece of plywood to keep the lumber dry and to protect it from surface damage. Adding weight atop the plywood will help restrain unwanted wood movement.

3
PREPARING
STOCK

THINK INSIDE THE BOX

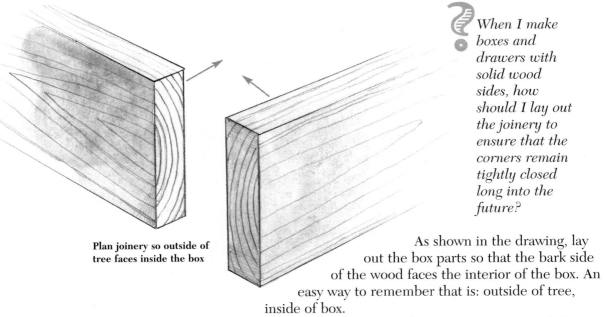

Plan joinery so outside of tree faces inside the box

？ *When I make boxes and drawers with solid wood sides, how should I lay out the joinery to ensure that the corners remain tightly closed long into the future?*

As shown in the drawing, lay out the box parts so that the bark side of the wood faces the interior of the box. An easy way to remember that is: outside of tree, inside of box.

When you follow this guideline, any distortion or cupping of the lumber will force the top and bottom corners of the box more tightly together instead of creating a gap. This is a case where thinking inside the box will improve your projects.

STRATEGIES TO REDUCE PLYWOOD CHIP-OUT

？ *When I cut plywood to size for a project, I often get chip-out of the veneer. How do I prevent or at least minimize that?*

Here are several strategies that will give you cleaner cuts. Always position the sheet so that the majority of the chipping will occur on the side of the panel that's less noticeable. With a handheld circular saw, cut the plywood with the good face down. On the table saw, the good face should be upward.

If both faces must be chip-free, put a zero-clearance insert into your table saw to better support both sides of the cut. (To see how to make your own zero-clearance insert, please refer to pages 208-209.)

You also can make scoring cuts on the plywood. To do that, raise the blade so the tips will make a cut $\frac{1}{16}$ in. deep into the panel. Then raise the blade high enough to cut through the entire sheet.

A strip of clear package sealing tape over the cut-line also helps reduce chip-out.

Of course, all these strategies work best when your table is properly adjusted for square cuts and you have a clean, sharp blade.

WITH 2 SQUARES, FIND CENTER

 I cut out some disks using a template so I wouldn't leave a mark on the wood. But now I need to find the center of a circle. How do I do that?

Team a combination square with a framing square as shown in the photo, and you'll get almost instant results. Hold or clamp the combination square so its blade is at the inner corner of the framing square. Position this assembly against the disk, and make a pencil line along the blade. Rotate the disk about 90 degrees (the exact amount is not critical), and make another line. The intersection of those two lines indicates the centerpoint.

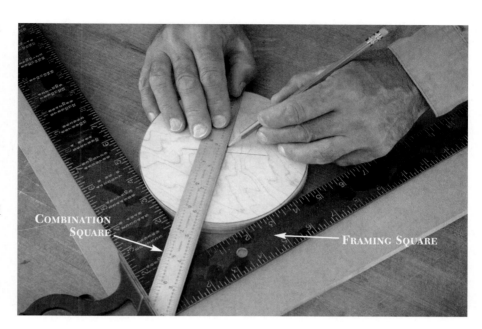

COMBINATION SQUARE

FRAMING SQUARE

If you don't happen to have two squares handy, here's another method that involves only a compass. Put the compass point on the rim of the circle, and set the pencil at a point you judge is less than halfway across the circle, as shown in the photo. Strike a small arc, and move the point to three other places around the rim. The four locations should be more or less equally spaced, but it's

not critical. Strike arcs from each of those spots. Connect the intersections of the arcs with diagonal lines to reveal the centerpoint.

CUT PLYWOOD TO LUGGABLE SIZE

Buying sheet goods is always a hassle. When I get them home, the first thing I have to do is cut them up into manageable pieces so I can maneuver the panels in my shop. How can I make handling these sheets a little easier?

To cut this problem down to size, have your lumber supplier slice the sheets into oversized blanks that you can transport easily and handle more efficiently.

When you plan your project, do a sketch of how the parts will lay out on the sheet of plywood. Arrange the pieces so an edge-to-edge cut will reduce the sheet into pieces you can handle. Take the drawing with you when you buy the plywood to reduce the possibility of mistakes.

Carry a crayon or marker with you, and make a scribble mark along each factory edge to identify these as cutting references in your shop instead of relying on a potentially out-of-square cut made at the lumberyard's panel saw.

Remember that your goal is to ease logistical problems, not to get parts cut to final size. Besides, most suppliers will rightfully balk at the idea of taking responsibility for cutting to precise dimensions. Allowing at least 1 in. of waste at each cut line is a good idea. Many panel saws at home centers have hopelessly dull blades and a misaligned cutting path — two factors that produce splintered veneer on plywood.

Some suppliers have an official policy against making rip cuts in sheet goods, but many employees cheerfully ignore the company's rules.

HAVE A TAILGATE CUTTING PARTY

There are some times when I just can't avoid hauling full sheets of plywood home in my pickup truck. My neighbor will give me a hand if he's home, but it comes at a high cost. His five minutes of work means that I get suckered into about an hour's worth of labor on one of his projects. How can I turn plywood handling into a one-man job?

Make yourself a pair of sawhorses that will support 2x2s about 1 in. below the level of your tailgate as shown in the drawing, and you'll be able to both unload the sheets yourself and cut them down to size conveniently.

As you pull the sheet of plywood out of the truck, hold it above the 2x2s until only a couple of inches of the panel still rest on the tailgate. Give it a yank, and the plywood will land squarely on the cutting surface. If you try dragging the sheet over the supports, you risk toppling the sawhorses. If you need to reposition the lumber strips, simply raise an end or edge of the plywood, and scoot the 2x2 where you want it.

Set your circular saw's depth of cut about ⅛ in. more than the panel's thickness, and you'll reuse the same set of 2x2 supports for years.

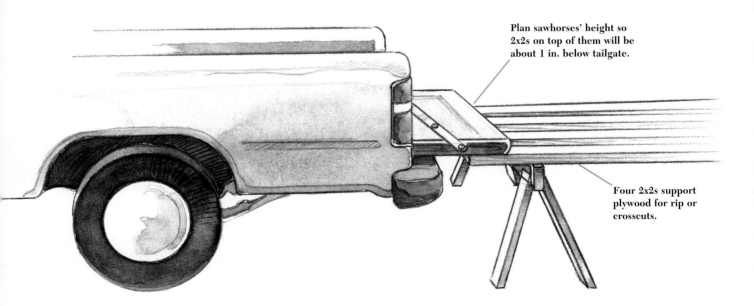

Plan sawhorses' height so 2x2s on top of them will be about 1 in. below tailgate.

Four 2x2s support plywood for rip or crosscuts.

MORE POWER: STRATEGY WITH A CHAIN SAW

 How do I chainsaw a log to reveal crotch figure, either for a turning blank or as a piece of flat lumber?

SAWING A LOG TO REVEAL CROTCH FIGURE

The following procedure works best when you can saw a log immediately after a tree has been felled. Serious checks (cracks) can begin to appear within a matter of hours, so if you won't be able to deal with the crotch immediately, leave all three portions long until you're ready to slice the log as shown in the drawing.

Prop the log upright, and make sure that you have a sharp chain in your saw. Aim your chain though the center of both legs of the crotch, and slice straight downward. When the log opens, you may see a beautiful feather or flame pattern caused by the interlocking grain of the tree. Or you may find bland-looking wood that you can toss onto your firewood stack.

If you're going to turn a bowl, you can bandsaw a blank immediately and rough-turn it. Plan the turning so the center of the tree aligns with the lathe's axis of rotation. If you mount the blank with the grain running perpendicular to the way the lathe spins, all the wonderful crotch figure will end up as shavings on the floor.

If you want to convert the wood into flat planks, chainsaw the cuts parallel to the one that opened the log. Before each cut, find a way to hold the wood securely. There's no log so good-looking that it's worth the risk of serious injury.

May be any desired length

RECYCLE YOUR SHAVINGS

 After running boards through my planer, I end up with a tremendous amount of shavings. It seems a shame to throw them all away, but what can I safely do with them?

Reuse shavings by laying them down as paths through your garden, as mulch around plants, or add them to your compost pile. Certain woods, such as cedar, also make good bedding material for small pets such as rabbits, hamsters, and gerbils. If you have any doubts about what woods are suitable, check with your veterinarian.

One wood that deserves particular caution is walnut. The shavings can cause damage to the hooves of horses, and the acid in the wood can wreak havoc with certain garden plants, especially tomatoes.

THE KNOTTY PROBLEM OF GETTING LUMBER HOME

 Sometimes I need to haul boards that are too long to fit in my pickup's bed. But when I prop them diagonally on top of the closed tailgate, they slide around. I wasn't in the scouts or Navy, so my knowledge of knots is a little short. How can I get a grip on this problem?

First, create an anchor point by cutting a stake to fit in the rear pocket of your pickup's fender. A projection of 18 in. is plenty. Drape an old bath towel around the stake to protect your paint.

Tie a length of ⅜-in. manila or sisal rope to the stake. These natural fibers grip each other more securely than nylon cord. A clove hitch is a sturdy knot, and it's easy to tie, as shown in the drawing. Make two underhand loops, put the right loop over the left, and slide both loops onto the stake. Pull on the ends of the rope to tighten the knot.

Load your lumber, snug it against the stake, and tie it with the free end of the rope. Then tie another clove hitch.

Secure a flag to the lumber with package sealing tape or the ever-popular duct tape. An old red towel or piece of fabric that's about 18 in. square should keep you out of trouble with the law, but check your local regulations to be sure.

After you unload the lumber, store the stake, rope, towel, flag, and tape behind the seat of your truck, so you'll be prepared for the next time.

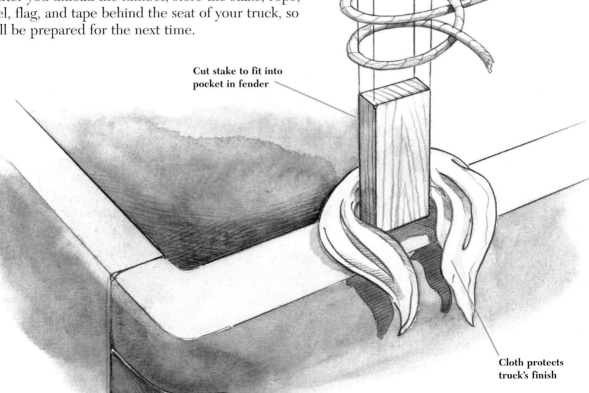

Tie clove hitch to stake; tie board to stake.

Cut stake to fit into pocket in fender

Cloth protects truck's finish

51

TAKING THE WAVE OUT OF PREMIUM VENEER

I bought some fancy veneer for the paneled top of a jewelry box, but the thin wood has become very wavy. How do I flatten it before gluing it in place?

If the waves are small and gentle, you may be able to skip the flattening process and glue the veneer directly to the substrate. To get major waves to relax, you need to condition the veneer with a softening solution. Although there are some commercial veneer relaxers on the market, you can easily mix up a batch of your own. Here's the recipe: three parts water, two parts white glue, one and one-half parts glycerin, and one part denatured alcohol. Purchase both the glycerin and the denatured alcohol at your local drugstore.

After you've mixed the ingredients, brush a liberal coat on both sides of the veneer or even dunk it in the mixture, and let the excess drip off for a minute or so.

Put a piece of sheet plastic (Plexiglas is one brand) onto a smooth work surface, lay down the veneer, and top it with another piece of plastic. Lay a piece of medium-density fiberboard (MDF) over the plastic, but resist the urge to press down because too much pressure too soon can crack the still-brittle veneer. Every four hours, add another piece of MDF (or an equivalent amount of evenly distributed weight) to increase the pressure. After one day of gradually increasing the

weight, you can double the weight of the stack by adding a toolbox or other heavy item.

After a total time of 48 hours elapses, unstack the pile and inspect the veneer. If it's not yet flat enough to glue, mist both sides of the wood with water, and reassemble the stack for another day of flattening. You can also increase the weight as further persuasion for the veneer.

When the veneer is flat, you don't necessarily have to dry it before gluing it in place. But if you do want to dry the veneer, replace the plastic sheets with pieces of brown paper and restack the pile. Change the brown paper every four hours until the veneer is dry. Store the veneer under weight to keep it flat.

HARNESS FLUSH-TRIM BIT TO TRIM DOOR EDGES

After I wrap solid-wood banding around the edges and ends of plywood doors, I always have a terrible time sanding the edges of the banding flush with the plywood. If I get in a hurry and remove too much stock, I can go through the face veneer of the plywood and ruin the door. How can I make this job quicker and more certain?

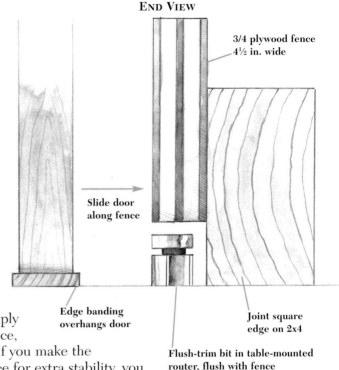

END VIEW

3/4 plywood fence 4½ in. wide

Slide door along fence

Edge banding overhangs door

Joint square edge on 2x4

Flush-trim bit in table-mounted router, flush with fence

Make the easy fence shown in the drawing, and you can harness the accuracy of a flush-trimming bit chucked into your table-mounted router instead of using a sander. When you clamp the fence to your router table, be certain that the bit's bearing is flush with the plywood fence. A small square will confirm the setting.

After the glue on the edge banding dries, simply run the face of the door against the plywood fence, and the bit will slice off the overhanging stock. If you make the plywood face wider to enlarge the contact surface for extra stability, you may need to switch from a 2 x 4 to a larger timber or add bracing so the fence won't flex.

NEED BETTER PLYWOOD? BE CREATIVE!

I'm building door panels and need some ¼-in. red oak plywood that has attractive veneer on both sides. My supplier's stock has a low quality veneer on the back-side. I've made a few calls, but I'm having a tough time finding better material. What can I do?

Order some ⅛-in. plywood that's good on one side, and glue the panels back-to-back to make the ¼-in. thickness you need. Be sure to align the veneer joints on both sides so the patterns will be centered no matter which side of the door you view.

SHORTCUTS TO BANDING DOOR EDGES

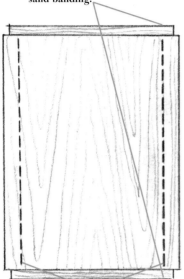

Start with a plywood blank 1 in. wider than the finished size. Band the top and bottom ends, trim, and sand banding.

Cut door to width

I want to apply solid-wood edge banding to a set of doors to hide the plywood's edge grain. Any suggestions on how to precisely mark and cut the banding?

Instead of squinting at layout lines and attempting to make perfect cuts, you can use a system that eliminates all of that tedious effort and gives you flawless results. Refer to the drawings, and you'll see how this system works.

Cut your plywood door blanks to height, but initially leave them 1 in. wider than needed. Prepare your banding — ⅛ in. is a popular thickness, but some people make banding as thick as ¼ in. Crosscut banding for the top and bottom of each door, and glue it into place, leaving it ¼ in. short of each corner. Masking tape is a good way to "clamp" the banding, as detailed on page 136.

After the glue dries and you trim and sand the banding flush, rip ½ in. from each side of the panel to make the plywood its final width. Now you can band the edges, leaving the strips long. The exact amount of overhang is not critical, of course, but you'll want at least enough projection to give the flush-cut saw a starting place. After you trim off the overhang, give the door its final sanding.

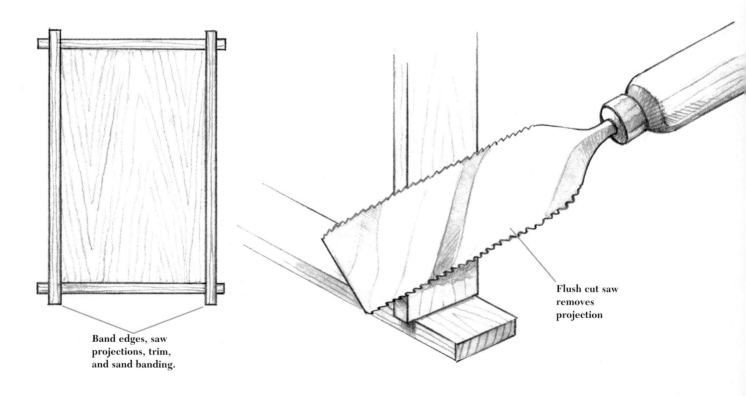

Band edges, saw projections, trim, and sand banding.

Flush cut saw removes projection

54

THE SQUARE STORY ON 3-INCH FURNITURE SQUARES

 I bought some 3-in.-square wood blanks to make table legs, but all four sides are rough. In addition, the blanks aren't really square. How do I establish a starting surface and square up the blanks?

You're correct when you refer to a starting surface, and the best way to establish that is with a jointer. Mark the end of each blank with the sequence of numbers shown in the photo, and run the Side 1 face over the jointer's cutter head until it is flat. For this series of cuts, direct your hand pressure downward, with only minimal pressure against the jointer's fence.

When Face 1 is flat and straight, you'll position it against the jointer's fence while you make Side 2 flat and square. This time, direct most of your pressure against the fence, not the cutter head, to ensure that you'll create a right angle.

Once you've set two faces that flat and square to each other, you can easily deal with the remaining two sides. True up those surfaces with a surface planer or table saw, keeping the smooth faces against the planer bed or the saw table.

CARPET PAD PROTECTS YOUR VALUABLE CARGO

 When I go to the lumberyard, I always load the plywood first, and put the hardwood lumber on top. But even when I drive carefully, the load will shift, dinging the edges of the lumber and scraping the plywood. How do I prevent this sliding?

Put even a relatively small non-slip router mat atop the plywood, and it will prevent damage because the lumber will stay put. If you want to cover the entire surface of the plywood, purchase a no-slip pad that's designed to go between a throw rug and a hard-surfaced floor. You'll find this very economical protection in the floor coverings section of your home center.

THE FLAT-OUT TRUTH
ABOUT WINDING STICKS

 I've read a little bit about how winding sticks can help a person judge whether a surface is flat. How does this procedure work?

Winding is a twist that can develop in a board or an assembly like a door. It is often difficult to detect because both edges may be straight and square.

(By the way, winding is pronounced like a baseball pitcher's preparation, not the breeze blowing toward left field.)

Mask and paint 1 in. long target 2 in. from each end

2"

Rout ¼ in. chamfer along outer face of each stick

Stub dowels align sticks during storage

½"

24"

Drill ¾ in. hanging hole 1 in. from end

To detect this defect, you'll need to make a pair of winding sticks like the set shown in the drawing. Carefully machine the sticks from a stable wood like mahogany, and apply a good finish to minimize the potential for twisting or warping. Inserting stub dowels into holes in the sticks will also minimize distortion to the set during storage. Mask around the target locations in the rear stick, and paint the targets white. Aerosol primer is a fast-drying and high-visibility choice.

To set up the sticks for use, place them on a board as shown in the photo. Squat down so your eye level matches the top of the sticks, and sight over the front one to the targets on the rear. Some people will close one eye, and squint through the other, but you'll be more relaxed and see much more clearly if you keep both eyes open and merely cover one eye with your hand.

In a world dominated by high-tech tools and gadgets, you'll be pleasantly surprised at how quickly and accurately a pair of shop-made winding sticks will check your work. If you discover wind in a board, move the rear stick forward in increments until you locate where the problem begins. Sighting from the other end of the board will confirm the results. Trim the board here to remove the section with wind. For minor wind, you may be able to salvage the whole board by jointing the twist flat.

56

HUNT DOWN SNIPE AT YOUR PLANER

 How do I prevent snipe at the beginning and end of a board that I run through a thickness planer? I've been saving a piece of wood for a special project, but if I lose much of its length I won't have enough.

Snipe is the scooped cut that appears at the beginning and end of a board that's been thickness-planed. The problem occurs when the planer's cutter head and feed rollers move up onto the stock at the front end and then drop off at the back. The challenge is to eliminate the rough take-off and bumpy landing.

Careful adjustment of the thickness planer will help minimize snipe, so start by dusting off your owner's manual. The next thing you can do will completely eliminate snipe from your good lumber. The method involves two pieces of scrap lumber that are each about 2 ft. long and the same thickness as your good stock.

Feed one of the scrap pieces into the planer, and butt your good stock against its trailing end. At the back end of your good board, butt the other piece of scrap stock. The first piece of scrap stock creates a launch pad, and the second one is a landing zone. Between these two, your board will glide on a smooth plane.

CHAMFER BIT STREAMLINES PROCESS FOR TABLE BANDING

For durability, I'd like to put laminate tops on a pair of square end tables I'm building for my family room. But for good looks, I'd like to put a band of solid wood around each top. How do I combine these two materials and get a good fit?

You don't have to settle for a good fit — you can get an excellent joint between the laminate and wood.

Begin by cutting a square of medium-density fiberboard (MDF), and miter your wood strips to fit around the perimeter. Cut biscuit slots to align the top and banding, and glue the strips in place.

Be careful to position the top edge of each strip flush with the surface of the MDF. Do any touch-up sanding after the glue dries.

Cut a piece of laminate that's large enough to cover both the MDF and the banding, and attach it by using contact cement. Chuck a chamfer bit into your router, and rout around the assembly to cut both the banding and the laminate at the same time for a perfect fit. Depending on the size of the chamfer, you may have to rout the profile in several passes, lowering the depth of cut each time.

MARK YOUR TABLE SAW'S SWEET SPOT

I put my table saw on a mobile base so I can get it out of the way when I don't need it. But when I try to move it back, it's always trial and error until I find a spot where it won't rock. Needless to say, my shop floor isn't the flattest surface on the face of the earth. Any good way to work around this problem?

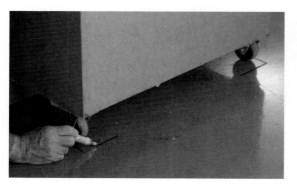

It's easy to cure a saw that wants to rock after you roll. When you find the solid landing spot again, draw lines on the floor by running a permanent marker around the corners of the base. An L-shaped mark of a couple of inches at each corner will identify the location. That way, you'll be able to quickly return to the spot with no fumbling.

If you have an outfeed stand for your table saw, mark its optimal position on the floor, too, for quick set-ups.

To Build a Rectangular Top, Assemble Backwards

I want to make a laminate-covered table with built-up edges. That's not the difficult part. What's difficult is, the piece of plywood I want to use doesn't have a straight edge on it, so I'm not sure how to cut the neat rectangular piece I need. What's the solution?

This really isn't a serious dilemma; in fact this problem gives you an opportunity to try out a technique that produces great results. The photo shows you how this method works.

Instead of starting with the plywood, begin with the build-up strips by cutting them to width and length. Crosscutting them in stacked pairs will ensure that they are precisely the same length. Attach the first long strip to the underside of the panel. Gluing and screwing is a good method, but glue and pneumatic-driven finishing nails are much faster. With a framing square to check your layout, position the remaining pieces, and fasten them.

Use a band saw or jig saw to cut the plywood to within ⅛ in. of the build-up strips. Chuck a heavy-duty flush-trimming bit into your router, and slice away the overhanging top so the edges are flush with the strips. If your bit's bearing is above the cutters, you'll rout the table top upside down, guiding the bearing against the build-up strips with the router base riding on the strips. If the bearing is below the cutters, rest the router on the top surface of the table top to trim the overhang flush.

4

MARKING,
CUTTING,
AND SIZING

SEEING RED WHEN SQUARING BLADES

Setting saw blades square to the table is a nightmare. At the table saw, the teeth interfere with my square. I have the same problem with the scroll saw. Plus, the blade is so short, it's hard to get an accurate reading. How much money do I have to spend to get an accurate gauge to help me set all of the blades in my shop?

The cost of absolute accuracy is absolutely zero — all you need is a piece of scrap wood. A straight length of 2x4 with parallel faces works great. Use your table saw's miter gauge to guide the cut as you slice a 2-in. piece from the end of the board, then turn off your saw. With both pieces of wood resting on the flat reference surface of your saw's table, turn over the offcut, and put the freshly cut surfaces against each other. Bend down so that you're looking straight at the end of the cut line. If there's a gap at the bottom of the joint, you need to tilt the top of the blade to the left. If there's a space at the top, adjust the blade to the right. The gap you see is twice the error, so alter the blade angle just a touch. Repeat the process until the flipped offcut fits perfectly, and your blade will be square to the table.

Squaring a band saw or scroll-saw table is even easier. Make a cut ¼ in. deep into the edge of a 2x4, and back out of the cut. Shut off the saw, turn the board over, and place it behind the saw blade. When the back of the blade goes into the cut line easily, the blade and table are square. Of course, the angle will be easier to see in a longer cut, so you may want to band saw into the wide face of the 2x4 instead of its edge.

CIRCLES FOR A SONG

I need to draw a circle that has a radius of 18 in., and I just can't get smooth results using a pencil and a piece of string. If the tension changes in the string or the angle of the pencil, I get a wobbly line. A set of trammel points would give me the accuracy I want, but I'm still trying to recover from the sticker shock of the catalog price. Are there any affordable methods?

Fortunately, there are at least two ways to solve this problem. Go to nearly any well-stocked art-supply store, and you'll find a yardstick compass for a fraction of the cost of the trammel set. As the name implies, the head and point of this compass fit onto a standard softwood yardstick, or you can cut a longer strip of wood for even bigger circles or arcs.

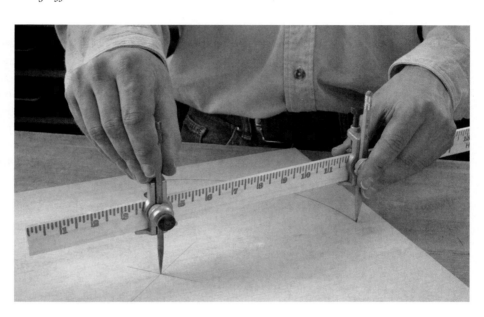

Replace the supplied lead with a craft knife blade if you prefer, to scribe the circle instead of drawing it. The yardstick compass is from Griffin Manufacturing (please see Resources, page 314.).

The other method is virtually cost-free. Simply rip ¼-in. plywood into a 1-in.-wide strip that's about 2 in. longer than the radius you need to draw. (For example,

11 in. for a 9-in. radius circle.) Drill a ¹⁄₁₆-in. hole about 1 in. from one end, and carefully measure the radius from that pivot hole. Drill another ¹⁄₁₆-in. hole, and your custom compass is complete. Tap a nail through the pivot hole, and insert the tip of a mechanical pencil through the other hole to draw the circle.

CENTERING VENEER PATTERNS

When I make cabinet door panels from plywood, I like to center the book-matched veneer design. But I hate doing all the calculations to figure out how much to cut from each side of the blank. I've even ruined a few panels by cutting them too small. Is there an easy way to get dependable results?

While there may not be a no-math approach, you can try this proven low-math method: All you need to know is the overall panel width, and that dimension divided in half. For this example, let's say you need a panel 12¾ in. wide, so 6⅜ in. is half the overall width.

To locate the center of the book-matched design, tilt the panel blank away from you so you're mainly looking at the end of the plywood, with your line of sight just skimming the face of the stock. Holding the wood like this makes it easier to see the veneer joint lines. Make a pencil mark on the end of the plywood indicating the center of the pattern. Measure 6⅜-in. to the left of the center mark, and make another line on the end of the plywood — this is the location of your first cut line. Take the blank to your table saw, and place the mark on the edge of the saw blade. Slide the rip fence against the other edge of the blank, and make the cut. Rotate the blank so that the edge you just cut is now against the rip fence. Reset the fence to the overall width of the panel — 12¾ in. — and make the second cut. This method ensures that the overall width of your panel will be perfect, even if your first cut is slightly off the mark.

FIGURE FRACTIONS FAST

 Whenever my cousin and I work on a project together and fractions need to be doubled or divided in half, it seems that he can instantly figure them in his head while I'm scratching my noggin. Everybody in the family knows he's no genius, so there must be some trick to it. Of course, I can't give him the satisfaction of asking, so what is it?

You may call it a trick, but your cousin is probably using a basic math principle to quickly figure the answers. In a fraction, the top number is called the numerator, and the bottom one is the denominator. For example, in the fraction ¾, 3 is the numerator and 4 is the denominator. To divide a fraction in half (two parts), you multiply the denominator by a factor of 2. So half of ¾ is ⅜. Other factors work just as quickly. To divide ¾ in fourths, the factor is four, so the answer is ³⁄₁₆.

To multiply fractions, divide the denominator by the factor. For example, use a factor of two to double ⅜ into ¾.

When you work with whole numbers and fractions, you'll avoid mistakes by treating them separately, then adding the individual parts together. For example, when you need to divide 7½ by two, you can easily figure that half of 7 is 3½, and half of ½ is ¼. Add them together, and you have 3¾.

RING AROUND THE CYLINDER

 I need to draw a line around a cylinder, but no matter what I try, the mark wanders around so it never ends at the starting point. How can I make an accurate line?

Your difficulty probably comes from trying to use straight tools on a curved surface. All you really need is a strip of paper about 2 in. wide and slightly longer than the circumference of the cylinder. Simply mark a pencil dot where you want the line, and wrap the paper around the cylinder so its edge touches the mark. When the paper is flat against the surface of the cylinder, its edge will be perpendicular to the axis of the cylinder. Simply draw your pencil along the paper to make your mark.

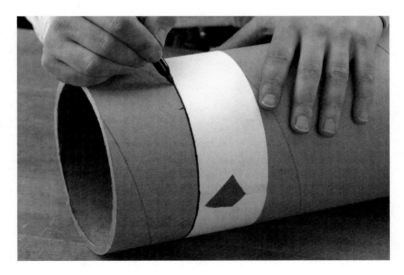

CLARIFYING MARKING GAUGE OPTIONS

 I was going to buy a marking gauge, but when I looked at my woodworking catalog, I got confused. There's a marking gauge, a cutting gauge, and one with a wheel cutter. Which one do I need?

The simple answer is: It all depends. The traditional rule of thumb is that the nail-like point of a marking gauge is for marking with the grain, while the knife of a cutting gauge usually produces a cleaner mark across the grain. Compared to these centuries-old designs, the wheeled gauge is the new kid, and it gives fine results both with and across the grain. Marking and cutting gauges usually have blocky heads, so they stay put on your workbench. The wheeled gauge has a circular head, so it may roll in a little circle when you set it down. But unless you set it right near the edge, there's little danger that it will roll off your bench.

PENNIES FOR PRECISION

 I enjoy going to flea markets and garage sales, and I sometimes see micrometers or dial indicators at bargain prices. Of course, I'd have to put a little work into cleaning away some surface rust or touching up chipped paint, but I don't mind that if it means saving money. Should I try them?

Many woodworking tools are worth the effort of restoration to put them back into service, but precision measuring tools can suffer permanent damage if handled improperly or dropped on a hard surface even once. If the tool's previous owner was so careless that he allowed it to rust, he might also have used it as a tack hammer. But even if you find a micrometer that looks new and operates smoothly, you should also check the anvils — the surfaces that touch the object being measured. They should be smooth and mirror-bright.

Don't be tempted so easily by price alone. Sometimes a cheap price tag means that the real value is zero.

TURNING CORNERS WITH STRAIGHT LINES

How do I transfer a line from the face of a board over to the end? When I move my square to the second position, the lines almost never meet perfectly.

Glue and screw together the simple face-and-end marking jig shown in the drawing, and use your miter saw to trim the ends perfectly square. Using the jig is simplicity itself — position its end with a starting point on the face of the board, then use a pencil or striking knife to mark both the face and end of the board. Be sure to hold your marking tool at the same angle on both surfaces.

If you want to purchase a solution to this problem, consider the Incra brand angled rule made by Taylor Design Group (please see Resources, page 314.). It simplifies layout if you need to make a series of accurately spaced lines on the face and end of a board.

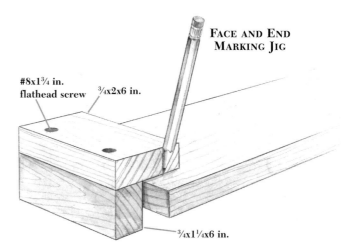

FACE AND END MARKING JIG

#8x1¾ in. flathead screw

¾x2x6 in.

¾x1¼x6 in.

STICK WITH THE CUT LIST

I bought some full-size plans for a project, but when I measure the parts on the drawings it's not the same as the dimension that's written. Sometimes the difference is only ¹⁄₃₂-in., but I don't want to goof up the project. Which do I believe, the written dimension in the cutting list or measuring off the drawing?

Many plans come with a disclaimer that reads something like: "Do not scale drawing." Translated, that means you should believe the written dimension, and there's a good reason for that. Most plans are printed on paper, which is a wood product. And just as wood changes in size in response to changes in humidity, paper also swells and shrinks. In the days before computer drafting, this paper problem was serious enough that the master "drawings" for new car designs were lines etched into a metal plate stored in a climate-controlled room.

GOOD TRADEOFF FOR TRACING

 For an upcoming project, I need to transfer some small designs to thin stock so I can scroll-saw them. But when I've gone shopping for carbon paper, the teenage clerks look at me like I've just landed on this planet. Surely, somebody somewhere still makes carbon paper.

Carbon paper isn't extinct yet, but it's probably not the best choice for your project. That's because it can leave a waxy residue that's hard to remove from wood. And worse, wax is a contaminant that causes adhesion problems for paint or clear finishes. Go to a crafts store, and look for a roll of graphite transfer paper. Black is the standard color, but you may also find it in several colors that will show up clearly on a variety of different surfaces.

But even with transfer paper, you still face the tedious job of tracing all the lines. Here's a shortcut: Skip that work and make a photocopy of the pattern and adhere it with a glue stick.

Make sure the glue stick is the type with removable adhesive — its tackiness is similar to self-adhesive notes, and just as easy to remove. Regular glue sticks have such a powerful adhesive that the paper simply won't release cleanly from the wood. Spray adhesive is even worse: it produces a too-tight bond and leaves sticky overspray everywhere.

Big Patterns Demand Savvy Solutions

 Are there any tricks to transferring large patterns to plywood for holiday yard decorations? I'd like to save the original in case I want to make a duplicate in the future.

Trying to maneuver transfer paper under a large paper pattern isn't a good solution. One alternative is to simply rub artist's charcoal on the back side of the pattern — not the entire sheet, but just along the lines. Tape the pattern to the glass of a large window or sliding patio door on a sunny day, and you'll be able to clearly see the lines on the back side of the paper. Take a piece of soft charcoal that's about 1 in. long, and use its edge to cover the lines. You also can use a charcoal pencil, but you'll need to scribble its point back and forth across the lines to ensure coverage.

After you've covered all the lines, tape the pattern sheet to your stock. Trace the lines with a colored pencil to keep track of your progress. If the transferred lines smear, you can set them with an artist's aerosol fixative, but hair spray works just as well. In fact, some people insist that the cheaper the hair spray, the better it works. That's because the cheap stuff has the holding power but skips the vitamins and fragrances that drive up the price without doing any useful work — at least not useful in a woodworking application.

TRY MICHELANGELO'S APPROACH TO PATTERN TRANSFERS

A friend told me that some people use a pounce wheel to transfer large patterns. Is that a real thing, or was my buddy pulling my leg?

A famous aviator once said, "I don't mind if someone pulls my leg as long as I'm taller afterward." In this case, your friend was giving you good advice. He's referring to a system based on fine powder and a small toothed wheel on a handle. It's essentially the same method that Michelangelo used to transfer his drawings to the ceiling of the Sistine Chapel.

Griffin Manufacturing (please see Resources, page 314) makes several varieties of pounce wheels.

Place your pattern on a slightly padded surface, such as a flattened corrugated box or several layers of newspaper over your workbench. As you roll the pounce wheel over the pattern lines, the points punch tiny holes through the paper. When you've rolled along all the lines, tape your pattern to your stock. To transfer the dots to dark-colored stock, you can sprinkle talcum powder or powdered chalk (from an art-supply store) onto the drawing, and then use a small balled-up cloth to pounce along the lines, forcing the powder through the holes. You also can put the powder into a small cloth bag or improvise with the toe of a discarded sock. To transfer the points to light-colored stock, buy some powdered charcoal at the art-supply store. A little bit of this black powder goes a long way, and you should wear latex gloves when handling it because its fine texture makes it difficult to wash off your skin.

Whether you use light or dark powder, set it with an aerosol fixative or hair spray to prevent smearing. After you fold up your pattern, store it in a large zip-top plastic bag.

MEASURE LESS, GAUGE MORE

I'm getting a little frustrated with my woodworking. I measure all of the parts as accurately as I can and cut them carefully, but when it comes time to assemble the project, the pieces never go together as tightly as they should — there's always a little gap here or there. Would investing in more accurate measuring tools help?

Don't take this answer the wrong way, but better measuring tools alone won't solve your dilemma.

You really need a completely different approach to woodworking. From your description of the way you work, you're trying to manufacture individual components to exacting tolerances, and then assemble them. That's a good way to build cars, but it's not really appropriate for the craftsperson building individual items, especially in wood. Even if you succeed in marking with absolute accuracy and then cut with zero tolerance, the material will betray you. Wood constantly changes size as it gains or loses moisture, so a part that's perfect one instant will be a different size in a few hours. In short, the quest for measured accuracy in woodworking is a doomed mission. Watch an experienced woodworker in his shop, and he's constantly cutting to fit, measuring as little as possible, and gauging the fit of one part against the next. Try this approach on your next project, and you'll probably get your best results ever.

MARK STUD LOCATIONS ON THE FLOOR TO SPARE THE WALL

 I'm going to install new base shoe molding after I paint the wall, but I hate to mar the fresh color coat with a pencil mark at every stud location. Besides, I'm painting the wall a dark color, so the pencil marks would barely show anyway. What's a good alternative?

Find the nailing locations with a stud finder, and put the marks on the floor with strips of masking tape. You could easily damage the fresh paint with ordinary masking tape — the adhesive might yank the color right off the wall. A low tack tape (see the varieties described on page 180) might work on the wall, but it's an unnecessary risk in this case.

If you're building a new wall, the best time to put the tape marks on the floor is after you finish the framing but before you hang the drywall. At that point, it's also a good idea to mark the location of every electrical box onto the floor. That eliminates the embarrassing problem of drywalling over an outlet or switch box and forgetting to cut its opening.

SHOW OFF YOUR SCRIBES

I've been practicing my hand-cut dovetails, and I am ready to build a chest of drawers. But I can't figure out the best way to remove the cross-grain lines I scribed with a cutting gauge. Should I plane or sand?

The best answer is: neither. Let the marks stand as evidence that you are serious enough about your craft to master a traditional technique. The scribe lines are a sign of craftsmanship, not a defect. Erasing them makes as much sense as trimming the grill marks off of a steak.

FINISH CARPENTER'S TRICK DRESSES UP QUARTER ROUNDS

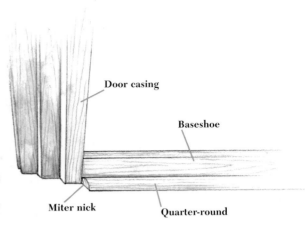

Door casing

Baseshoe

Miter nick

Quarter-round

 I decided to install new baseboards and quarter-round molding after we had our hardwood floors refinished. I did a trial run to see how it will look, and the baseboard fits fine against the door casing, but the end of the quarter round sticks way out. How can I make it look better?

Here's an old trim carpenter's trick: Miter a tiny nick out of the end of the quarter round so that its end matches the thickness of the door casing. You'll be surprised how this small cut will make a big improvement in the way that the trim looks. The quarter round will then visually make a smooth transition into the casing, eliminating the abrupt look you see now.

By the way, you'll save a lot of bending if you apply the finish to the trim before you install it. That way, you'll merely have to fill the nail holes with color putty. To conceal the raw wood exposed by the tiny miter cut in the quarter round, use a touch-up stain marker available in the paint section of your hardware store.

DIAGONAL DIVISION

 Whenever I need to divide a board into equal parts, my math almost always produces a nasty dimension like $1\,^{23}/_{64}$ in. If I try to multiply that a few times, and then find all those marks on a ruler, I'm pretty sure my brain will explode. I'm not sure my insurance will cover that sort of injury. Isn't there an easier way?

There's a really easy way. Let's say you have a board that's $6\,^5/_{16}$ in. wide, and you want to divide it into eight equal parts. Simply take your rule, and position it diagonally across the board with the "zero" end at one edge of the board and the 8 in. mark at the other edge. Make a dot at every even inch mark, then use a square to extend from each point to the end of the board.

If you want to divide the same board into five parts, you won't be able to use the 5 in. mark because that's narrower than the stock. So use the 10 in. point on your rule, and make a dot every 2 in.

LINING UP MITER CUTS

 Marking the line for an accurate cut is one thing, but how do I get my miter saw to cut right to the line I made on the wood?

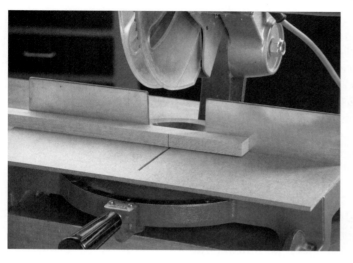

Use double-faced tape (sometimes called carpet tape) to attach a piece of scrap hardboard to the base of your miter saw. Then you'll see exactly where each side of the saw kerf will be when you make the cut. Instead of marking your cut line on the face of your stock, mark the edge so that you'll be able to position it exactly on the kerf in the hardboard.

If you own a miter saw with a fixed base, you'll be able to make square and miter cuts without the hardboard getting in the way. But if you have a saw where the cut line in the base moves when you change angles, you'll have to replace the hardboard when you shift.

Making a little scribble mark on the waste side of the stock is another good idea. That will help prevent the mistake of cutting to the wrong side of the line.

TRIANGULAR SOLUTION TO ACCURATE PARTS ASSEMBLY

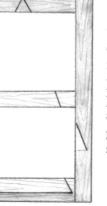

Whenever I lay out parts for assembly — whether for edge-gluing a tabletop or assembling a cabinet door — I get parts mixed up. I've tried lettering and numbering, but isn't there an easier system?

Triangle marks guide
tabletop glue-up

Marking a door
for easy assembly

The triangle marking system is time-tested, fast, and easy. And while it's not completely foolproof, it's highly nitwit-resistant. The basic concept is that every piece of an assembly gets a mark that's part of a triangle with its point at the top and the base at the bottom. The drawings give a couple of examples of how the system works.

SAVE YOUR BACK ON WEEKEND PROJECTS

 It's a good thing I have an office job, because a Saturday of cutting framing lumber wore me to a nub. By the end of the day, I could barely bend over to pick the circular saw off the ground for the umpteenth time. I don't figure I'm going to find the Fountain of Youth, so is there anything else I can do to save my back?

Picking a saw up off the ground all day made your weekend harder than it had to be. If you have a large worm-drive saw, simply rest its base against the leg of your sawhorse between cuts. If you use a smaller saw, make yourself an elevated platform to reduce the bending to a minimum. This platform can be as simple as an overturned five-gallon bucket or trash can — anything to limit the distance that you have to bend.

When you do need to reach down for something, try to keep your back straight and bend at the knees. The muscles in your legs are among the largest and strongest in your body. By contrast, bending at the waist puts tremendous strain on the relatively small and weak lower back muscles — that's why it's so easy to get a back strain.

If you have to hold a tool in your hand for any length of time, relax your elbow and let your arm hang straight down at your side. This is a much more relaxed position because it relieves stresses on the muscles and tendons in both your upper and lower arm.

ROUTER SOLUTION TO IDENTICAL CABINET OPENINGS

I'm building a home office, and I need to cut several 3-in.-dia. circular openings for wire-management grommets through the desktop. The cabinet I'm building needs holes for vents that are rectangular with rounded corners. I hate to shell out the money for a huge hole saw I'd probably never use again. I could possibly cut one neat hole with a jig saw, but doing it a number of times would be a pain. How else can I get neat results?

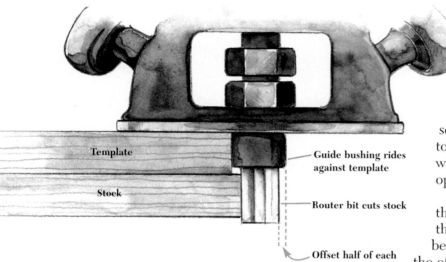

Template

Stock

Guide bushing rides against template

Router bit cuts stock

Offset half of each side of bit

By investing a few minutes into making router templates, you'll be able to quickly cut as many holes as you need, and all of them will be absolutely identical. Refer to the drawing, and you'll see how a guide bushing attached to your router's baseplate teams up with a straight bit to make an opening.

You'll notice that the diameter of the bushing is larger than the bit that fits inside it. The difference between the two diameters is called the offset. For example, if you have a ½-in. bushing and a ⅜-in. bit, the offset is ⅛ in. If you rout a circle, you'll have to add ⅛ in. to the diameter of the template. That results in a 3⅛-in. template to rout a 3-in. hole.

The same arithmetic applies to rectangular openings. For a 4- x 6-in. opening, make a 4⅛-x 6⅛-template.

Make the template from plywood that's slightly thicker than the length of the bushing's collar. Take some care in shaping the template because every little irregularity in it will be duplicated onto your workpiece. Making a test cut into scrap stock is a good idea. You may want to tape or clamp a piece of scrap wood under your stock so the waste you cut doesn't splinter the edge of the hole when it falls away.

To use the template, clamp it to your stock. If clamping is impractical, use double-faced cloth carpet tape. Don't overload your router — make the cut in several passes, advancing the bit ¼ in. between cuts. Or cut out most of the waste material with a jig saw first, then refine the cutout by routing with the template in place.

REPLACE TRIM THE PROFESSIONAL WAY

I'm replacing some window trim because of water damage. I can't figure out what the original trim carpenter did because no end grain shows on the stool, and the casing under the stool carries the front profile around the end. How do I duplicate this look so this window will match the others in the house?

The original carpenter created mitered returns on those pieces, and it's a sign of high-quality work. Once you learn how it's done, you'll be able to easily duplicate the look effortlessly. The drawing gives the easy three-step process, but there are a few other tips that will help you.

One of the most challenging steps is cutting the small returns with a power miter saw. Accuracy isn't the real culprit — it's that the saw blade sometimes sucks up the small piece and shatters it. If that happens to you, stop the cut right before the piece falls free. Break off the return, and shave away the stub with a utility knife.

To glue the return in place, brush a thin film of woodworker's glue on both parts, and rub them back and forth until the glue grabs. Wipe off any glue squeeze-out right away with a damp rag. For extra security, you can use masking tape to hold the return in place until the glue dries. After you remove the tape, use sandpaper in a block to bring the back of the return flush with the rear of the trim, if necessary.

You can easily apply the same technique to the stool and other molding profiles. The procedure for creating returns is the same, whether you're dealing with tiny quarter-round or massive crown molding.

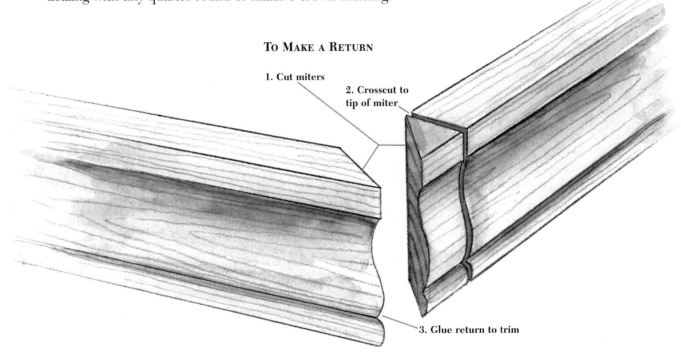

To Make a Return

1. Cut miters

2. Crosscut to tip of miter

3. Glue return to trim

TO MARK WOOD, REVISIT YOUR CHILDHOOD

How do I make assembly identification marks that are easy to see but simple to remove from lumber? Softwood dents when I write on it, and pencil marks are nearly invisible on dark woods like walnut.

Different woods present a variety of challenges, but here are some ideas that will help you cope with a wide range of materials. White chalk works great on mahogany, walnut, and other dark woods.

A black lumber-marking crayon is a good choice for lighter woods if planing or sanding steps will follow. To color-code a number of assemblies, buy a box of children's crayons.

For easily damaged softwoods, make the marks onto masking tape, and then stick strips of tape onto your stock. If you put the tape onto the stock first, avoid using a pencil or ballpoint pen because they could compress the wood fibers. Instead, choose a fine felt tip marker (Sanford's Sharpie is one brand). These markers come in a variety of colors, enabling you to color-code each door or other component for easy identification.

SUPPORT GROUP FOR MITER SAWS

Cutting long pieces of trim with a miter saw is a real hassle. I spend so much energy simply holding the stock in place that it's difficult to concentrate on lining up an accurate cut. I've seen miter saw stations that would solve the problem, but if I bought one I wouldn't have any money left to do woodworking. Is there some jig I could build?

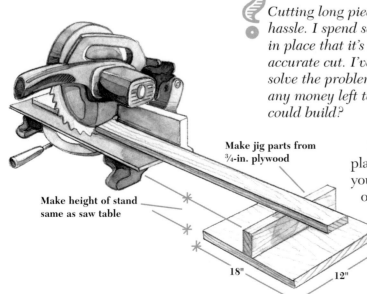

Make jig parts from ¾-in. plywood

Make height of stand same as saw table

18"

12"

Build a pair of the jigs shown in the drawing, place one on each side of your miter saw, and you'll be able to effortlessly support long runs of trim or lumber. In fact, the lengths you can go to are virtually unlimited. The jigs are easy to make from ¾-in. plywood that you simply glue and screw together. Take the jigs to the job site, and you'll simplify chores ranging from mitering door casing to building a deck.

FIND A PLACE FOR A FOLDING WOOD RULE

 I've never had much luck using a tape measure for measuring the distance between two fixed points, such as inside a box. It's only vaguely accurate at best. Isn't there a better way of measuring inside dimensions?

Buy a folding wood rule with a brass extension scale, and your troubles are over. Some people think that folding rules are a quaint relic from the days when carpenters used handsaws and carried metal lunch boxes. But several companies still make this tool because it remains incredibly useful.

Transfer rule to stock to be cut

Mark cut-line at end of slide extension

Using the rule is a snap. Unfold enough sections to nearly fit within the space you wish to measure, then extend the brass scale until it completes the end-to-end contact. The slide has enough friction built into its operation that it will hold its setting.

Now for the best part: you don't even have to read the measurement, you can simply use the rule as a gauge to mark the piece of lumber you want to cut. Put the wood end of the rule flush with the end of the board, and make a pencil mark at the end of the brass extension. It's easy and dead-on accurate.

FOR A BETTER FIT, WORK UPSIDE DOWN

 Whenever I miter the casing around a door, the last piece is always a real pain. I keep nibbling away at the miter to get a perfect fit at both the top and the floor, but it rarely comes out just right. All I want is better results faster. Is that possible?

Mark for the final square cut after you cut the miter. Then invert the final piece against the installed trim as shown in the drawing, and you'll get a great fit. To keep the miters tight, apply glue to the joints, and drive a 4d (1½-in.) nail downward though the long edge of the top piece across the joint and into its mate, which locks the joint. These pointers should give you exactly what you want — an improved fit in less time.

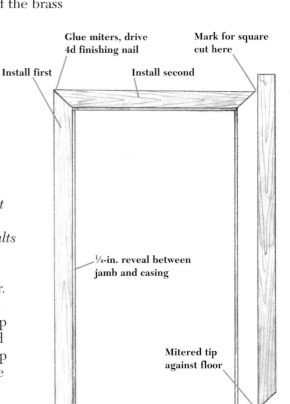

Glue miters, drive 4d finishing nail

Mark for square cut here

Install first

Install second

¼-in. reveal between jamb and casing

Mitered tip against floor

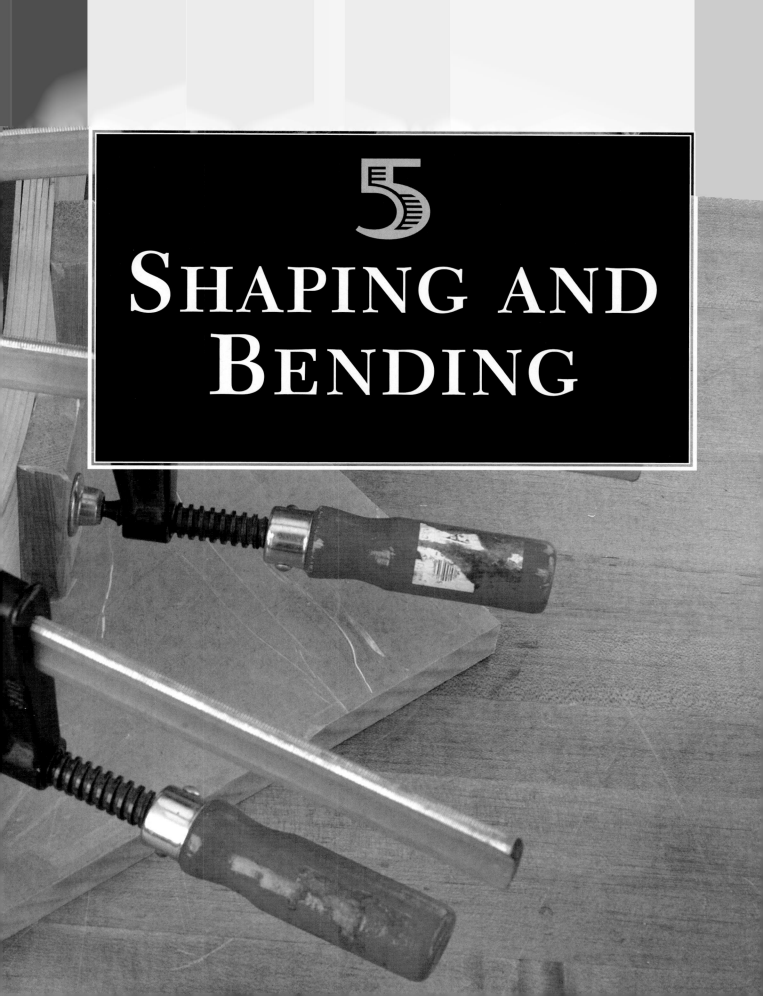

5
SHAPING AND BENDING

OUTFEED SHIMS ARE A GODSEND WITH SOME ROUTER PROFILES

 I want to put a bullnose profile along the edge of a straight board. How do I guide this cut?

Whenever you rout with a bit that shapes the entire face of a board, you need to compensate for the removed stock by shimming the outfeed (left) half of your router table's fence. The shim will support the stock after it leaves the bit.

Begin by chucking the bit into your table-mounted router and setting the height. Create a cutout in the fence for the bit, and position the fence as shown in the Step 1 drawing to control the bit's projection. When the thin metal rule touches the deepest part of the bullnose's curve, the rest of the rule should slightly rock between the right (infeed) half of the fence and the left (outfeed) half. Make a test cut along two inches of test stock as shown in the Step 2 drawing, and turn off the router. The gap between the cut edge and the outfeed half of the fence is the thickness of shim you'll need to add. The shim can be a piece of wood, metal, or plastic laminate that's attached with double-faced tape. (Don't forget to allow for the thickness of the tape.)

Fine-tune the thickness of the shim by adding strips of a durable tape, such as package sealing tape. Don't rely on masking tape because its rough surface makes it likely that the wood will snag on it instead of sliding.

STEP 1

Fence

Bullnose bit

Thin metal rule

**STEP 2
(TOP VIEW OF ROUTER TABLE)**

Fence

Left (outfeed) half | Right (infeed) half

Bit

Thickness of shim required

Stock

Feed

STEPPED TABLE-SAW CUTS SAVE SERIOUS CHANGE

 To make part of an apron for a table, I need to shape a sweeping curve along a piece of stock 1¾ in. thick. I can't find a cutter that will make the profile I want, but that's all right because I wouldn't be able to afford it anyway. How can I make this shape?

A series of stepped cuts at the table saw will get you very close to the desired shape, and you'll be able to quickly complete it with hand tools. For stability and ease of handling during the cuts, start with a wide piece of stock, and then rip the part to its final width later.

Mark the curve on the end of your stock as shown in the drawing, and set your rip fence for the first cut. Push the board over the blade, and check the results. If necessary, raise the blade slightly to come closer to the line. Needless to say, you don't want to overshoot the mark. Move the rip fence by the thickness of the blade, crank the blade slightly higher, and make the second cut. Continue making stepped cuts to remove the bulk of the waste.

Clamp the stock to your workbench, and remove the facets with a plane to smooth the curve. For the best results, make long planing strokes. Scrape or sand the wood to final smoothness.

This edge against rip fence

Rip to width after shaping

Raise table saw blade to remove waste

Waste

NAIL THE SOLUTION FOR STACKED SCROLL-SAW CUTS

 Whenever I stack-cut with my scroll saw, the double-faced tape between layers sometimes breaks delicate portions of the finished design as I try to separate the pieces. How can I detach the parts more easily?

When you stack up the pieces, drive brads or finishing nails into waste portions of the stock, as shown in the photo. A pneumatic (air-powered) driver makes this an easy task. Simply select fasteners that are slightly longer than half the thickness of the stack, and drive them from both the top and bottom. For example, if you're cutting six thicknesses of ⅛-in. plywood, the combined thickness will be about ¾ in., so ½-in. brads driven from both the top and bottom will secure the stack.

BAG YOUR BOWL BLANKS TO SLOW THE DRYING PROCESS

 I'm going to turn some bowls from fresh-cut wood after my neighbor cuts down a tree. How do I prevent the bowls from drying too rapidly and splitting?

Some people like to turn green bowls to a thin wall and live with the natural deformations that the wood assumes as it dries. But if you want a perfectly round shape, you'll have to do the turning in two stages.

First, rough out the bowl to its general shape, but leave the walls a consistent thickness — about 1 in. thick for a medium-size bowl of up to 10 in. in diameter. For larger bowls, increase the wall thickness.

Weigh the bowl on a scale, and write the date and weight onto the rough turning with a marking crayon. Double up two paper grocery sacks, and pack the bowl inside, completely filling and surrounding the bowl with its own shavings. The paper and shavings will help prevent uneven drying and abrupt moisture loss that can lead to cracks. Put the sack in a cool dark area, away from drafts and direct sunlight.

Now for the hard part: Wait two weeks. Unpack the bowl, weigh it, record the weight, and repack it. Repeat this process every week until the bowl's weight stabilizes. Now you can place the bowl on an open shelf but continue to shelter it from direct sunlight. Repeat the once-weekly weighing until there's no further change, and you can then turn the bowl to its final size.

The drying process can be unpredictable, and you must expect a certain number of failures. Keep a record of what works and what doesn't in a notebook — call it your logbook. Feel free to experiment with procedures that can improve results. For example, you may want to give a bowl a generous coat of paste wax before packing it in order to further slow the drying rate.

MDF Helps You Trim Dollars from Your Trim Budget

I have a newer house with generic interior trim, but I'm thinking of giving the dining room an elegant look with wide baseboards and fluted casings around the doors and windows. When I priced out this trim at the lumberyard, it blows my budget. Is there an affordable way to get the look I want?

If you like the look of painted trim, you can create impressive-looking moldings from inexpensive medium-density fiberboard (MDF). Used alone or in conjunction with standard molding profiles, you can create a truly custom look. Take a look at the drawing for one example of a baseboard that's easy to make.

MDF cuts cleanly at the table saw, and you can easily rout flutes, beads, and roundovers. MDF is widely available in ¾-in. thickness, but with a little searching you can also find it ½ in. thick. You'll need a good-quality primer because the material drinks up paint until the surface is sealed. A pneumatic (air-powered) nailer makes installation fast.

One drawback of MDF is that machining it produces clouds of powdery dust. Crank up your dust-collection system and wear a dust respirator.

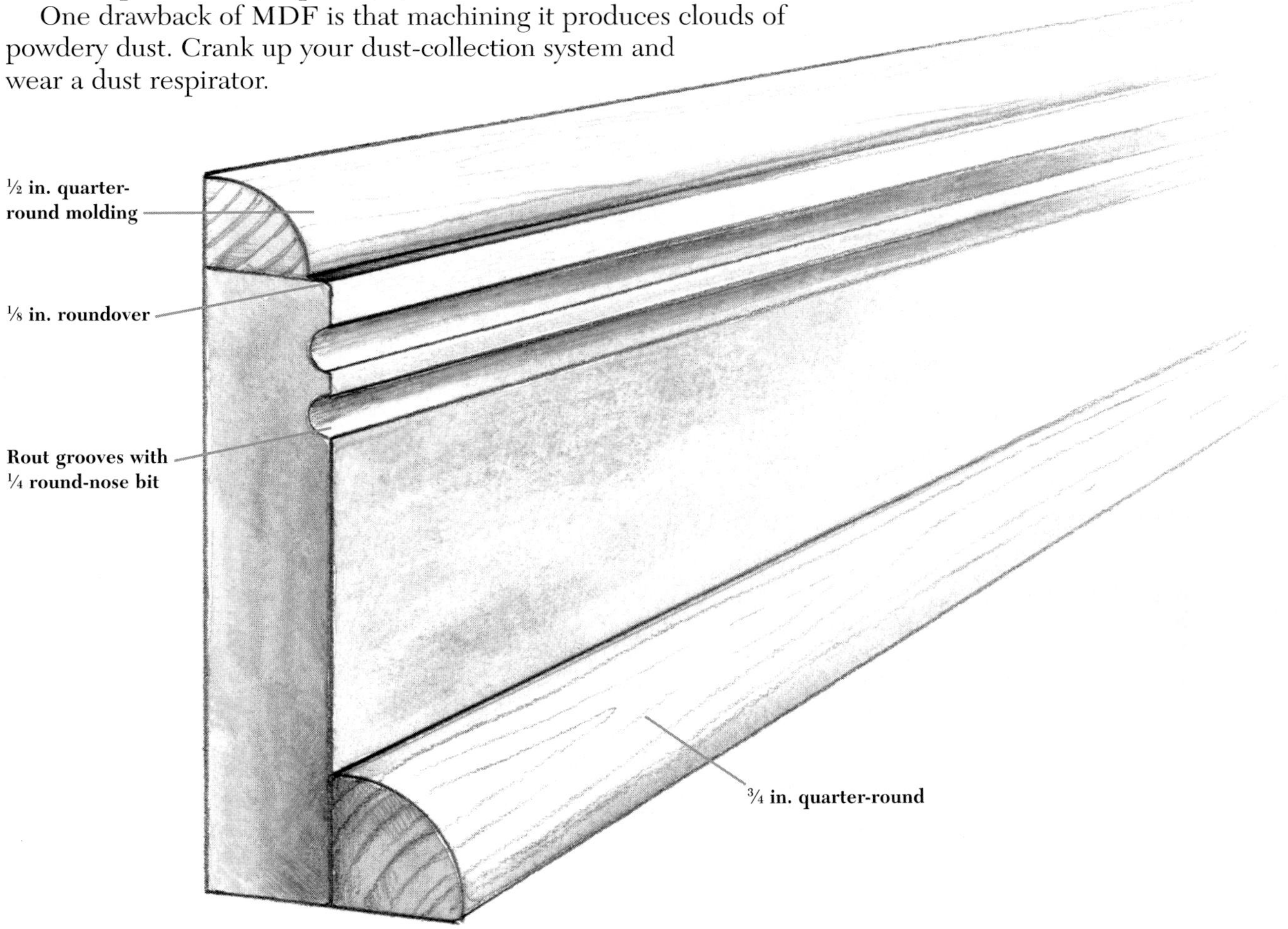

½ in. quarter-round molding

⅛ in. roundover

Rout grooves with ¼ round-nose bit

¾ in. quarter-round

THE UPS AND DOWNS OF SPIRAL FLUTES

 I was getting ready to order a new mortising bit for my router, and thought I would try a spiral flute design. But the catalog has up-spiral and down-spiral bits. Which one do I want?

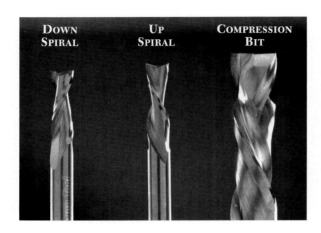

The spiral flute is an excellent choice because it continuously slices the wood fibers instead of chopping them as a straight bit does. The up-spiral design is usually the better choice for cutting mortises in solid wood because it efficiently ejects the chips from the cutting site. A down-spiral meets the demands of cutting through brittle manufactured materials, such as plastic laminate, and leaving a chip-free edge. A downside of the down-spiral is that you may need to stop the cut to blow out chips with compressed air.

If you need to leave an unblemished edge on both sides of a panel, choose a specialty cutter called a compression bit. Part of its length cuts downward, and part cuts upward. You can purchase this style of bit with a point to create its own starting hole when plunged through plywood, or with a bearing to template-rout edges of plywood or solid stock.

When you're shopping for up-spiral bits, don't overlook firms that supply metalworkers. A machinist's end mill, although originally designed for metal cutting, also performs well as a mortising bit.

A RULE FOR RULE JOINTS

 I'm making a rule joint on a drop-leaf table, but I can't figure out how to shape the roundover (beaded edge). By the time my bit cuts the full profile, the bearing will be off the edge of the wood. What's the solution?

Add a piece of scrap stock below the edge of the tabletop to create a bearing surface. As shown in the photo, this technique allows you to choose how large to make the fillet — the vertical flat above the roundover.

The procedure works whether the edge you're routing is straight or curved, and you can even go all around a workpiece.

BEHIND CLOSED DOORS, SHAVE FOR A GREAT FIT

 I've made a cabinet with a pair of inset doors that meet at the middle. I was able to get consistent ¹⁄₁₆-in. gaps all around the doors. But where the two door stiles meet, they rub against each other every time I open a door. How can I fix this problem?

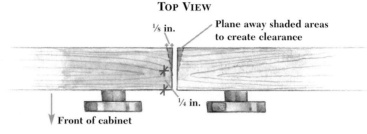

TOP VIEW

⅛ in.

Plane away shaded areas to create clearance

¼ in.

Front of cabinet

This clearance problem can occur with inset doors of all sizes, from cabinets to the front door of your home. Carefully check the architectural doors in your house, and you'll discover that the usual solution is beveling the entire latch edge of the door. But doing that with cabinet doors can be somewhat tricky because of the tight tolerances involved. It's all too easy to accidentally reduce the overall width of the doors, ruining the fit.

Try the approach shown in the drawing, and you'll make a clearance bevel without compromising the fit. To avoid the possibility of mistakes, mark the doors before removing them. You'll see that the taper starts ¼ in. from the front face of the door so that the door's front edge doesn't change.

If the taper suggested in the drawing doesn't fix the problem, take a few more shavings off each door and test the fit again.

THE BOTTOM LINE ON BOTTOMING ROUTER BITS

I read an article that says you're supposed to chuck as much of the bit as possible into your router, and the next article says you're not supposed to bottom out the bit. Which one is right?

In a way, both answers are correct because you should chuck as much shank length as possible without bottoming out the bit.

The reason is that the act of rotating the locking nut tends to move the shank slightly downward into the chuck. If the bit is already bottomed out, you'll have to exert more force to overcome that resistance. This can make the bit difficult to remove when you need to swap it for a different one.

When you insert a bit, push it in until it hits bottom, withdraw it about ⅛ in., and tighten.

CENTERING CUTS SIMPLIFIES DOOR CONSTRUCTION

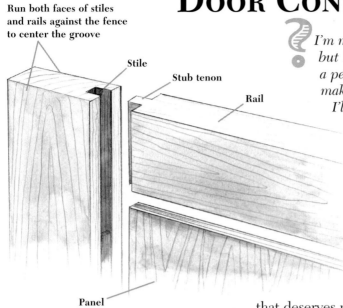

Run both faces of stiles and rails against the fence to center the groove

Stile

Stub tenon

Rail

Panel

I'm making some doors with stub tenons, but I've found out that it's easier to design a perfectly centered groove than to actually make it. If I can't center the groove, then I'll have to make tenons that are offset by the same amount. How do I get out of this nightmare?

Most people would never dream that the solution is as easy as running both faces of the rails and stiles against the fence of your table saw or router table. This simple procedure ensures that the groove is perfectly centered.

By the way, you made a good choice by selecting the stub tenon. It's a joint that deserves more respect. It's fast, has a neat appearance, and it's surprisingly strong with today's adhesives.

INSERT PLATE THE CULPRIT FOR ROUTER QUALITY

When I rout a profile onto a length of wood at my router table, I often get inconsistent results. The cut starts out fine, but then it goes shallow, and then the last few inches are fine again. What's going on?

A sagging insert plate probably causes your problem. At the start of the cut, your downward pressure on the stock forces it down into the trough, giving a satisfactory profile. But as soon as the board spans the depression, the cut becomes shallow, increasing only at the end when the board again dips downward.

The solution is relatively obvious — make or purchase a new insert plate. To prevent the new insert from suffering a similar fate, you need to take the weight of the router off the insert when you're not using it. A low-tech but effective way to eliminate stress is to put the idle router "up on blocks" as shown in the photo. Simply slide wood scraps under the router's body to elevate it.

Yes, ½-Inch Shanks Do Make a Difference

? *What's the big deal about router bits with ½-in. shanks? Are they really any better than the ones with ¼-in. shanks?*

The larger shank diameter provides an enormous advantage in reliability and strength. A quick review of basic geometry reveals why.

Doubling the diameter of the shank also doubles its circumference, so that means twice as much surface area where the shank meets the collet. That translates into double the holding power, so the bit is much less likely to shift or loosen.

But the real bonus is that doubling the diameter increases the cross-sectional area of the bit by a factor of four. You can see that in the end view photo of two bits that are identical except for shank size. (If you want to do the calculations yourself, the formula for the area of a circle is the radius squared times pi — approximately 3.14.)

The shear strength of a metal rod is proportional to its cross-sectional area, so a ½-in. shank has four times the strength of the ¼-in. size. That means a bit that's far less likely to deform or transfer vibration into the cutters. It will spin more smoothly, producing a cleaner cut.

A Gap-Avoidance Turning Strategy

? *When I combine turned pieces in a project, it seems that there is always a visible gap. How do I fix the fit?*

There are several areas you can check. First, examine the parting cuts at the ends of the pieces. If they are even slightly humped, you'll get a poor fit at the rim. To avoid this problem, always turn a small undercut on pieces that will be joined. In the drawing, the undercuts are exaggerated for clarity.

The second thing you can check is the depth of the hole for the tenon. Always make the hole at least ¹⁄₁₆ in. deeper than the length of the tenon to prevent the tenon from bottoming out before the joint fully closes. (This is a good practice with rectangular tenons, too.)

The third step you can take is cutting a pair of V-grooves along each tenon. Like the grooves in manufactured dowels, these channels allow trapped air and glue to escape. Otherwise, the powerful piston effect may prevent the joint from seating.

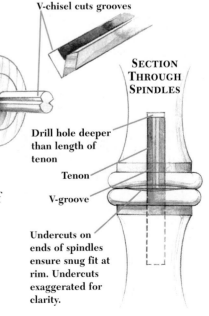

V-chisel cuts grooves

Section Through Spindles

Drill hole deeper than length of tenon

Tenon

V-groove

Undercuts on ends of spindles ensure snug fit at rim. Undercuts exaggerated for clarity.

ROUT YOUR OWN HARDWOOD DOWELS TO MATCH

Every so often, I need hardwood dowels. But when I get them by mail order, their color doesn't match the rest of the lumber for my project. Is there any way that I can make my own dowels? By the way, I don't have a lathe.

No lathe, no problem. Here's a method that will enable you to make dowels by using your router. Although the following example deals with a 1-in. dowel, you can easily adapt the idea to different sizes.

Begin by ripping a length of wood into a 1⅛-in. square rod. Chuck a ½-in. roundover bit into your table-mounted router, and set the fence so its face is flush with the rim of the bearing. You can verify this by holding a straightedge along the fence.

To round the central portion of the rod, run each edge along the router bit. As you can see in the photo, leaving a 1 in. flat at each end of the rod lets you register the stock to the table and fence. For the smoothest results, raise the bit in small steps until the center of the rod is round. Push blocks will help to keep your fingers away from the bit. Cut away the square ends and the transitional curves, and your dowel is complete.

To make dowels longer than your router table can handle, consider capping the table with a larger auxiliary top for more bearing support.

EASY STEPS FOR LATHE INLAYS

 At a gallery show, I saw a turned bowl that had an inlay around it. Is this a technique I can do in my own shop?

The pattern of the inlay banding makes it look complicated, but if you purchase the strip, you can sidestep all of that work. Actually inlaying the strip into your bowl is easier than you might think. Begin by selecting a relatively flat portion on your bowl, and cut a groove that matches the width of the banding with a sharp parting tool. The banding may not be absolutely uniform in width, so it's a good idea to check the fit at several spots along the strip. The depth of the groove should be just slightly less than the thickness of the inlay so you can sand it flush after installation. A difference of $1/64$ in. or so is plenty.

Brush a thin coat of glue onto the bottom and walls of the groove, and press the banding firmly into the groove with your fingers or a wood block. A strip of masking tape across the banding near the starting point will keep it from slipping in the groove as you press it into place.

When you get back to the beginning, overlap the inlay strip onto itself, and push a sharp chisel through both layers of banding to create a perfectly flush joint. Remove the scrap you just trimmed from the beginning of the groove to make room for the other cut end. Add a strip of masking tape across the completed joint.

Give the glue a day or two to completely cure before sanding the inlay flush with the surface of the bowl.

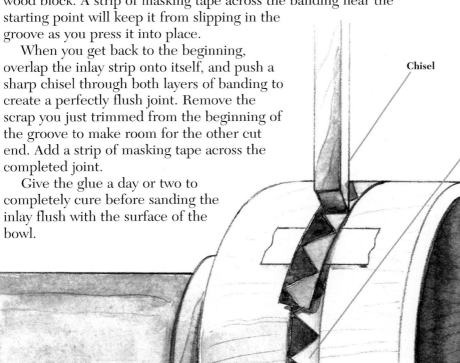

Chisel

Inlay band

INLAY SCROLL-SAW WORK
JUST A MATTER OF DEGREES

To make a cabinet really special, I would like to inlay a scroll-sawn design into the door panel. I know it can be done, but I'm not sure about the technique. What's the setup?

The secret behind this technique is simultaneously cutting two layers of contrasting wood at an angle so the inlay seamlessly seats itself into the ground like a tapered plug.

Surface two pieces of wood to identical thickness, stack them face to face, and tape them securely along their edges and ends. The piece on top will be the inlay, and the bottom piece is the ground.

Two pieces of scrap from these panels will help you determine the correct tilt angle for your scroll saw. The thickness of the stock determines the angle, and the easiest way to find it is with a few test cuts. Tilt the table about 2 degrees, and make a test cut. Remove the scrap from the ground, and test-fit the inlay as shown in the photo.

If the surface of the inlay goes past the surface of the ground, add more tilt to the table, and try again. If the inlay stops before it is flush, you've set the table at too steep an angle. Subtract some tilt, and try again.

The amount of adjustment required is usually quite small, so make your correction in tiny steps. When the inlay fits perfectly, drill an angled starter hole with a 1/16-in. bit through the stacked stock. The hole should tilt in the same direction as the blade.

Insert your blade through the hole, and carefully cut the stock, avoiding side pressure on the blade. Apply glue to the perimeter of the cut in the ground, and press the inlay flush. After the glue dries, sand the surface of the inlaid panel.

EVEN A LOWLY RASP DESERVES SOME MAINTENANCE

 How often should I clean a file or rasp, and what's the best way to do that?

The right tool for this cleaning job is called a file card, a set of stiff wire bristles attached to a wood handle. As shown in the photo, you simply hold the card so its angle matches the rows of the teeth, and pull it across the file. Some file cards include a stiff fiber brush on the other side of the handle.

It's always important to clean wood particles from files and rasps before storage because the wood can hold moisture that can promote rusting.

Rub the clean teeth of files and rasps with chalk, and particles will be less likely to stick, extending the time between cleanings.

ROUTER SPEED CONTROL CRITICAL WITH MONSTER BITS

 I'd like to try one of those big panel-raising bits in my router, but frankly I'm a bit skeptical about spinning that large a chunk of metal at such high speed. Is there any way to slow it down?

This is a job for a router speed control or switching to a variable-speed router. By dialing the speed downward, you'll bring the cutter's pace into a safer operating range while still retaining the power required to make the cut. If you buy a speed control, make sure the unit you purchase is compatible with your router's horsepower and amperage ratings. Unfortunately, some speed controls don't work with routers that have a "soft-start" feature.

Never try to use a huge bit like this freehand — always chuck it into a table-mounted router.

FACTS ON FILES

Can I smooth wood with a file? Do I want a single-cut or double-cut file?

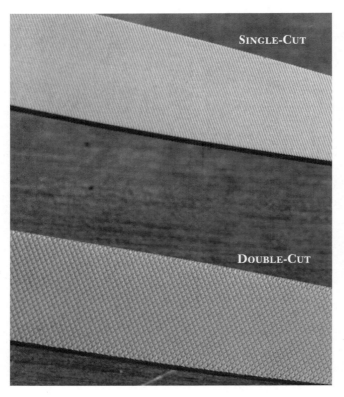

SINGLE-CUT

DOUBLE-CUT

In a single-cut file (top), each row is an individual tooth that extends from one side of the file to the other and functions like a wide chisel. A double-cut file gets its name from the fact that it has an intersecting cut that divides the wide tooth into a series of individual points. The photo makes the difference between the two types very clear.

The double-cut file (bottom), will remove stock more quickly, but it doesn't leave as smooth a surface as the single-cut file.

In addition to choosing between single- and double-cut, you also need to select the spacing between the teeth. The six main categories are: rough, coarse, bastard, second-cut, smooth, and dead smooth. To further complicate matters, the spacing varies with length. For example, a rough cut on a small file may be equivalent to a second-cut on a large file. When you shop for a file, pay more attention to the tooth spacing you see than to the name designation you read.

A LESSON ON STEAM AND BOILING WATER

Some articles on wood bending advocate a steam box, and others suggest boiling water. Which one is better?

Both methods can make wood flexible enough to bend, and each one has its advantages and drawbacks. Steam is hotter than the boiling temperature of water, so it will plasticize the wood more quickly. On the negative side, however, the higher temperature makes steam more dangerous to work with.

A steam box can easily accommodate strips longer than you could conveniently immerse in water. But when you want to bend only a portion of a workpiece — the upturned nose of a toboggan, for example — boiling water is a superior solution.

WASHER-SCRIBING FOR WAVY WALLS

 I want to attach a long shelf to the wall, and it's low enough that everyone will be able to see the uneven gaps between the straight back edge of the shelf and the waves in the wall. How can I get a tight fit?

Getting a great fit isn't difficult if you use a methodical approach to scribe the shelf to the wall. In this process, you'll cut away the back edge of the shelf to make its shape match the wall.

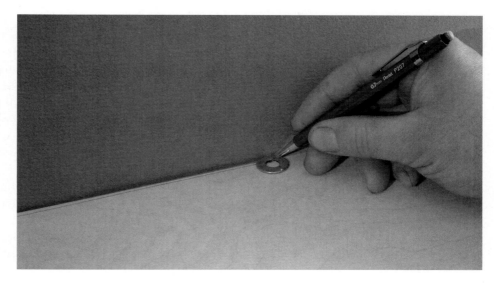

Begin by positioning the shelf, and make registration marks on both the wall and shelf so that you'll be able to replace it in exactly that same position later. Next, place a flat washer on the shelf, hold a mechanical pencil vertical inside the opening, and draw it along the wall as shown in the photo. If you don't get an unbroken line because the pencil's tip falls off the back edge, switch to a larger washer, and mark again.

The next step is to remove the waste at the back of the shelf. If there is a considerable amount to eliminate, cut away the bulk of it with a band saw or jig saw. Complete the stock removal with a belt sander held a few degrees past vertical to create the back bevel shown in the drawing. The clearance at the bottom of the shelf will help ensure a tight fit at the top.

Wall

Back bevel at bottom ensures tight fit at top.

DOUBLE-CHECK MOISTURE BEFORE DOUBLING YOUR LAMINATIONS

 I want to do a bent laminated assembly that has a strip of a contrasting wood in the middle. Is there anything special I need to consider when I'm choosing the woods?

There are several things for you to think about, but probably the two most important are the moisture content of the wood and the bending characteristics of the two species.

A moisture meter (about $140) can help you ensure that the two pieces of lumber have similar moisture contents and are within the moisture content range specified by the glue manufacturer. If you don't have a meter, place both boards in your shop for an acclimation period of a week or two. (This is probably a good idea even if you do have a meter.)

You'll also want to ensure that a strip from each species will curve to the bending form without splitting. Checking that is as easy as ripping some test strips and flexing them onto the form. If the strip splits, cut another one that's thinner and try again.

START INSIDE AND WORK OUTSIDE WITH SCROLL-SAW CUTS

 When I cut a design with the scroll saw, do I cut the perimeter of the shape or the inside cuts first?

There are several good reasons why you should begin with the internal cutouts — you'll have more material to grasp as you guide the board, and you prevent possible damage to the perimeter if it accidentally makes contact with the saw's arm.

Another reason is more psychological than practical. It's a better feeling of accomplishment to complete the project by slicing the outline than by removing the last, small internal piece.

SUCCESS IS AROUND THE BEND WITH LAMINATIONS

 *I've never done a bent lamination before. What are the basic steps?*

The first step is to design and build a bending form. One of its key qualities is that its curve must be tighter than the desired final line of the laminated part to allow for springback after it's released from the form. That raises the question of how much tighter, and that's difficult to answer. It depends on a variety of factors, including the thickness of the individual strips and the strength of the adhesive. The only way to know for sure is to do a test assembly. It also helps if your furniture design can accommodate some leeway. For example, if you're gluing chair leg assemblies, the ability to tolerate an angle of 93 degrees instead of a perfect right angle will increase the size of your success target.

The form should have provisions for easily attaching clamps — holes sized to fit your clamps is a good solution. If possible, use clamping blocks to distribute the pressure. Apply a couple coats of finish to the bending form, and also add a coat of paste wax to ensure that the glue-up won't accidentally bond to the form.

Glue selection is an important factor, so please refer to the chart on page 143 for advice. You'll want an adhesive that provides a long open time to complete the assembly plus a resistance to creeping. You could select ordinary yellow woodworking glue or even white glue for simple assemblies that you can clamp quickly. But also take a look at the structurally

sound bonds you can achieve with a urea-formaldehyde adhesive. As you'll quickly discover, this is a formulation you want to use in a well-ventilated area.

A rehearsal of the procedure, doing everything but applying glue, will alert you to any potential problems. If possible, recruit another pair of hands to help ensure that you'll be able to complete the assembly before the glue grabs.

THE KEYS TO ROUTING DOVETAIL KEYS

 I want to inlay some dovetail keys into a tabletop as both a functional and decorative element. How can I easily do it?

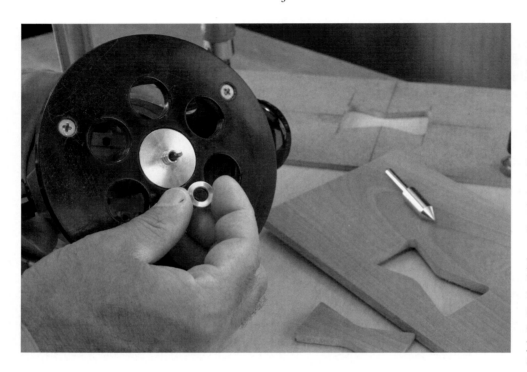

Purchase a router inlay kit, and you'll take a big shortcut from the traditional scribe-and-fit method. You'll also need a template that's used to shape both the recess and the inlay.

You can purchase templates in a few standard shapes, but it's easy to make your own from sturdy ¼-in. stock. You can get by with hardboard for a short-lived pattern, but sheet plastic is much more wear-resistant. The outer guide bushing has a ⁵⁄₁₆-in. diameter, so your pattern must accommodate that size all around. It also means that the outside corners of the inlay cannot be sharper than a ⁹⁄₃₂-in. radius. Inside corners will have a minimum radius of ¹⁄₁₆-in. because of the ⅛-in. bit. When you make the template, you can cut the corners to a point; the bushings will automatically produce the radii.

Be certain to make the template large enough so you can easily clamp it to your workpieces and have enough clearance for the router.

Loosely install the threaded bushing and nut onto your router's baseplate, and chuck the centering tool into your plunge router. Poke the centering tool through the hole in the bushing, and tighten the nut. Some inexpensive inlay kits omit the centering tool, but without it you may have a tough time ensuring that the bushing and the bit have the same centerpoint. And if there's any offset, you'll get an inlay that fits sloppily or not at all.

Replace the centering tool with the ⅛-in. carbide bit, and set the depth of cut to match the thickness of the inlay stock. Don't forget to allow for the thickness of the template itself when you lock in this setting.

With the template clamped to the workpiece and with the ring snapped or screwed onto the nose of the bushing, rout clockwise around the perimeter. The down-spiral bit (see page 86) produces a clean edge. Then clean out the waste in the central portion of the design. If you're doing a large scale inlay, you'll save time by using a second router equipped with a bigger bit to clear the recess.

Remove the ring from the bushing's nose, and clamp the template above the inlay stock. It's a good idea to secure the inlay material to a scrap substrate with double-face tape. That will prevent possible damage to the inlay when it's cut free. With the bushing's nose against the edge of the template, plunge down into the inlay, and rout clockwise around the pattern.

If the inlay is too tight, sand a slight bevel along its leading edge to ease its entry into the recess. Be careful with your test-fitting — once it's too small you'll have to cut a new one.

TAKE A CLOSER LOOK AT RASP DIFFERENCES

 What's the difference between a rasp and cabinetmaker's rasp — besides the fancy price tag for the second one?

A common wood rasp has teeth that are aligned in straight rows, while the teeth on the cabinetmaker's version has its teeth raised in a random fashion. The difference between the two is easy to see in the side-by-side close-up photo.

When you use a common rasp, it can leave furrows in the wood that require a considerable amount of work to remove. As a result of its non-pattern, the cabinetmaker's rasp leaves a smoother surface.

If you want to extend the life of your cabinetmaker's rasp, you can do the bulk of the stock removal with an ordinary rasp, and save your more expensive one for the final shaping. Of course, you'll increase the longevity of any file by making sure it doesn't clunk against other metal tools and by brushing the teeth clean after use (see page 93 for file-cleaning tips).

6
CUTTING
JOINTS

THE LONG AND SHORT OF GLUING STRENGTH

I read an article on woodworking joints that made a big deal out of end-grain and long-grain surfaces, but it didn't explain why this was so important. How does this figure into my thinking when I'm choosing which joint to select for a project?

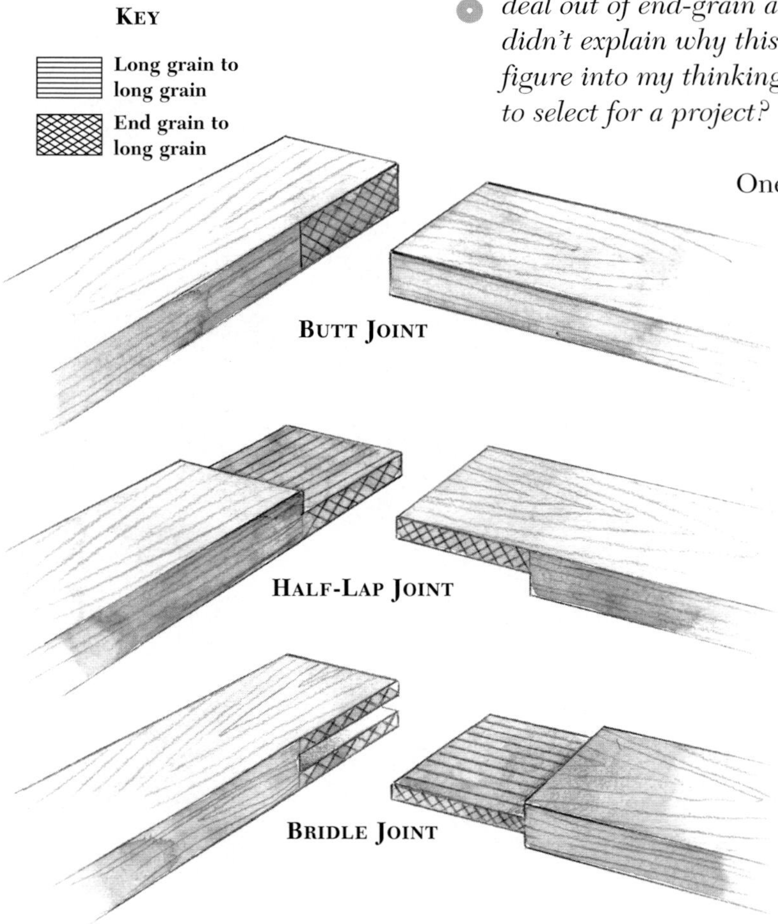

BUTT JOINT

HALF-LAP JOINT

BRIDLE JOINT

One fundamental consideration that underlies the design of a woodworking joint is structural. A dovetail joint, for example, will hold wood together even if the glue fails. The other main consideration is the amount of glue surface in the joint, especially long-grain to long-grain surface.

That's important because glue makes an excellent bond between long-grain surfaces, but a weak bond when one or both of the surfaces is end grain. Look at the joints in the drawing, and you'll see how the design of a joint influences the amount of end-grain to long-grain contact, as well as the overall amount of glue area.

To illustrate this concept with an example, consider making each joint with two boards that each measure $3/4$ x 3 in. The chart below summarizes the results:

Joint	End-Grain Area	Long-Grain Area	Total Joint Area	Percent Long Grain
Butt	$2^1/4$ sq. in.	-0-	$2^1/4$ sq. in.	-0-
Half-lap	$2^1/4$ sq. in.	9 sq. in.	$11^1/4$ sq. in.	80%
Bridle	$2^1/4$ sq. in.	18 sq. in.	$20^1/4$ sq. in.	89%

The butt joint is the weakest in three categories, having the smallest total joint, no long-grain gluing surface, and therefore a zero percentage of long-grain gluing area. The half-lap is better, with a substantial long-grain area and a respectable percentage of long-grain surface to the total joint area. But of these three, the bridle joint is clearly the winner. It has double the long-grain gluing area of the half-lap joint and a higher long-grain percentage.

BISCUITS ARE YOUR FRIENDS FOR CABINET FACES

 When I glue the face frame to a cabinet, do I need biscuits or screws to reinforce the joint? Should I consider that plywood is a good long-grain glue surface or a weak end-grain surface?

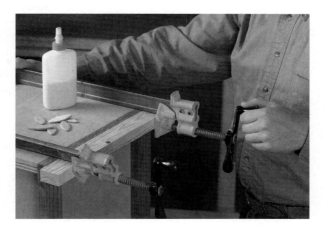

The edge of plywood presents alternating layers of long grain and short grain, so gluing solid wood to ¾-in. plywood is more or less equivalent to a joint with a ⅜-in. thickness of solid wood. Actually it's more than that because the end-grain surface has more than zero holding power. So you could rely on a glue-only joint, but there are other good reasons why you should consider adding biscuits or pockethole screws.

In this example, biscuits will be helpful for alignment during glue-up. Assembling and squaring even a medium-size cabinet can quickly turn into a wrestling match, so don't be shy about taking any advantage that will help you subdue your opponent. You might also consider using pockethole screws in conjunction with the glue assembly. As soon you drive the pockethole screws, you can remove the clamps, freeing them to help you assemble the next cabinet.

APPRECIATING HAUNCHED TENONS

 I saw plans for a chair that recommends haunched tenons to join the aprons to the legs. What's the purpose of the haunch?

The haunch provides some structural support to the joint, helping the apron resist twisting forces. The haunch is easy to cut — you form a tenon with shoulders on both sides and the bottom. Then, you simply measure and mark the waste at the top of the tenon.

If you're making only a few haunched tenons, it's easy to remove the waste with a handsaw or band saw. But if you're making a roomful of chairs, it would be worth your while to create a setup with a dado blade at your table saw.

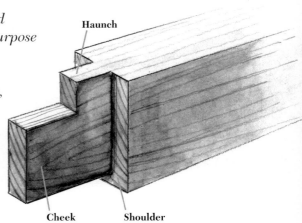

Haunch

Cheek   Shoulder

TRY SOME NEW JOINERY

I saw plans in a magazine for a project I'd like to build, but I've never made the type of joint they suggest. What risks do I run by switching to a joint that I'm confident in making?

From a strictly functional perspective, there is rarely one perfect joint for a particular application, so the piece of furniture probably won't fall apart if you alter the joinery. However, the style of the project may dictate the vocabulary of joints.

For example, Arts and Crafts furniture often includes through-tenons, and if you change that joint to something different, you'll compromise the stylistic integrity of the piece.

A well-made joint, even if it is relatively simple, will usually be stronger than a sloppily made complex joint. So you might want to stick with joints you already know how to build.

But on the other hand, part of the fun of woodworking lies in experimenting with new techniques and challenging yourself to learn something different. Grab some scrap lumber, and try your hand at actually making the new joint before you make your final decision.

TINY ERRORS ADD UP QUICKLY WITH MITERED CORNERS

 Whenever I make a box with mitered sides, I can get three tight joints, but the last one doesn't want to go together snugly. What can I do to fix this corner?

It's not really about fixing one corner — you have to make a tiny adjustment in every miter cut for a tight fit. In a four-sided mitered box, you need to make eight precise cuts to get a perfect fit, so even a tiny inaccuracy is multiplied eight times. Trying to see a small error in a single cut is extremely difficult, but making a quick test box from scrap stock will clearly show you the path to the correct angle.

After making your series of test cuts, align the pieces along a straightedge, and tape them together. Roll up the box, and you'll see that three corners automatically close. If the fourth one is also closed, you've hit the perfect angle on your first try. After you recover from your astonishment, make the cuts in your good stock.

But it's more likely that you'll see one of the two conditions in the drawings. Whether you need to increase or decrease the angle, remember that the misalignment you see in the final corner is the result of eight angles, so make your correction in extremely small steps.

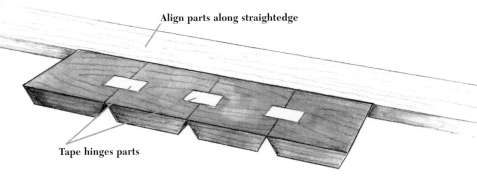

Align parts along straightedge

Tape hinges parts

Untape the test pieces, recut the angles, and again examine the results until you have the precisely cut angle. Save this test piece and use it as a reference for setting blade angles the next time you need to cut a perfect miter.

One other tip — if you're making a mitered assembly that will only be seen from the outside, you can allow yourself a slight gap on the inside of the final corner. This will help ensure four crisp outside corners.

Need to increase cut angle

Need to decrease cut angle

DEGREES OF PRECISION

I'm making an octagon frame for a clock, and to get a perfect fit, I'll need to make 16 cuts at exactly 22½ degrees. How can I hit that level of accuracy?

TOP VIEW OF TABLE SAW

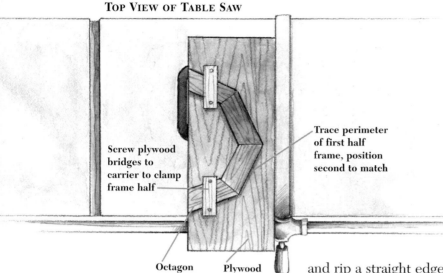

Screw plywood bridges to carrier to clamp frame half

Trace perimeter of first half frame, position second to match

Octagon frame half

Plywood carrier

When accuracy is hard to achieve honestly, it's time to cheat. In this case, the solution is to glue up two half frames, then trim them to exactly the same size. This procedure creates a straight line across the frame that will ensure easy assembly. Mark the cut lines on the two unglued ends of each frame half, but leave them long.

Referring to the drawing, make some plywood bridges to serve as clamps to hold the half frame to the carrier, and rip a straight edge along a plywood carrier that will comfortably hold a half frame. Don't move the rip fence after you make that cut.

Carefully align the cut lines of the half frame with the straight edge of the carrier, clamp your stock in place, and make your cut. Before you unclamp the frame half, trace its perimeter onto the carrier with a pencil. This will enable you to quickly position the second frame half.

COPING WITH GOOD CUTS

Whenever I run base molding around rooms, I do fine with the right-hand coped cuts, and that's probably because I'm right-handed. But when I need to do a cope on the left end of the stock, I feel completely uncoordinated. At times like that, I'd give my right arm to be ambidextrous. How can I make these cuts successfully?

If you plan your work correctly, you should be able to almost completely avoid left copes. In your case, work around the room or closet from right to left, and you'll always cut the cope on the right end of the stock. The first cut you make should be a cope cut, so the last cut is a butted end that fits underneath the first cope. Southpaws would simply work in the opposite direction to consistently cut left copes.

FLAT SAWBLADES MAKE BEAUTIFUL SPLINE SLOTS

 When I cut spline slots with my table saw blade, the bottom of the cut isn't flat, so the spline can't completely fill it. How can I correct that?

Your problem is caused by a grinding pattern called alternate top bevel (ATB) that's commonly used on circular saw blades called "combination" blades, designed for both rip and crosscutting. Although you might be able to track down an off-the-shelf answer to your quest for a flat-bottomed cut, you'll get quicker results by going to a sharpening shop and having a blade custom-ground.

Don't let the thought of requesting a special service scare you, because an experienced shop should be able to suggest a blade that can be easily modified and quickly handle the job without any exorbitant charges. Call several shops, if possible, to find the best service at a reasonable price. Reserve the blade for the sole task of cutting splines, and it will last a long time.

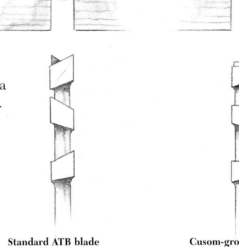

Standard ATB blade produces cut with "ears"

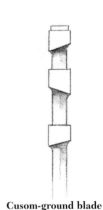

Cusom-ground blade cuts flat-bottomed kerf

GO ACROSS THE GRAIN WITH SPLINES

 I can never remember whether the grain of a spline should go across the joint or parallel with it. What's the rule?

The grain of the spline always goes across the grain of the parts being joined. A simple test with a piece of veneer will dramatically demonstrate why. If you hold onto edges of the veneer and pull, it's easy to tear or split it down the length of the grain. But if you hold veneer along the grain and pull, all you're going to do is make yourself tired.

Another way to remember: Martial artists can easily split wood along the grain, but they prudently stay away from cross-grain attempts.

FIND PERFECTION WITH EDGE-TO-EDGE JOINTS

 How can I get edge-to-edge joints that fit perfectly?

Whether you prepare edge joints with a hand plane, a jointer, or straight from your table saw's blade, here's a technique that will give you seamless results, even if the angle isn't precisely 90 degrees.

When you plane boards by hand, clamp them face to face as shown in the photo, and plane them at the same time. After you plane, unfold the boards as if there's an imaginary hinge at the planed edges. The angles on the two boards will be complementary, meaning that the two of them add up to 180 degrees. For example, if one angle is 88 degrees the other one will be 92 degrees, ensuring a tight fit.

To get the same result at your jointer, run alternating board faces along the fence. With a table saw, run one board face up and the next one face down.

By repeating the process, you can edge-join as many boards as you require.

COPING WITH NEW BASE SHOES

 I'm going to replace the base shoe molding in a room. A friend suggested that I should cope the joints instead of simply mitering them. Is there any good reason for going to that extra work?

When you cope a corner, you'll produce a joint that automatically adjusts to out-of-square inside corners and accommodates future movement. Mitering would be acceptable if every corner of your home were exactly square and none of your house's parts would ever shift or settle in the future. But if your home is like virtually every other house on the planet, there's not a square corner in it.

The coped corner consists of a piece of molding that is butted into the corner, and the other piece has the profile of the molding cut into its end. Accomplishing that is easier than you may think. Begin by making a miter cut along the end of the molding. Now all you have to do is cut along the edge of the mitered line. If you're working with unfinished molding, you can make the line more visible by dragging the side of a pencil point along it. Clamp the molding firmly to your work table.

Make the straight portion of the cut with a fine backsaw, and the curved portion with a coping saw. Although you can make both cuts with the coping saw, it's difficult to make the long cut straight with the short blade of the coping saw. Switching saws is quicker than touching up a wavy cut.

With both cuts, back-cutting at an angle, as shown in the drawing, helps ensure a tight fit at the face of the joint. You can easily refine the cut profile with a sharp utility knife or a rattail file.

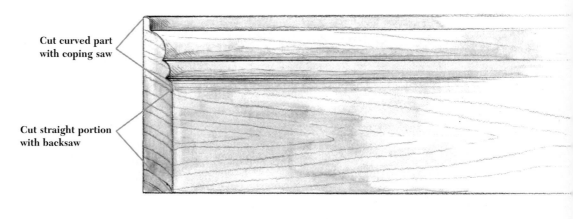

Cut curved part with coping saw

Cut straight portion with backsaw

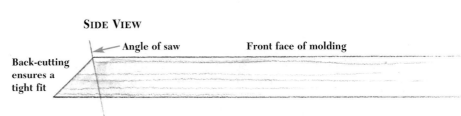

SIDE VIEW

Angle of saw

Front face of molding

Back-cutting ensures a tight fit

AN ADVANCED DEGREE IN MITERED CORNERS

 As a variation from the usual rectangular boxes I make, I was considering making some with an unusual number of sides, such as five or nine. How do I figure the angles to cut at the end of each piece?

Assuming that you're dealing with sides of equal length, here's the formula: multiply the number of sides by two, and then divide that number into 360 to determine the angle of each cut. For a five-sided box, for example, you divide 360 by 10, resulting in a cut of 36 degrees at the end of each side.

This information is also handy for staves for cylinders or for "tile" construction of bowls. You'll save a lot of money compared to purchasing solid wood blanks, and you have the option of combining different species of lumber to expore that decorative effect

By the way, here's why the formula works. Multiplying the number of sides by two gives you the number of joints, and 360 degrees represents the total of all angles in a closed figure.

Number of sides	3	4	5	6	7	8	9	10
Angle of end cut	60	45	36	30	25.7*	22.5	20	18

*rounded to nearest $^1/_{10}$ degree; all other angles are exact

A HANDSAW TIP GRANDPA NEVER TOLD YOU

 Whenever I make a freehand cut, my careful layout work is wasted because the saw chooses its own starting point, and that's seldom where I had planned it. How can I gain control over the saw?

Make a starting place for the saw blade with a utility knife. Hold the knife at a 45-degree angle to the corner of the board's edge, then push into the wood to make a cut at the edge of the line. Now hold the knife at the opposite angle, and slice toward the first cut to remove a chip. Start the blade at the base of this chip, and your cut will be right on target.

Eye-Appealing Joints, Courtesy of Veneer

I've seen jewelry boxes where it looks like the maker inserted strips of veneer into the mitered corners. Does this have any real strength, or is it simply decorative?

Using a contrasting species of veneer and angling the cuts can make spline joint eye-appealing, but it's also surprisingly strong. A good deal of the strength comes by adding a long-grain gluing area to the joint.

Making the slots for the veneer splines is as simple as using a fine-toothed saw to cut down to depth lines marked with strips of tape on the sides of the box, as shown in the Step 1 photo. Clamping the box with a corner pointing straight up as shown makes the cutting easy. If you've never attempted this before, you may want to experiment with a piece of scrap first to shore up your courage.

If your saw blade is slightly thinner than the veneer, don't worry. Simply put the veneer on a steel surface and give it a few taps with your hammer to compress it slightly. When the glue absorbs into it, the veneer will expand for a snug fit.

Cut all your strips to size, and work the glue into a slot with a thin metal blade (an artist's palette knife works great). Quickly slide a veneer strip into position, as shown in the Step 2 photo. As you probably already figured out, you can't apply the glue to the veneer because it will quickly expand wider than the slot.

After the glue dries, remove the tape, trim the veneer splines with a flush-cutting saw, and sand inward from the corners to avoid splitting the veneer.

STEP 1

STEP 2

MIRROR-IMAGE BOOKCASE SIDES

I'm making a bookcase where some of the shelves will be housed in dadoes, and the others will be adjustable. How do I make sure that the sides turn out identically?

A slight clarification: You actually need sides that are accurate mirror images of each other, not identical. That can be a real challenge. One way to avoid mistakes is to put the back edges of the sides next to each other, as shown in the photo.

Clamp a straightedge to the sides, and rout dadoes — through or stopped — across both sides at once. That way, the dadoes are guaranteed to line up.

FIVE WAYS TO IMPROVE PICTURE FRAME CORNERS

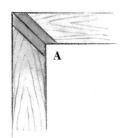

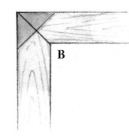

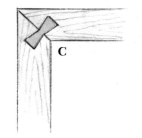

How can I reinforce the mitered corners in a batch of picture frames I'm going to make?

There are several great ways to do that: You can cut a spline slot in the ends of both mitered pieces before assembly (A), or after assembly (B). (See the jig in Chapter 10, page 206, that helps you cut the spline slots after assembly.) A dovetail key (page 98) is really just a shaped spline (C), and it inserts diagonally across an assembled joint to add both strength and decoration. You can drill holes through an assembled joint, and glue in dowels to reinforce the miter (D). With a plate joiner, you can insert a completely concealed biscuit (E) into the joint at assembly. If you choose wide, flat molding for the frame, you can drive pockethole screws across the joint. And don't forget about finishing nails — they may seem like a low-tech reinforcement method, but they are still effective. Drill pilot holes for the nails so they they won't shift the joint or split the wood when you hammer them.

TWO OPTIONS BEAT MORTISE AND TENON JOINTS

 I'm planning to build a set of kitchen cabinets using traditional face-frame construction. But the thought of making all those mortise and tenon joints in the frames is really dampening my enthusiasm. What's an easier joint?

You're making the project more complicated than it needs to be. The mortise and tenon is an excellent joint for structural applications, such as joining aprons to table legs or rails to chair legs. But with a face frame, you really don't need that much strength. Consider using pockethole screws or biscuits instead. Both of these methods allow you to immediately cut face-frame pieces to finished length instead of adding the allowance for the tenon. Either fastening method is also faster to make and install than mortise and tenon joints.

SPARE THE GLUE AND SAVE SOME TIME

 When I assemble a face frame with pockethole screws, should I also put glue between the parts when I assemble them?

This is a little bit like wearing a pair of suspenders with two belts — it can't really hurt, but it's not necessary. Before the glue could contribute any strength to the joint, both screws would have to lose their grip, and that's extremely unlikely. Besides, it takes extra time to spread glue between the parts and to clean up any extra that squeezes out.

SIMPLIFY YOUR DAY: CUT MORTISES BEFORE TENONS

 Which comes first, the tenon or the mortise?

The answer to this question is considerably easier than the riddle involving the chicken and the egg. The mortise comes first, and there's a good reason for that.

When you consider the various ways that you can form a mortise, each of them involves tooling that's a fixed size — whether it's the width of a mortise chisel, the diameter of a drill or router bit, or the cutter in a mortising machine. While you can choose from a variety of mortise widths, they are usually well-defined incremental measurements, such as ¼, ⅜, or ½ inch.

It is much easier to fine-tune the stock removal of the tenon to arrive at a desired measurement than it would be to slice the walls of the mortise.

THE HOLE STORY ON DRILL PRESS DIMPLES

 Whenever I need to set up my drill press for a critical operation, such as doweling, it takes forever to get the fence set just right. Is there a shortcut that will save me some time?

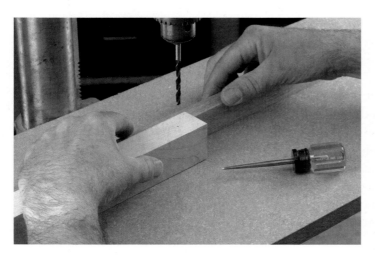

After you mark the hole's centerpoint on your stock, press a shallow dimple into the stock with a scratch awl. Loosen the drill press fence so that it slides easily. Chuck a brad-point bit into your drill press, and lower the bit until its point just enters the dimple in the stock. Gently slide the fence against the edge of the stock, and hold it securely with one hand. Let the bit rise out of the dimple, and clamp the fence in place. This technique also works nicely with Forstner bits.

A Unique Angle for a Routing Solution

 I cut a long groove in a piece of plywood by guiding my router against a 1x2 straightedge. But the straightedge flexed, ruining the cut and the lumber. How do I avoid making that mistake again?

Finding a dependably flat and straight piece of lumber for a fence is always a challenge. Of course, you can buy sturdy commercial clamps that will do the job, but they can be pricey.

Instead, consider an inexpensive length of L-shaped angle iron from your hardware store that you can simply clamp to your stock. It isn't going to flex or warp, and it's virtually indestructible.

After you purchase the angle iron, you'll probably need to degrease it by giving it a bath with a scrub brush and dishwashing soap. Also carefully inspect the metal for bumps that could disfigure your wood when the angle is clamped into position. A belt sander will quickly erase any imperfections, and a quick coat of metal primer will help prevent rust.

If you have lots of plywood scraps on hand, you can also make a more stout straightedge by choosing a wider piece. A 4-in.-wide or wider plywood straightedge won't flex like a 1x2 will.

Eliminate Sawdust from Tenon Tight Spots

 I cut tenons with an auxiliary fence screwed to my miter gauge. But I spend a lot of time clearing out the sawdust in the tight corner between the stop block and the fence. How can I eliminate this nuisance?

Buildup at the stopblock could prevent the end of your workpiece from accurately registering, and that would defeat the accuracy of the setup. You can neatly sidestep the problem by resting your stopblock on a ⅛-in. spacer when you clamp it in place. When you remove the spacer, you create an escape route for the sawdust.

By the way, you may find it easier to use a handscrew clamp as a stopblock instead of juggling a block and separate clamp.

DON'T FLIP YOUR LID
OVER CUTTING A LID

What's the best way to cut a lid from an assembled box?

There's always more than one way to skin the proverbial catfish, so here are three methods and two variations, and you can choose the one that you like best. The first involves the band saw, so the box size is limited to the maximum dimension you can guide under the blade guard. Make certain that you start with a sharp blade that's properly tensioned, and that the saw table is square to the blade. Even under the best of circumstances, you'll face some touch-up sanding on the mating surfaces of the base and lid. On the plus side, you can create an angled cut or intentionally wavy line that will add visual interest to the box.

The next two ways involve the table saw, and the basic setup is the same for both methods. Attach a high plywood face to your table saw's rip fence to help stabilize the box when it's on end. Set the height of the blade about ⅛ in. higher than the thickness of your box's sides. With the base of the box firmly against the rip fence, make cuts into both ends. Keep the box moving at a brisk pace to reduce the risk of a burned cut.

Get some spacers that are the width of the blade's kerf, and tape them in place as shown in the photo. The thickness of the spacer must match the width of the kerf as closely as possible, so add a thickness or two of tape to the spacer until it's just right. Slice along the two long edges to separate the lid.

The next method is very similar to the one just described, except that you set the saw blade about 1/32 in. less than the thickness of the stock. That way, you can skip the spacers because the tiny bit of remaining wood keeps the lid from collapsing inward as you complete the cut. To finish separating the lid, slice down the middle of the kerf on all sides with a sharp utility knife. Be sure to resist the urge to twist the lid free from the last fibers because that could leave an unsightly rip in the base, lid, or both. Use a hand plane and sandpaper to smooth the mating surfaces (see page 156 for sanding suggestions).

Use could also use a table-mounted router and straight bit as the cutting tool instead of the table saw. Adjust the height of the bit to either completely separate the lid or to leave it attached by a sliver.

TRY A LIPPED LID ON YOUR NEXT BOX

I'd like to make a batch of small boxes as gifts, but the price of any hinge worth having is positively astonishing. Is there an easy way to create a lift-off lid that would eliminate the need for hinges?

Check out the drawing and the photo for a box design that lets you create lipped lids quickly and easily. Rout three grooves on the inner faces of the box's sides and ends: one for the lid panel, one for the bottom, and one for the inner half of the interlocking lid. Assemble the box with mitered corners.

When the glue has dried, set up your table-mounted router to separate the lid. The photo shows how a scrap from the side can help you accurately gauge this setup. Be sure to insert spacers into the first two grooves you cut so the lid won't be damaged when it's cut free. (Please see the techniques for separating lids on page 116.)

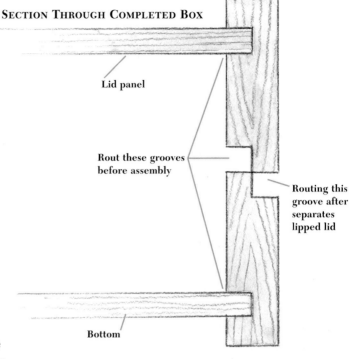

SECTION THROUGH COMPLETED BOX

Lid panel

Rout these grooves before assembly

Routing this groove after separates lipped lid

Bottom

ROUTER SHORTCUT MAKES FINE TENONS

I'm going to build a quilt rack, and I need to reduce the ends of the 1-in. dowels to ¾-in. tenons. What's the fastest and most accurate way?

Set up your router table as shown in the photo, and you can quickly make accurately sized tenons. Clamp the fence so the distance from the bit's centerpoint to the fence equals the radius of the dowel. In this case, that's ½ in.

Clamp a stopblock to the fence to set the length of the tenon. To do this, simply measure from the right side of the bit to the block. Raise the straight bit slightly above the surface of the table, turn on the router, and advance the dowel into the bit. As soon as the bit makes contact with the wood, rotate the dowel. It's not necessary to cut a full-length tenon merely to check this setting.

Raise the bit in tiny increments, remembering that the distance you raise the bit will reduce the size of the tenon by twice that amount. For example, raising the bit ¹⁄₁₆ in. will make the tenon ⅛ in smaller.

Verify the size of the tenon by inserting it into a hole drilled into a block of wood. This gauge block is easier and more accurate than measuring each tenon. By the way, it's a good idea to check every tenon because the diameter of the dowels may vary, and that will affect the size of the tenon.

When you have your adjustments locked in, you'll be able to cut all the tenons quickly.

This method is also an expedient way to replace round chair rungs.

STRENGTHEN JOINTS WITH THIS ADAPTATION

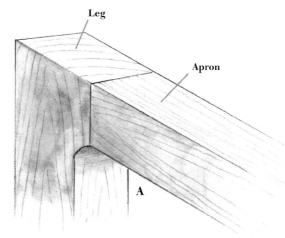

Leg

Apron

 I want to build a coffee table that has a smooth curve where the legs meet the rails. But in the test joints I've made, the curve in the rail has delicate places that break easily. How can I get the look I want and the sturdiness I need?

Make the curve in the leg, not the rail, to avoid weak short-grain areas that break easily. The assembled joint, marked Drawing A, will give the smooth uninterrupted line you want. Band-saw the waste from the leg before assembly, but leave a little extra material at the curve so you can complete the smoothing after assembly for a seamless look.

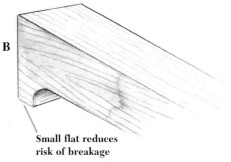

A

B

If that approach sounds like too much work, you can compromise slightly by adopting the shape shown in Drawing B. A flat area of ⅛ in. or more at the bottom of the curve will let the wood retain enough strength so it won't be broken easily.

Small flat reduces risk of breakage

THE SECRET TO LAPPED JOINTS

 Whenever I need to make a lapped joint, it never fits quite as snugly as I want. Is there some trick to achieving a perfect fit?

There are actually several techniques that will help you achieve a snug fit with a minimum of trouble. Instead of measuring the width of the cuts, directly gauge them from the stock itself, and score the line with a striking knife or utility knife. Also, make sure that your saw blade is set at exactly 90 degrees so that the walls of the joint will be perfectly vertical.

Turn the top piece upside down to test-fit the joint. If it doesn't easily slide together, don't try to widen the cuts. Instead, plane or sand one edge of the top piece until the fit is right. After you have the top piece fitted, repeat the procedure for the bottom piece.

GAUGE BLOCKS SAVE TIME AT ROUTER AND TABLE SAW

I often need to set the bit on my table-mounted router at a standard height above the table: ¼ or ⅜ in., for example. Is there an easy way to measure this height so I don't have to fool around with so many test cuts?

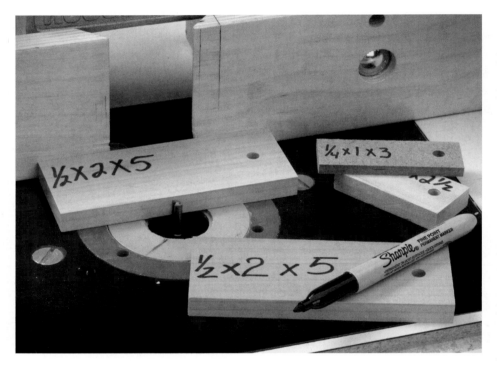

Take a few minutes to make yourself a set of gauge blocks, and you'll quickly zero in to exact settings at the router table, drill press, and your saws. For example, cut a block that's exactly ¼ in. thick, 1 in. wide, 3 in. long, and drill a ¼-in. hole though it. To set your router bit ¼ in. above the table, you simply raise the bit through the hole until its tip is flush with the upper surface of the block.

To set your table saw's rip fence exactly 1 in. from the inner edge of the blade, put the block flat on the saw table, and gently slide the fence up to it. You get the idea. Make a set of blocks that feature standard measurements plus any specialized settings your work requires.

By using the blocks in combination, you can make accurate setups amazingly fast. For example, combine the 1-in. width of one block with the ⅜-in. thickness of another, and you have an accurate measurement without even picking up a ruler.

Clearly label both sides of each block with its dimensions, and give the wood a fast finish with aerosol lacquer to slow down seasonal dimensional changes. A small cardboard box will store the blocks in one location and help keep them from becoming shims.

NOT ALL MITER GAUGES ARE THE SAME

 I was following the directions in a magazine article about building a picnic table. I set my miter gauge to the angle they stated, but the cut came out completely wrong. Was the magazine article wrong, or is it my mistake?

Always beware when an article in a book or magazine gives you an angle setting for your table-saw's miter gauge. In the crosscut position, some miter gauges read 90 degrees, and some read zero degrees. As a result, the setting on one gauge will read as the complementary angle on the other. In this case, a complementary angle means that adding settings from the two gauges will always result in 90 degrees. For example, a 70-degree setting on one will be the same as a 20-degree setting on the other. The only time they will be identical is at the 45-degree position.

You may have to study the drawing to verify the setting because you don't know whether you and the writer have gauges that are calibrated the same.

One other caution about building projects based on magazine articles. Each issue of a magazine may contain hundreds of dimensions, and even with careful editing and checking, an occasional error slips into print. If you have the patience to wait until the next issue of the magazine comes out, you can check whether any corrections are noted. Alternatively, you can contact the magazine's office or Web site to see if any other readers found mistakes before you start making sawdust.

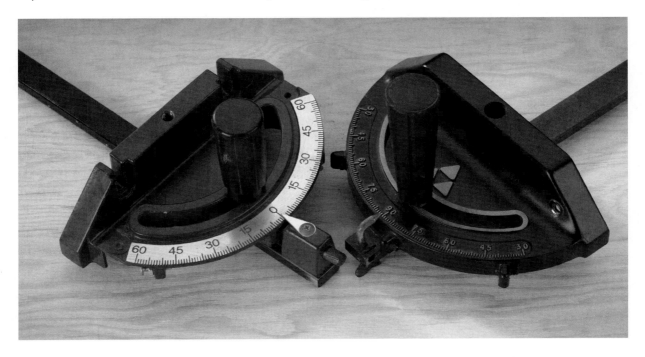

7

GLUING AND CLAMPING

WIPE AWAY THOSE SQUEEZE-OUT PROBLEMS

What's the best way to clean up glue that's squeezed out, such as when I'm edge-gluing boards for a tabletop?

First, give the glue a chance to "skin over" before you try to remove it. There are a couple of ways to check if the glue has started to dry on the surface enough to form a skin. It will lose its wet look, and have more of matte appearance. Also, when you touch the glue lightly with your finger, your skin won't get wet.

Now's the time to scoop as much of the glue as possible with a plastic putty knife while smearing it around as little as possible. Frequently clean the putty knife with a rag or paper towel. You can apply quite a bit of pressure with a plastic putty knife. Unless you're working with extremely soft wood, there's little chance that you'll mark it.

Take a clean, soft rag that you've soaked in water and then hand-wring as dry as you can get it. Go over the joint, scrubbing at stubborn glue spots. After you've cleaned a 12-in. length of the joint, follow immediately with a dry soft cloth. Keep switching to clean areas on both rags as you continue the process.

Resist the temptation to flood the joint with water because this will have two harmful side effects. First, it will dilute the glue, allowing it to flow deeply into the pores of wood. As a result, you'll have to scrape and sand for a long time to keep it from showing up under a stained or clear finish. Second, too much water can also dilute the glue in the joint, weakening it.

DRIED GLUE: ENEMY OF SHARP TOOLS

 Why do I have to go through all of the trouble of carefully cleaning a glued joint? I've always wondered why I can't just let it dry, then plane or belt-sand it out of existence.

When yellow woodworker's glue dries, it gets hard enough to nick a plane blade, whether it's hand-powered or a motor-driven planer. Dried glue also wears down a sanding belt faster than its abrasive can cut away the glue.

While cleaning up glue joints isn't much fun, it is certainly far less work than the alternative — changing planer blades and sanding belts.

STARVED JOINT DEFINED

 I've heard of a "starved" joint. What is it?

That's when a joint doesn't have enough glue between the parts to develop full strength. You may be surprised to learn that most starved joints start out with plenty of glue. But then the woodworker squeezes the joint closed too tightly with clamps and the glue disappears into the pores of the wood or becomes wasted as squeeze-out.

For maximum strength in a glue joint, you need to apply enough pressure to bring the wood pieces into intimate contact, then stop. Don't be tempted to use clamps as strongarms for correcting joints that don't fit properly in the first place. Fix the joint with more sanding, jointing, or chisel work.

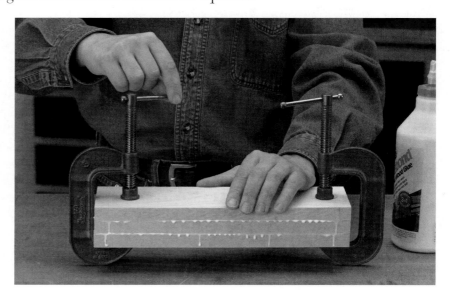

EPOXY: WORTH THE INVESTMENT

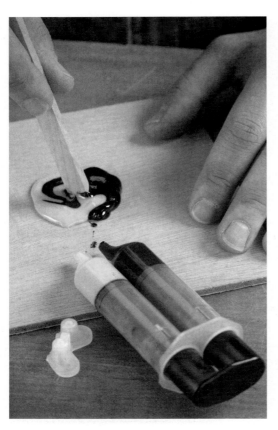

 Why do I need to shell out money for epoxy? I can squirt a bunch of yellow glue into a gap, and it will hold just fine, won't it?

Nope. Epoxy and yellow glue work in completely different ways. Epoxy adheres well to a wide range of materials and it also sticks well to itself. That second property is why it can be used as gap-filling adhesive.

And although yellow glue may also fill up the hole, it won't offer much in the way of real strength. Here's why: Yellow glue adheres well to both pieces of wood in the joint, but the molecules of glue in between these two surfaces rapidly lose their holding power when the distance between the two pieces exceeds a few thousandths of an inch.

Epoxy and yellow glue also are completely different in the way that they cure: Yellow glue loses its solvent through evaporation, while epoxy undergoes a chemical transformation.

STRETCH YOUR PIPE CLAMP INVENTORY

 Every so often, I need an extra-long pipe clamp or two, but I don't want to buy jumbo pieces of pipe for only occasional use. What's the solution?

When you buy pipe for your clamps, have them threaded at both ends so that you can add inexpensive pipe couplers (also in the plumbing department) to make any length you'll need in the future. Instead of looking for a place to store the couplers, simply spin them on the ends of the pipe. That tactic eliminates a storage problem and also protects the threads on the pipe.

ADHESIVE TERMS DEFINED

 A while back I read an article on adhesives, and the writer mentioned "drying," "setting," and "curing." Was he just exercising his vocabulary, or is there a real difference among these terms?

In the case of common woodworking glues, drying simply means that enough solvent has evaporated that the joint is no longer wet to the touch. Setting refers to the time required before you can safely handle an assembly. But curing refers to the more complicated and time-consuming process of developing strength. To the naked eye, not much seems to be happening, but the molecules are working nonstop to develop a joint that is usually stronger than the wood itself.

Comparing it to the process of laying a concrete road may make all this easier to understand. Within a day, you can walk on it and not sink in, and with each passing day it doesn't look or feel like it's getting any harder. But the project engineer won't let any vehicles on it for a long time — even weeks — until the concrete cures enough to endure the strain of traffic.

In the same way, you need to give wood joints sufficient cure time before you subject them to stresses of further machining or you may compromise the strength of your project.

There's another good reason that you should wait a day or so between glue-up and flattening the panel. In the drawing, you can see (A) how the moisture from the adhesive in a freshly-glued panel swells the wood along both sides of the glueline. If you remove this ridge when smoothing the panel, the initial results (B) will look good. But as the moisture level eventually equalizes itself within the wood, you'll get a valley along the joint (C).

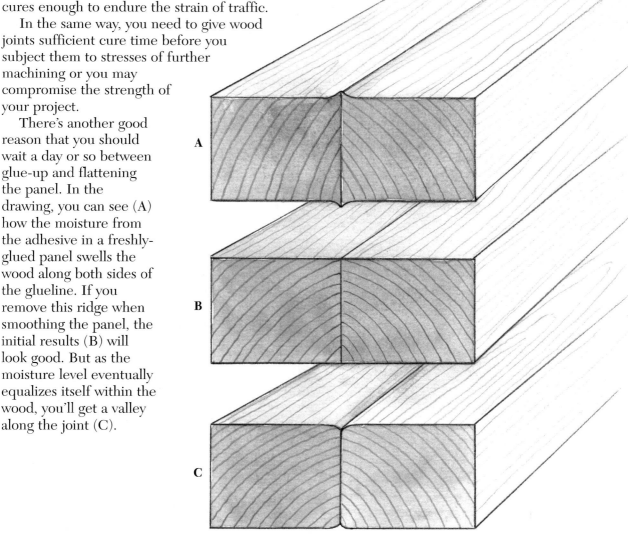

GLUE CREEP SPOILS MANY A PROJECT

I carefully glued up an assembly, and put it on my workbench. When I came back from lunch, the joints had slipped out of position somehow, ruining the fit. What in the world happened?

Your project was the victim of glue creep — the tendency of a joint to move in order to relieve built-up stresses. Creep is especially prevalent during and immediately after assembly and while the glue is still slippery. Any stresses — within the wood itself or from clamp pressure — can initiate a slide that won't stop until a larger force overcomes it. By that time, your assembly could be ruined.

Apply these tactics to control the problem in the future:

- Machine joints that fit tightly.

- Avoid excessive clamping pressure.

- Position clamps to prevent parts from sliding during the first few hours after assembly. Check the joint occasionally.

- Make sure the assembly is under as little strain as possible.

- As soon as you feel confident that the glue has grabbed well enough, back off clamping pressure or even remove the clamps.

- But even after the glue has cured, creep can still attack joints that are under load. Over time, this problem — sometimes called cold flow — can produce unsightly misalignments. If you see this problem developing in a completed project, reduce the load or reinforce the joint.

KEEPING PANELS FLAT DURING GLUING

? *What's a simple and effective way to keep panels flat during glue-up?*

Check out the photos, and you'll see how to modify a handscrew clamp and then use it to keep panels flat. Carefully close the jaws of an 8-in. clamp (the dimension refers to the length of the wood jaws), keeping the wood's ends and edges flush. Chuck a 1-in. Forstner bit in your drill press to drill a hole centered between the jaws and with its centerpoint 3-in. from the tip of the jaw.

After clamping across the boards and cleaning up the glue that squeezes out, add a handscrew clamp across the end of each pair of boards, centering the semicircular cutouts above and below the glueline. Carefully snug the clamp so it makes firm contact along its entire length, but don't overdo the pressure. The cutouts prevent the clamp from sticking to the joint and also permit access for further joint cleanup if needed.

The modification to the clamp doesn't interfere with its ability to clamp other assemblies, so you're improving your tools, not sacrificing them.

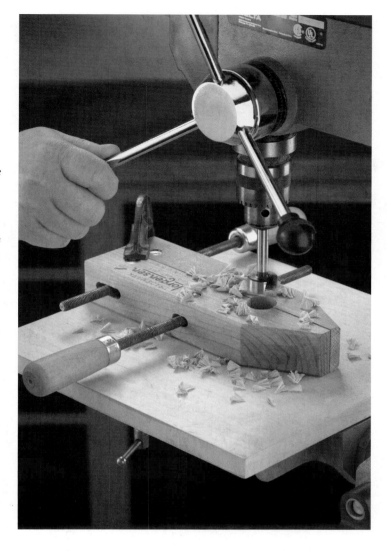

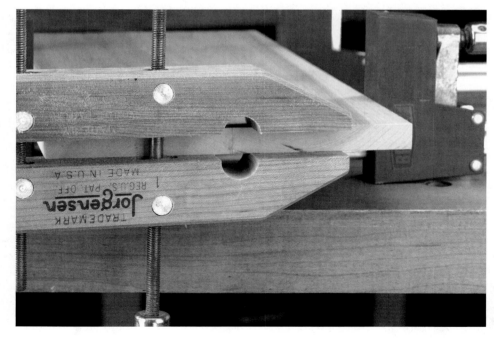

A Quiet Approach at Your Drill Press

? *I rely on C-clamps at the drill press to attach a plywood table and to secure the fence. The vibration of the running motor sets all of the adjustment rods rattling in their holes. If I'm drilling only one or two holes, I can tolerate it, but during any extended drilling session the racket threatens to drive me cuckoo. How can I silence this annoyance?*

If you figure that your sanity is worth at least two dollars, you can solve this problem with a package of Plasti-Tak available at a hobby shop, art-supply store, or office-supply center. The product is most often used for non-mark mounting of posters to walls. Following the directions on the package, stretch a wad of the material into a ribbon, wrap it around the rod and threaded post, and pinch it in place.

You can re-use the adhesive many times by stretching it before each use to re-activate it. Store the unused material in a zip-top sandwich bag to keep it dust-free.

Plasti-Tak is distributed in the United States by Brooks Manufacturing (please see Resources, page 314.).

Take Care With Clamps

? *I carefully prepare my stock before glue-up because afterward it's such a nuisance to try to get into the corners. But despite my best efforts and careful handling, I often find small dents in my project when I unclamp it. What's the cause of that?*

Check the jaws of your clamps for blobs of dried glue, wood chips, or any other debris. Clamping pressure can force this foreign material into your wood, producing the dents you mention. Also check that the contact surfaces of clamping cauls or blocks are clean.

Make it a habit to rub your hand over both jaws of the clamp each time you grab it and before you apply it your work. Do this and you'll sidestep this problem in the future.

THE TRICK TO OPENING HANDSCREW CLAMPS

 I've seen guys who twirl a handscrew clamp with both hands, opening or shutting it in a matter of seconds. When I try it, sometimes the clamp opens when I want it to shut or vice versa. Every time I pick up a clamp, I don't know which way it's going to go. How do I eliminate the trial and error?

The answer is as simple as picking up a handscrew clamp in an identical way each time. For example, grab the clamp so your right hand is always on the handle at the end of the clamp and your left hand grips the handle of the rod that passes through the middle of the jaws. Now, hold the clamp in front of you at chest height.

When you rotate the jaws toward you, they will open; rotate them away from you to close.

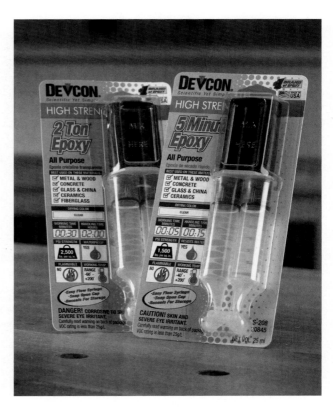

EPOXIES COME IN DIFFERENT SPEEDS

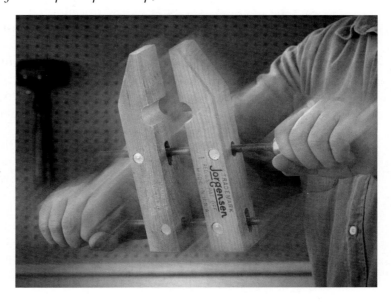

At the hardware store, I saw epoxy that sets in five minutes and another type from the same manufacturer that takes hours to set up. Am I missing something, or why would anyone pick the slow one?

There's a trade-off that's going on: if you want a quick grip, you'll sacrifice some strength in the fully cured bond. If you can afford the time — or if achieving strength is more important than time — choose the slow-set version.

KEEP GLUE AWAY WHEN FITTING PANELS

 I understand that I'm not supposed to glue a solid panel door into the grooves in the frame. I followed that advice, but during periods of low humidity — especially in the winter — the panel floats around so much that it moves off center and rattles. How can I fix this problem in existing doors and prevent it in the future?

To fix the existing door, lay it face down on your workbench, and carefully center the panel in the grooves. Near the inner edge of the upper and lower rails, and centered in their length, drill pilot holes for brads and drive them to secure the panel. Drive only one brad into the upper rail and one into the lower rail. For door rails made of ¾-in. stock, a ½-in. brad usually does fine.

This procedure will keep the panel centered but still allows it to expand on both sides of its centerline. Solid wood changes very little in length due to changes in humidity, so restraining it in that dimension is no big deal. You can also apply this solution to future cabinets you make. If you're building a lot of doors, consider getting a power assist by using a pneumatic (air-powered) brad driver. You can also select a headless pinner, a pneumatic tool that drives special small-gauge fasteners that are nearly invisible when installed.

There are several strategies you can adapt to control this problem in the future. Consider making the panels from quartersawn stock because it expands and contracts less in width than lumber that's sawn in other ways. You can also place Space Balls, rubber spheres that have a diameter of .026 in. for a snug fit into a ¼-in. groove. The balls are firm enough to keep a panel centered, but soft enough to compress when the wood panel expands. Space Balls are inexpensive and are usually sold in bags of 100 by woodworking specialty stores and catalogs.

DON'T GET STUCK ON JUST ONE GLUE

Every couple of years, some manufacturer trots out a new "wonder" adhesive that is said to be better, faster, and stronger than anything else on the market. But to me, the real miracle is that none of the old adhesives ever leaves the marketplace. I'll admit that the ever-expanding number of choices confuses me. Isn't there one glue I can stick with for everything?

No, there isn't one adhesive that will meet all of your needs all of the time. Sometimes you'll want an adhesive that gives you an extended open time so you can complete an intricate assembly, while other times you'll want glue that grabs quickly. Water resistance may occasionally be important, or you may need a structurally sound bond for a load-bearing architectural application.

The fact that a large variety of adhesives can coexist in the marketplace is proof that each one of them is meeting a need. Refer to the chart of Glue Facts on page 143 for information that will help you match your needs with available products.

PROCEED CAUTIOUSLY WHEN GLUING PAINTED WOOD

I'm building a project that will be painted a number of different colors, and it would be much easier to paint it before assembly to eliminate tedious masking. Is there any glue that will work on painted surfaces?

The best solution is to leave the joint surfaces unpainted so you can apply regular woodworking glues that are designed to soak into the wood's structure. After you've sealed the surface with paint or stain, the effectiveness of most wood glues drops dramatically. You can apply polyurethane glue or an epoxy on painted surfaces, but you also have to bear in mind that the strength of the joint can't be any greater than the grip the paint has on the wood. If the paint leaves the wood, the adhesive goes with it.

DON'T LET SQUEEZE-OUT SPOIL YOUR PROJECTS

Every time I glue up a box with mitered corners, I get glue squeeze-out along the inner corners, which is a nasty clean-up job. But my next project is a jewelry box where I cut the lid off the base after the assembly has dried, so there's no way to clean up the inside joint surfaces. How do I avoid a mess?

The photo shows how a strip of masking tape along each miter can solve your problem. Position the strip near the miter, but keep it at least $\frac{1}{32}$ in. away from the cut line so it doesn't accidentally get caught in the joint and spoil its fit.

While the strips don't keep glue from squeezing out along the joint, they do prevent it from sticking to the wood, and that's good enough to solve your problem. You can adapt this concept to a variety of other joints, such as mortise and tenons or edge joints when gluing up wide panels.

A SQUEEZE PLAY PROTECTS GLUE INVESTMENT

Polyurethane glue is handy for many applications, but I hate the way that it dries out in a partially empty container. Sometimes it seems I throw away as much as I use.

Before you store polyurethane glue, put a few drops of mineral spirits into the container to form a shield between the glue's surface and the air. Actually, air itself isn't the culprit — it's the moisture in the air that's catalyzing the glue and making it set.

You might also consider buying your glue in containers that aren't as large. Although the cost per ounce is greater for the smaller containers, throwing glue away is no bargain.

PUT SOME PRESSURE ON YOUR GLUING OPERATION

I need to glue two pieces of 16- x 24-in. plywood face to face. How do I apply even pressure to the middle of the panel?

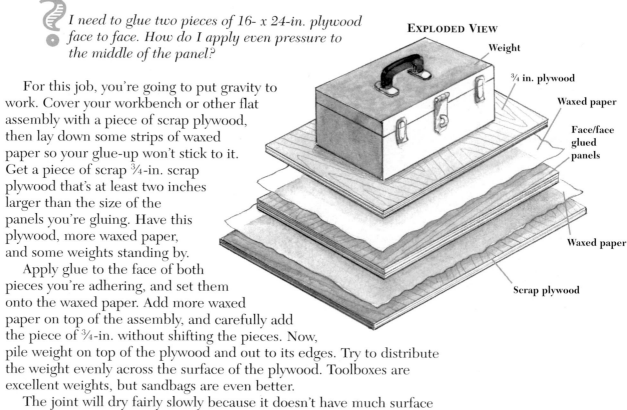

EXPLODED VIEW

Weight

¾ in. plywood

Waxed paper

Face/face glued panels

Waxed paper

Scrap plywood

For this job, you're going to put gravity to work. Cover your workbench or other flat assembly with a piece of scrap plywood, then lay down some strips of waxed paper so your glue-up won't stick to it. Get a piece of scrap ¾-in. scrap plywood that's at least two inches larger than the size of the panels you're gluing. Have this plywood, more waxed paper, and some weights standing by.

Apply glue to the face of both pieces you're adhering, and set them onto the waxed paper. Add more waxed paper on top of the assembly, and carefully add the piece of ¾-in. without shifting the pieces. Now, pile weight on top of the plywood and out to its edges. Try to distribute the weight evenly across the surface of the plywood. Toolboxes are excellent weights, but sandbags are even better.

The joint will dry fairly slowly because it doesn't have much surface area exposed to promote evaporation, so give the assembly at least a full day to dry.

AN EXTRA HAND FOR CLAMPING PROJECTS

Is there an easy way to align the parts of a mitered box during glue-up? By the time I'm ready to lasso the box with a band clamp, the glue is half dried.

Hinge the components of the box to each other with clear package sealing tape, then turn the strip over so the joints face upward. Roll up the assembly to check the fit of the joints. When you're satisfied with the fit, brush on the glue and roll it up again. As always, go easy with the clamping pressure.

A SCIENCE TO SPREADING GLUE

What's the big deal with people carefully spreading glue along both boards of a joint? I just wiggle a line of glue along one board, clamp it up, and I'm finished.

If you haven't had any glue joints fail, it's been more a matter of luck than good technique. One of the essentials of a good bond is establishing a wet surface on both pieces of wood so the glue molecules can chemically interact with the cell structure of the wood. With the uneven coverage you apply to the first board, you've already taken a big step backward from creating a strong joint. The glue transferred to the second board will have even sketchier coverage, further compromising the joint.

Creating a sound glue joint may take a few more minutes of work, but repairing a separated joint can be an extremely difficult — sometimes nearly impossible — chore.

SPARE THE CLAMP: TRICKS TO APPLY EDGE BANDS

I want to edge-band some plywood with ⅛-in.-thick strips of solid wood that I'll cut. How can I clamp the banding without using a half-ton of clamps?

Skip the clamps and space pieces of masking tape about 2 in. apart along the strip. You'll be able to exercise fine positioning control and get adequate clamping pressure. Instead of picking up and setting down the roll of tape dozens of times during the project, go to an office-supply store and buy a tabletop tape dispenser that will handle masking tape. It will save you lots of time. One other point: When you smooth out the tape, leave at least ½ in. unstuck at the end of each strip of tape. That way, when it's time to remove the tape, you'll be able to easily grip and rip.

PLAN AHEAD FOR GLUE ADHESION

 How do I best prepare a surface for maximum glue adhesion: sawing, planing, or sanding?

The ideal surface for wood-to-wood joints is cleanly sliced wood fibers, so planed is better than sawn. Sanding makes the surface fuzzy, so it's a poor choice. Contrary to what you may have heard in the past, roughing up the surface does not make the glue stick better. The exception to that statement is when you're dealing with nonporous materials, such as plastic or metal.

If you can run down the entire edge of a board with a single handplane stroke, you'll have the optimal surface. Next best is the surface produced by sharp jointer knives. Keep the wood moving over the jointer cutters or you'll risk glazing the surface, a condition that reduces the glue's ability to effectively interact with the wood.

Some woodworkers believe that a sawn joint adheres better if you use a feed rate at your saw that is quicker than usual. The truth behind this belief is that a faster feed rate produces a surface that is less likely to be glazed. If there are any burn marks on the cut line, try again.

Freshly machined surfaces accept glue best, so assemble them the same day if possible. If a delay is unavoidable, wiping the mating surface with a cloth dampened with acetone will remove surface contaminants. Acetone is also a good surface prep for oily woods such as teak, or woods high in tannic acid, such as cedar or redwood. Make sure the solvent evaporates before you apply the adhesive. Be even more certain that you dispose of solvent-soaked rags in a safe manner to avoid spontaneous combustion. (See page 249 for safe disposal tips.)

A Professional Approach: Tinted Glue

I'm building a blanket chest using walnut lumber. I'd like to minimize the appearance of glue lines by tinting the adhesive. What's the best way to do that?

You have two choices: Purchase a glue that's already tinted, such as Titebond Dark, manufactured by Franklin, or mix your own custom color using water-soluble aniline dyes. If you choose to mix your own, you'll prevent possible lumping by dissolving a small amount of dye into a few drops of water before adding it to the glue. Make a trial batch by adding the mixture to the glue, and stirring thoroughly to evenly distribute the dye. Perform a test assembly, and allow the glue to dry so you can accurately judge its color.

After you've achieved the color you want, mix a batch of tinted glue large enough for the entire project.

Glue Won't Last Forever on the Shelf

A few years ago, I bought a gallon of yellow glue because it was cheaper than buying the small bottles. But now it's starting to get thick. Can I just add water to thin it down?

When glue starts to get thick or stringy, that means it's past the end of its storage life, and you need to throw it away. Even with fresh glue, adding more than 5 percent water will weaken the bond.

You can make liquid hide or polyurethane glue easier to spread by putting the bottle into a container of warm (not boiling) water.

If you buy a gallon in the future, you can improve its longevity by transferring the contents into bottles that taper at the neck. Fill these small bottles, and you'll dramatically reduce the amount of glue surface area that's exposed to air. By contrast, a half-empty gallon jug presents an enormous surface area that can speed evaporation. Store the bottles in a cool location out of sunlight. The discussion of surface area also reveals one good reason that glue is often sold in tall cylindrical bottles. It's a shape that can hold a large volume of liquid while presenting a minimal evaporation surface.

NOT ALL GLUES LOVE THE OUTDOORS

Various glues are labeled as weatherproof, water resistant, or waterproof. Is there a real difference, or is this just a word game?

If you imagine yourself floating in a small wooden boat out of the sight of land, you'd want to make sure that your craft is held together by a glue that's waterproof — immune to the effects of prolonged immersion. For a cutting board that you'll quickly wash by hand and dry, water resistant is good enough. If you're building a trellis, weatherproof is important.

Match the adhesive to the project's requirements and your performance expectations. You can certainly upgrade a cutting board's adhesive to waterproof, but you'll pay more for it. You'll have to decide if spending a few dollars more is worth the extra insurance.

GET A LEG UP ON GLUING CHAIRS

I'm repairing some chairs, and I'm nearly ready to glue the leg assemblies together and attach them to the seat. The only thing holding me back is that I can't figure out how to attach any clamps to the round parts. The fact that the legs slant inward makes it even more difficult. How can I get a grip?

This is an ideal job for surgical tubing, a stretchy material you can purchase by the foot at many hardware stores and some pharmacies. Tie one end of the tubing to one leg, and put some tension on it by stretching it to another leg. Take a wrap or two around that leg, and continue the process until you have everything held firmly.

Surgical tubing is also good for other oddball assembly jobs, such as gluing up a hollow staved cylinder for a table base. Make a loop around the assembly and tie it, then put tension on the tube as you spiral around the assembly.

CRACKING THE GLUE BOTTLE'S EXPIRATION DATE

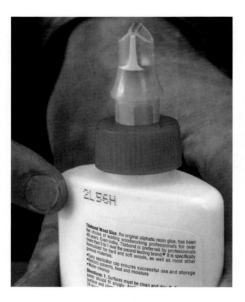

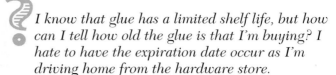

I know that glue has a limited shelf life, but how can I tell how old the glue is that I'm buying? I hate to have the expiration date occur as I'm driving home from the hardware store.

Some glues have the expiration date clearly stamped on the bottle, and others require you to crack the manufacturer's code. But you don't need to hire an undercover operative — anyone with a telephone or Internet access can unlock the secret. Franklin, the manufacturer of Titebond, explains their code on the company's Web site.

For that firm's products, look for the series of letters and numbers printed on the container. The first digit is the last number in the year of manufacture, and the second character in the code is a letter that represents the month of manufacture. A represents January, B for February, and so on up to the letter M. (The letter I is skipped because it could be confused with the numeral 1.) For example a code sequence that begins with 4H tells you that the glue was made in August, 2004.

For other glue manufacturers, call the company's customer service telephone number or visit its Web site.

After you've deciphered the date of manufacture, refer to the Glue Facts chart (on page 143) to figure the expiration date. Write this date on the glue bottle with permanent marker.

BLACK PIPE: SMART INVESTMENT FOR CLAMPS

What's better for pipe clamps — black pipe or galvanized? What's the difference, anyway?

Black pipe, which is intended for natural-gas lines, is less expensive so many woodworkers choose it. Galvanized pipe, designed for water lines, costs more because of the corrosion-resistant coating but some people believe it's worth it for improved looks.

Strength is not a significant issue because both types will bend if you apply excessive force. Generally speaking, black pipe is the better choice. The galvanized coating can crumble under the stress of the clutch plates and cause the clamp head to slip.

HIDE GLUE HAS A PLACE IN TODAY'S SHOP

I saw some liquid hide glue at the hardware store the other day. I thought this was only available in a dry form. Is this stuff just a curiosity, or does it still have valid uses in a modern workshop?

The dry form of hide glue requires you to mix it with water and heat it before use. You can purchase a thermostatically controlled water bath glue pot for this purpose through specialty woodworking catalogs. The prepared form of hide glue requires no mixing or heating, and has a longer open time.

Both forms are fine for general assembly tasks, but they excel at adhering veneers because glue squeezed out onto the surface of the wood does not affect stains or finishes. By contrast, most other woodworking glues block stains, so glue squeeze-out can result in a splotchy appearance.

Hide glue has a low resistance to water, but musical instrument makers consider this property a virtue. That's because they want joints that can be disassembled, if necessary, by future generations to make repairs to the instrument.

CLAMPING DOWN ON A SOLUTION

I place little plywood squares under the jaws of my C-clamps so that they won't dent my project. But juggling all of those parts, plus tightening the clamp, and keeping everything lined up is a real pain. How can I simplify this process?

At the hardware store, you can buy self-adhesive circles of cork that stick to the jaws of your clamp. You can still apply plenty of clamping pressure, but you'll reduce the risk of denting. Purchase a diameter to fit your clamps, or buy a sheet of the cork and punch the disks yourself.

ONE-HANDED ADJUSTMENTS FOR C-CLAMPS

 Is there a trick to quickly adjusting C-clamps? When I have a long adjustment to make, I don't know which wears out faster, my finger or my patience.

Hold the adjustment rod along your fingers, and grip the end of the threaded rod between your thumb and forefinger as shown in the photo. Moving your hand in a small clockwise circle will put the C-shaped frame into motion and open the clamp. Reversing the direction of the spin will, of course, close the clamp.

DOGGONE GOOD TIPS FOR WORKBENCH CLAMPING

Every so often, I need to clamp down something onto my workbench. If it's near the edge, I can use regular bar or pipe clamps. But what if I need to apply downward pressure in the middle of the bench?

If your bench has a line of dog holes, you can take the head off some bar clamps, and reassemble it after you've inserted the bar through a hole. You can easily perform the same trick by using a pipe clamp, but you may need the ½-in. pipe size. If your bench doesn't already have a line of holes, consider creating at least one hole in your bench to take advantage of downward clamping.

This is a very handy setup to apply when driving screws using a pocket hole system. The clamp keeps the parts aligned while you drill or drive the fasteners.

Glue 101: Understanding Adhesives

Glue Facts

Adhesive/ Example	white glue/ Elmer's Glue-All	yellow glue/ Titebond	yellow, water resistant/ Titebond II	resorcinol/ Weldwood Resorcinol	plastic resin/ Weldwood Plastic Resin	quick-set epoxy/5-Minute Epoxy	long-set epoxy/2-Ton Epoxy
Type	polyvinyl acetate (PVA)	aliphatic resin	cross-linking polyaliphatic	Resorcinol formaldehyde	urea formaldehyde	two-part epoxy	two-part epoxy
Open Time*	10 min.	5 min.	5min.	30 min.	20-30 min.	5 min.	20 min.
Set Time**	40 min.	1 hr.	1 hr.	10 hrs.	12 hrs.	1 hr.	8 hrs.
Solvent***	water	water	water	water	water	lacquer thinner	lacquer thinner
Water Resistance	low	medium	high	high	high	high	low
Shelf Life****	1 year	2 years	5 years	1 year	1 year	3 years	3 years
Typical Applications	general purpose, interior	general purpose, interior	general purpose, interior and exterior	suitable for marine applications	bond has high structural strength	interior and exterior	interior and exterior
Notes	gives longer assembly time than yellow glue	typical woodworking adhesive	grabs quicker than regular yellow glue	observe safety and ventilation cautions	long open time aids in complex assemblies and veneering	fills gaps, ultimate bond not as strong as slow-set epoxy	bonds dissimilar materials; good ability to fill gaps

* Open time = the duration for spreading glue and getting the assembly clamped
** Set time = minimum duration before gently handling, not machining, the assembly
*** Solvent = cleanup medium when adhesive is wet
****Shelf life = duration between date of manufacture and disposal

Adhesive/ Example	polyurethane/ Gorilla Glue	contact cement-solvent	contact cement-water-based	instant glue/ Hot Stuff	instant glue/ Cypox	hide glue-dry	hide glue-liquid
Type	polyurethane	solvent-based neoprene	water-borne neoprene	cyanoacrylate (CA)	ethyl cyanoacrylate	dry form of hide glue	prepared hide glue
Open Time	20 min.	1 hr.	1 hr.	5-10 min.	5 min.	2-3 min.	30 min.
Set Time	1 to 4 hrs.	immediate	immediate	1 min.	1 min.	2 hrs.	2 hrs.
Solvent	denatured alcohol	lacquer thinner	water	acetone	acetone	water	water
Water Resistance	high	high	high	good	good	poor	poor
Shelf Life	6 mo.-1 year	1 year	1 year	1 year	2 years	unlimited when stored dry	1 year
Typical Applications	interior and exterior	plastic laminate application	plastic laminate application	quick repairs	quick repairs	interior, veneers, musical instruments	interior, veneers, musical instruments
Notes	low odor, quickly cures to maximum strength	hazard of fire and explosion; observe safety and ventilation cautions	easy application and clean-up; low odor	standard and gap-filling types; observe cautions	wider range of materials than regular CA; add your own fillers	mix with water and heat; glue takes stain evenly	ready to use; glue takes stain evenly

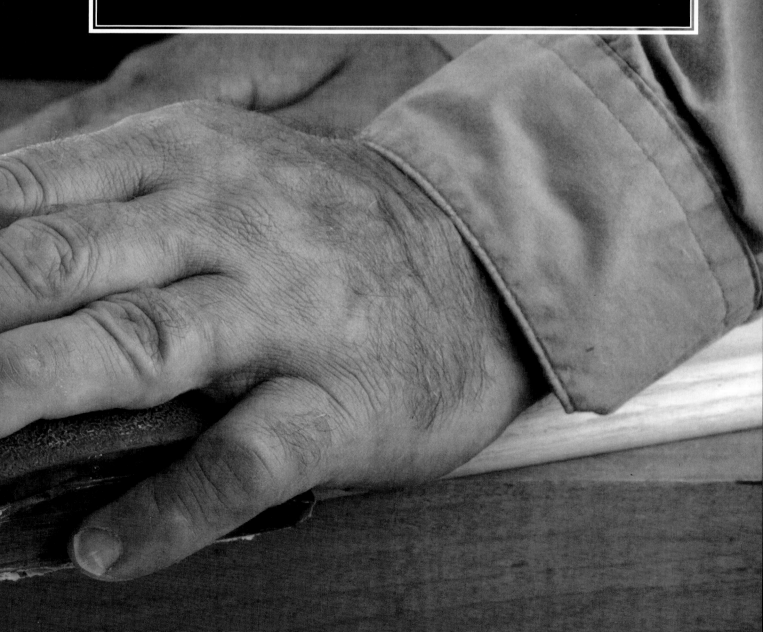

8
SANDING

ABRASIVE SHOP HELPERS —
YOU NEED BOTH TYPES

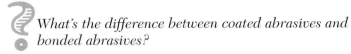

What's the difference between coated abrasives and bonded abrasives?

A coated abrasive is what most people call sandpaper — an abrasive attached to a flexible backing. Bonded abrasive takes a solid form such as a grinding wheel or sharpening stone.

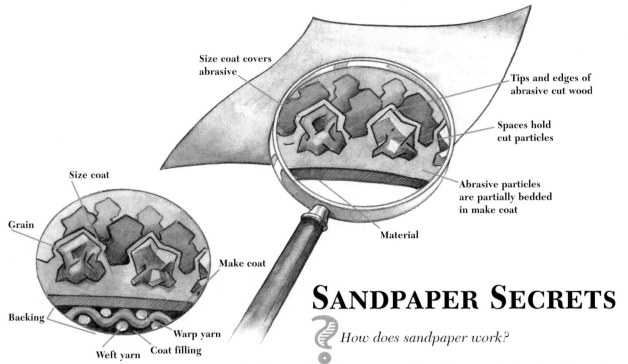

Size coat covers abrasive

Tips and edges of abrasive cut wood

Spaces hold cut particles

Abrasive particles are partially bedded in make coat

Material

Size coat

Grain

Make coat

Backing

Warp yarn

Weft yarn   Coat filling

SANDPAPER SECRETS

How does sandpaper work?

Take a look at the construction of a coated abrasive sheet in the drawings, and you'll see why abrasives are correctly classified as cutting tools. The tips and edges of the mineral granules act like saw teeth, slicing away pieces of wood. The spaces between the grains act like the gullets of a saw blade, temporarily holding the particles of wood until suction or gravity removes them.

The coarser the abrasive, the bigger the cutting "tooth" is, so it removes relatively large pieces of wood and leaves behind scratches where the wood used to be. As you move to finer grits of abrasive, the mineral teeth get smaller, so the scratches diminish in size, eventually reaching the point where you can no longer see them with the naked eye. At this point, the surface appears smooth.

A coated abrasive wears at least two coats — the make (or making) coat partially imbeds the minerals, holding them to the backing material. A size coat covers the abrasive minerals, further securing them to the sheet. When the backing material is cloth, there's an additional layer beneath the make coat, called the coat filling. Its function is to bridge the gaps in the cloth's weave, creating a smooth starting surface.

RATING ABRASIVE MATERIALS

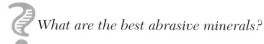 *What are the best abrasive minerals?*

Here's a quick rundown on the various abrasives you may encounter at your hardware store, home center, or through catalogs:

- **Aluminum oxide (AO)** is the most widely used abrasive material, and it spans the grit spectrum from 24 to 1500. This material is sometimes simply called alumina.

- **Silicon carbide (SC)** materials usually start no finer than 220 grit, and move upward to 1200 and beyond. Silicon carbide materials are usually employed by woodworkers to smooth sealers, between coats of varnish, or to wet-sand a finish before polishing it.

- **Alumina zirconia (AZ)** is a form of aluminum oxide, but it also has some of the characteristics of silicon carbide. This abrasive is principally employed for abrasive planing, so it starts at the coarse end of the spectrum and usually gets no finer than 120 grit. AZ is a premium material, typically costing 15 to 40 percent more than SC.

- **Emery** is a natural mineral that's been a smooth performer for hundreds of years. It's not as sharp, hard, or durable as either AO or SC. Some distributors sell emery abrasives as "shop" grade for woodworking, but it is more commonly employed for smoothing metal than wood.

- **Garnet** is another natural mineral that's been mined for its abrasive properties for more than 200 years. Garnet paper is best suited for hand-sanding, and it gives fine results in that role.

- **Crocus** is a very fine abrasive that's better suited for polishing metals than for woodworking applications. Sheets of this abrasive are usually called crocus cloth. The typical grit you'll find is about 800.

UNDERSTANDING FRIABILITY AND HARDNESS

 A metalworking friend of mine told me that silicon carbide is harder than aluminum oxide, and asked me why woodworkers don't choose it instead of the softer abrasive. What's the answer?

In woodworking, the relative softness of aluminum oxide is an advantage because of a property called *friability*. That means that the mineral particles fracture as you sand, exposing fresh sharp surfaces to continue the cutting action. In fact, abrasive paper is the only self-sharpening tool in your shop.

Silicon carbide is less friable than aluminum oxide — in fact, wood isn't hard enough to make the mineral crack. As a result, as soon as the first sharp facets dull, the abrasive paper won't cut any more wood.

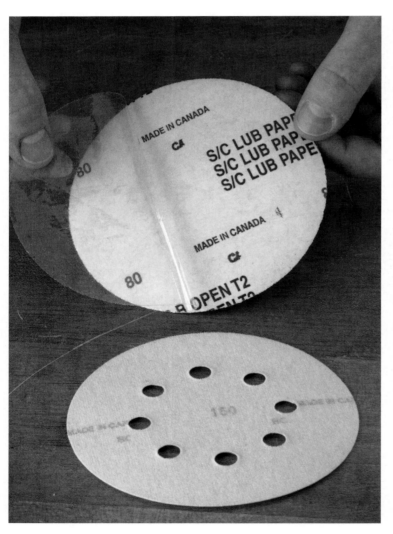

SORTING OUT SANDING TERMINOLOGY

 The catalog of sanding products lists sanding disks as PSA, H&L or plain. I understand plain, but what are the other two abbreviations?

PSA stands for pressure-sensitive adhesive, and H&L is hook-and-loop. Many people commonly refer to hook-and-loop fasteners by the brand name of a single product: Velcro™.

THE GRIT ON ABRASIVES

I've heard that abrasives have different grading systems. What are these systems, and how do they compare?

The chart on page 309, shows a side-by-side comparison of some of the more common abrasive grading systems so that you'll see what grits are equivalent. Here's a little bit of background on the various systems:

CAMI stands for the Coated Abrasives Manufacturers Institute. If you're a woodworker in the United States, this is probably the system you know best. Abrasives graded according to the CAMI system have a larger tolerance range than in the FEPA system. This means that a single grit designation has a wider scale of permitted particle sizes.

FEPA is the Federation of European Producers of Abrasives. If the abrasives you buy are imported from the European continent, they were probably manufactured and graded by this system, which puts the letter P before the number. Numbers in the FEPA (or P-graded) system and the CAMI system are similar up to approximately grit 220. In finer grades, the numbers in the FEPA accelerate more rapidly.

Micron-graded abrasives have a narrow tolerance range for consistent performance — a quality that can be important for demanding applications such as leveling finishes. The substantially higher cost of micron-graded products, which are usually mounted on polyester film instead of paper, means that they are probably not your most cost-effective choice for everyday wood-sanding chores. The abbreviation for micron is the Greek letter mu, which looks like a lower case (small) u.

Trizact Abrasive Grade refers to a proprietary engineered abrasive manufactured by 3M. These abrasives are popular with countertop installers who work with solid core materials like DuPont Corian™.

JIS is the Japanese Industrial Systems scale.

Jethro scale is an old-fashioned grading system that uses a number and zero combination to describe the grit, for example, 3-0 grit. You may find references to this system in old woodworking books, but it's sometimes still employed to refer to abrasives for finishing wood floors.

GET THE ABRASIVE BACKING YOU NEED

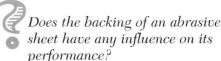 *Does the backing of an abrasive sheet have any influence on its performance?*

Absolutely — an abrasive on a thin paper will handle differently from the same grit on a heavyweight cloth belt. Your choice is influenced by whether you need a paper that will conform to a shape while smoothing it or whether you want the sander's platen to transfer its flatness to your workpiece.

Paper backings range from lightweight A to heavyweight F. Generally speaking, you'll see light backings teamed with fine grits on papers intended for sanding by hand. When you see products designed for machine sanding, particularly with coarser grits, the paper backing is heavier.

Backing referred to as fiber is essentially a super-heavyweight paper composed of multiple layers that are bonded under heat and pressure.

Cloth backings include the lightweight "J", the medium "X", and the heavy "Y". When the suffix "F" is added to the J or X weight, that means the cloth flexes easily to conform to a surface.

AVOID THAT GLAZED-OVER LOOK

 What is my final grit for sanding hardwoods? Is it a different grit for softwoods?

A final grit for hardwoods can be in the 150 to 180 range, although some people go as far as 220. For softwoods, 120 or 150 can be the final stage.

Oversanding can burnish the wood and close its pores, inhibiting penetration of stains and finish. To check for burnishing, hold the wood near your eye level, and sight along its surface toward a light source. A properly prepared surface will be smooth and free from scratches, but a burnished surface will appear glazed.

RANDOM THOUGHTS ON BUYING RANDOM-ORBIT SANDERS

 I'm thinking about getting a random-orbit sander. What are some of the points I should consider when shopping around? Should I get an electric sander or air-powered?

One of the key considerations is the diameter of the orbit — other factors being equal, smaller orbits will produce less noticeable scratches. Adaptability to a dust collection system is often another key consideration.

Many professional cabinet shops prefer pneumatic (air-powered) sanders because of their lighter weight, dependability, and ease of maintenance. Although a pneumatic sander may initially cost more than an electric sander, it can be restored economically. A worn-out electric sander has a one-way ticket to the landfill.

If you do work both in the shop and at a job site, an electric sander is your wisest choice. But if you're able to purchase a second sander, consider the pneumatic variety.

GET TOP PERFORMANCE FROM YOUR RANDOM-ORBIT SANDER

 Any tips on operating a random-orbit sander?

"Start on, stop off" will help you get better performance from your sander. This phrase means that you should start the sander while the pad is resting on the wood. Otherwise, you risk scratching the wood by a less than perfect landing on the panel. When you're ready to stop sanding, lift the sander straight up before flipping off the switch.

Set the sander on a soft pad when it's not in use — a carpet remnant or a retired computer mouse pad are good choices. Setting the disk onto a hard surface can crack the abrasive particles, particularly if you don't wait for the motor to stop turning.

GO ON SCRATCH PATROL

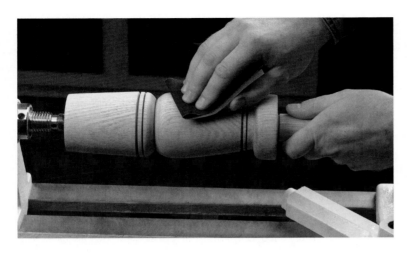

I just turned some table legs on my lathe, and was pleased with them until I applied the finish. At that point, all of these sanding scratches appeared, ringing each leg. How do I prevent this in the future?

It sounds like you stopped sanding with too coarse a grit, or skipped grits to try to complete the project more quickly. When you skip a grit, it can mean incomplete removal of the scratches of the previous grit. Further sanding smoothes the surrounding wood, accentuating the appearance of the deep scratches.

One further tip: Shut off the lathe to do the final sanding with the grain on any long surfaces that are straight or gently tapered.

WHY REAL WOODWORKERS PREFER OPEN COATS

What's the difference between an "open-coat" abrasive and one with a "closed coat"?

The terms "open" and "closed" refer to the percentage of coverage that the abrasive has on its backing. For woodworking, you want an open-coat abrasive because the unoccupied spaces provide room for the stock that was abraded from the surface. Abrasives suitable for woodworking usually have 50 to 70 percent coverage of the backing. If you try to sand wood with a closed-coat abrasive, it will quickly clog the paper and stop the cutting action.

The exception occurs when you're wet-sanding a finish. In that case, you'll choose a closed-coat abrasive (probably silicon carbide), and the lubricant will help float away the particles that could otherwise block the abrasive's cutting action.

EVERY GOOD VARNISH NEEDS A TOOTH

 Why do I need to sand between coats of finish?

When you're applying a varnish, sanding between coats provides "tooth" in the previous coat so the next coat will have a good mechanical grip and not simply slide away. In this case, the build occurs like layers of sedimentary rock — one distinct layer on top of another.

There is no real necessity for sanding between coats of lacquer or shellac. That's because those finishes bond in a completely different fashion — each new application partially dissolves the coat before it to create a chemical connection. As a result, the final film is a single unit even though it was applied in successive layers. You could compare this build to layers of snowfall that form a glacier — each layer melts into the previous one.

FRAMED UP WITH A BELT SANDER

I'm looking for a new belt sander. Some come with an accessory called a sanding frame. What's the purpose of that?

Even in experienced hands, a belt sander can tip during the smoothing process, and if that occurs, you may create damage that requires even further sanding. A sanding frame acts like a set of training wheels to keep your sander from losing its balance.

You can use the sanding frame as a temporary help until you become more proficient with your sander, or you can bring it into action whenever you want the extra security.

GRIT-SKIPPING: A NO-NO

 When people suggest that a person shouldn't skip grits when sanding, do they really mean to use every single grit? That seems like it will take too much time.

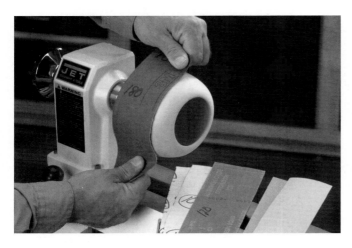

Not skipping grits really does mean not skipping grits. For example, let's say that you just stopped sanding with 100-grit, but instead of picking up 120-grit paper next, you grab the finer 150-grit in an attempt to save time. Unfortunately, your strategy will backfire, and here's why.

The purpose of using the next grit is to remove the scratches of the prior abrasive. The proper tool to remove the 100-grit scratches is 120-grit; 150-grit is engineered to remove nothing larger than the scratches left behind by 120. The 150-grit paper will eventually do the job, but it will take more time, more energy, and more materials.

Skipping grits means that you're forcing a smaller tool to do the job of a bigger one. It's like trying to cut down a tree with a dovetail saw — with enough time and energy, it's theoretically possible, but there's no reason to make your work so difficult.

CARVERS AVOID SANDING

 I'm just getting into carving, and am having trouble figuring out when the carving ends and the sanding begins. How far should I go with the sanding?

Many carvers believe that the best surface comes from a sharp chisel or gouge, and that any sanding at all degrades the crispness of the surface. They also cite the fact that sanding can deposit abrasive into the pores of the wood, and that those tiny chunks could dull the tools employed for subsequent carving.

Other carvers are somewhat less dogmatic, stating that sanding is permitted, but that it should be reserved as the final operation. But even then, they say, sanding should done with discretion, a light touch, and paper that's 220-grit or finer.

AVOIDING SCRATCHES AT THE INTERSECTION

How do I avoid cross-sanding scratches at a mitered corner?

While you're in the process of bringing the edges flush, some cross-grain sanding is unavoidable. But the final smoothing should eradicate all traces of these stray scratches. The drawings show two proven tactics.

In the method shown in the first drawing, hold your cabinet scraper's blade midway along one mitered piece, positioning the blade at a 45-degree angle to match the miter. Pull the blade up to the corner, and without changing its position, pull away from the miter. The arrows on the drawing indicate the direction of travel.

In the second method, put sandpaper into a block that's held at an angle to match the miter, and sand up to the joint. Until you gain experience in this method, you can protect the other half of the joint with a strip of masking tape. This technique also works well with parts that meet at a 90-degree angle, as in the face frame of a cabinet.

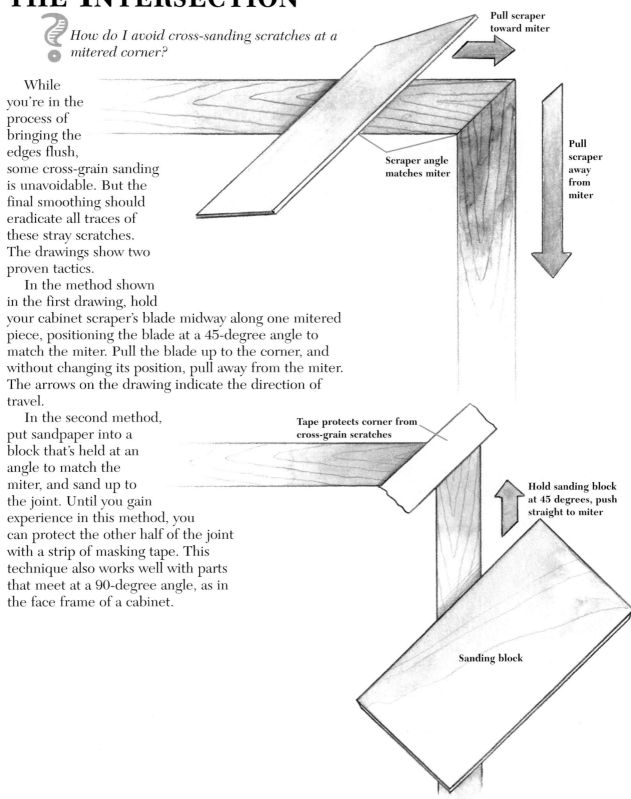

Pull scraper toward miter

Pull scraper away from miter

Scraper angle matches miter

Tape protects corner from cross-grain scratches

Hold sanding block at 45 degrees, push straight to miter

Sanding block

WORST CASE: ACCENTING SCRATCHES

 What's the correct technique for spot-sanding a scratch from a piece of wood?

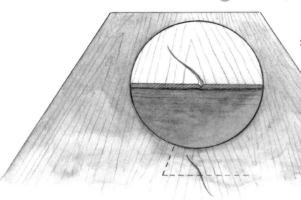

Attempting to obliterate a mark by concentrated sanding in one area will simply replace a scratch with a dished-out area — hardly an improvement. Deep dish is great for pizza, but not a good idea for wood finishing.

You need to reverse your thinking about the scratch. To make it disappear, you need to lower the level of all the other wood until it matches the level where the scratch was. In effect, you want to sand everything except the scratch.

SEAMLESS SANDING

 I make small boxes as a single unit, then cut the lid free at my table saw. But a couple of corners will almost always show a slight cutting error that needs to be sanded. How can I smooth these parts and keep the base and lid even for a seamless look?

Get a flat piece of plywood or medium-density fiberboard (MDF), and attach full sheets of sandpaper to it with spray adhesive. Depending on the amount of stock you need to remove and the density of the wood, you can start at 80- or 100-grit.

Move the box in a small circular pattern while applying only light downward pressure. After about a dozen strokes, rotate the box one-fourth turn to make certain you don't concentrate the stock removal in any one area. You'll have to stop every so often to brush away or vacuum the dust so the paper won't clog.

After you've leveled the lid and base with the coarsest grit, move to a finer abrasive and sand with a lighter touch to minimize the scratches.

Complete the process by sanding with the grain. See page 155 for two techniques that help you eliminate cross-grain sanding scratches at mitered corners.

WORKING THROUGH THE GRITS

 When I switch from one sanding grit to the next, do I need to bother clearing away all the sawdust?

A horsehair bench-cleaning brush is a great tool for clearing away sawdust, but you could also suck up the debris with a vacuum or push it away with a rag.

If you leave the dust on the wood, it will quickly clog your sandpaper, reducing its ability to cut. The dusting also removes bits of the previous

abrasive. If left on the wood's surface, they would continue to make large scratches while you're attempting to make smaller ones.

ENOUGH SANDING IS ENOUGH – OR IS IT?

 My grandpa told me to sand until the sweat runs UP my arm. But I really never know when I've sanded enough. Is there any rule of thumb that will help guide me?

Until you have a lot of experience with sanding, counting strokes can be a good guide. For example, say that you're trying to remove milling marks from a board's edge. After 15 strokes, it looks like the marks are gone. Now, sand 15 more strokes to make sure. In other words, when you think you're finished you're usually halfway there.

SANDPAPER STORAGE SECRETS

 Are there any guidelines for storing sandpaper? It seems that it could survive anything.

Manufacturers often suggest keeping abrasive sheets in their original packaging until you're ready to put them to work, and protecting the material from extremes in humidity and temperature.

Sheets with paper backing can curl unless they are held flat, and temperatures that freeze or fry can damage the coatings that hold the abrasive to the backing material. So if you have an unheated shop, it's a good idea to bring the abrasives into the house during freezing weather.

When you have abrasive belts, you can condition them to your shop's environment by hanging them on a peg or dowel for a day before putting them in your machine. Don't hang a belt on a nail because that could puncture the backing.

3M'S SYSTEM FOR SCOTCH-BRITE™ PADS

 I've seen different colors of Scotch-Brite™ abrasive pads at the hardware store, but they don't have a grit number listed. How do they rate in terms of coarseness?

The manufacturer, 3M, doesn't assign numbers to these sheets that compare them to any equivalent grade of coated abrasive. Instead, the company ranks them in terms of the aggressiveness of their cut. The white sheet is the least assertive, and is called ultra fine. It's followed by the super-fine gray sheet. The green sheet is next in texture, but it's handier in household cleaning than in the workshop. The maroon sheet is the most abrasive, but it's not commonly found in hardware stores. Look instead in auto-paint supply shops because this sheet is better suited to metal prep than woodworking.

POWER SANDING AT THE LATHE

 I've heard that some people use a sanding disk to smooth the inside and outside of a bowl on the lathe. How does this work?

Power sanding with an abrasive disk in a drill against a spinning bowl in the lathe is an excellent way to refine both the interior and exterior surfaces. It's also a great method of raising clouds of dust, so be sure to wear breathing protection and exercise every dust extraction strategy you know.

Choose a disk that's small enough to fit inside the bowl without making contact above the horizontal centerline. When you're working on the outside of the bowl, you can usually choose a larger disk, but again you'll need to work below the centerline.

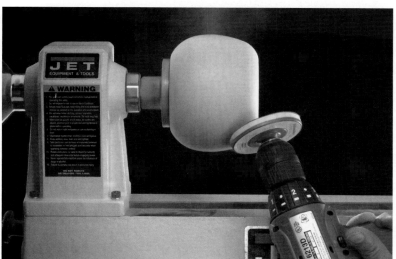

Feedback from the lathe will quickly teach you how far you can move the disk. If you stray into an area where the disk doesn't belong, the lathe will let you know.

By the way, power sanding is not a cure for poor turning technique or damage inflicted on the bowl blank by dull gouges or scrapers. But when you're contending with unruly grain, power sanding will give you a real advantage.

HAND-SANDING STILL REQUIRED

 Will proper use of a random-orbit sander completely eliminate hand-sanding?

The quick answer is: no. You can cut way back on the drudgery of sanding, but even the best random-orbit sander makes random scratches. The only way to finally eradicate them is by hand-sanding with the grain of the wood.

ROUTING YOUR WAY AROUND SANDING CHORES

I want to make some curved brackets for a shelf, and that means cutting multiples of a shape that's 1½ in. thick. But the cutting isn't the hard part — smoothing the edges is the part that looks like it's going to take forever. This is way beyond the capability of any flush-trim router bit I have, much less the router to power it. Any smooth ideas?

The setup shown in the photo will make the smoothing an easy job. The first task is selecting the size of the sanding drum. Choose the largest one that will fit the curves in your workpiece by placing possible drums atop a full-size pattern of the shape made from ¾-in.-thick stock. Take care making your pattern because you will duplicate any irregularity on every part you make.

Cut a ¾-in.-thick disk that is the diameter of the sanding drum and the paper sleeve, but minus the thickness of the abrasive particles.

To prevent the guide disk from rotating, drive two flathead screws to fasten it to a plywood auxiliary table. After you've chucked the sanding drum into your drill press, position the guide disk under it, checking for flush alignment with a square. Clamp the auxiliary table to your drill press.

Fasten the pattern to the bottom of a blank that you've band-sawn as close to the waste side of the line as you dare. Cloth double-faced carpet tape is the best choice if you need an unmarked surface, but screws are another fast and reliable method of joining the stock and pattern.

When you sand the stock, work the entire perimeter evenly instead of trying to jam the pattern against the guide disk. If you need to slightly increase the size of the disk, give it a wrap or two of clear plastic tape. Masking tape is too soft, and may tear easily.

There is also a commercial version of this concept that attaches a guide bearing to the bottom of the drum, making it function like an oversized flush-trim router bit.

MUSCLE-LESS SANDING

 How much downward pressure should I put onto a sanding block or random-orbit sander?

With a random-orbit sander, the weight of the tool itself provides enough downward force. Pushing harder will merely inflict excessive wear on both the motor and your arm. The same principle applies when you sand with a block. Simply rest your hand on the block, keep your elbow relaxed, and use the muscles of your shoulder and back to move the block in long, even strokes.

NO PUZZLE TO SMOOTH SQUARE RODS

 I want to make some smoothly sanded square rods as blanks for puzzles and toy parts. How can I get the precision I want without spending a lot of money on a specialized sander?

The setup shown in the photo will work to tight tolerances even if you have a very tight budget.

Set up the distance between the drum and fence to remove as little stock as possible while still smoothing the entire surface of the rod. Referring to the photo, write numbers on the end of each rod to indicate the sanding sequence. With Side 1 against the table, run each rod past the sanding drum. You can complete the sanding by pulling the rod through, or by pushing it with the next rod. Next, run Side 2 of each rod against the table.

Shut off the motor, and make a pencil line on the router table indicating the position of the fence. Slightly loosen one of the fence clamps, and tap the back edge of the fence with a light hammer blow until you see the fence barely move in relation to the mark. Tighten the clamp, and run sides 3 and 4 against the table.

The end result is a smooth and perfectly square rod.

KEEP THINGS MOVING WHEN SANDING JOINTS

 How do I smooth the joints of a cabinet face frame with a random-orbit sander?

To avoid concentrating the sanding action directly over the joint, keep the sander in constant motion, sweeping at least two times the diameter of its sanding disk in each direction away from the joint. The drawing conveys this concept.

If you sanded on only the joint itself, it would produce a scooped-out area that could be very unsightly and would also be a poor matching surface for the cabinet door.

Smooth joint by working random-orbit sander 2x its base diameter from joint

THE BENEFITS OF SANDING BLOCKS

 Loading paper into a sanding block is a nuisance. Why should I bother?

Using a sanding block will give you superior results because the firm backing bridges small irregularities in the wood's surface, flattening the stock instead of merely following its contours. In addition, the block distributes pressure over a larger area, speeding the sanding process.

So the few seconds that it takes to load paper into a commercial sanding block pays immediate dividends by shortening the amount of time you need to sand.

If your local hardware store doesn't carry firm rubber sanding blocks, check at a professional paint store or an auto-body supply store. The standard block takes one-fourth of a sandpaper sheet cut across its width. You'll also find jumbo blocks that take a strip the full length of a sheet.

UNCORK A GREAT SANDING SOLUTION

 I've heard that cork-backed sanding blocks are good. Can I make my own?

Yes, you can, and it's very easy. Start with a scrap piece of medium-density fiberboard (MDF) and a piece of sheet cork. Many hardware stores and hobby centers sell sheet cork to make bulletin boards. Glue the cork to the MDF using virtually any adhesive: contact cement, spray adhesive, white glue, or woodworker's glue. With the cork against a flat surface, put weights on the MDF, and wait for the adhesive to dry.

With the cork facing upward on your table saw, cut the panel into blocks of any size or shape that you desire. Although you can hold the edges of the paper, you'll get better results by using sandpaper with pressure-sensitive adhesive (PSA rolls). Simply cut a strip and stick it to the cork.

If the sandpaper doesn't remove cleanly from the cork, it's no big deal. Making the blocks is so fast and inexpensive that you can consider them disposable.

CUSTOM SANDING BLOCK

 I need to smooth the inside curve of some large cove molding I made with my table saw. How do I make a sanding block that fits the shape?

Custom-form a sanding block by band-sawing a scrap of rigid foam insulation to the curve of the cove. The insulation can be a scrap from a construction project or a piece of packing material.

SAVE YOUR MANICURE

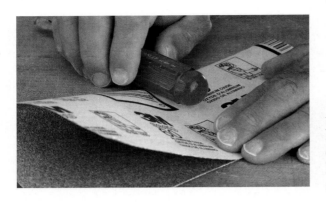

? *When I need to tear sandpaper into strips, I end up abrading my fingertips trying to fold a sharp crease in thin paper. Is there a better way?*

Fold the sandpaper so grit faces grit, and run the handle of a screwdriver along the folded backing paper. This pressure will sometimes cause the paper to separate cleanly along the line. But if you do have to tear, you'll have a strong guideline.

EASING THE EDGE

? *Woodworking project instructions will sometimes suggest to "ease all the edges before applying the finish." What exactly does that mean, why is it necessary, and how do I do it?*

Easing the edges simply means reducing any potential sharpness at corners and edges, and there are several good reasons for doing that. First, it makes a project friendlier to handle by reducing the possibility of cuts from intersections that are too crisp. Second, it provides better adhesion for the finish, especially if it is the film-building variety, such as varnish or lacquer. If the corner is too sharp, the film becomes very thin along that edge.

The key concept is that you want to eliminate sharpness without making the corner mushy. So do the easing with the final grit of paper in your sanding schedule. Ease edges with three light strokes, as shown in the end view drawing.

At the corner of a box, you can use the technique shown in the side view drawing. As the end of the sanding block goes over the end of the corner, tip its back end upward while maintaining firm contact with the wood. The first few times you try this movement it may seem awkward, but with a little practice it is quick and easy.

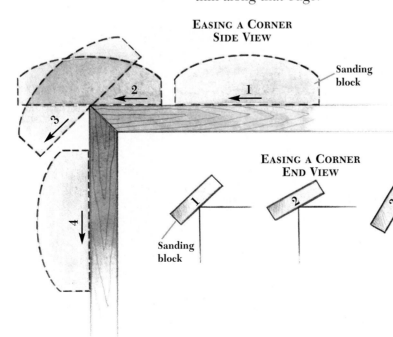

EASING A CORNER SIDE VIEW

Sanding block

EASING A CORNER END VIEW

Sanding block

WASHBOARDS TO AVOID

 I wanted to get an oak tabletop nice and smooth, but as I continued to sand, the wood took on a washboard feel. What happened?

Certain woods like oak and pine have distinct differences between the soft growth area that the tree adds early in the season (early or spring wood) and the harder subsequent portion of the growth ring (late or summer wood). If your sander has a soft pad behind the abrasive, you'll sand away the early wood, creating gullies, while hardly affecting the late wood, which then remains as ridges.

To avoid the problem, choose a firm backing pad and don't sand any more than necessary.

UNDERSTANDING STEARATE

 What is stearate?

Stearate is an oil-based lubricant applied as a topcoat to abrasive sheets, belts, and disks in order to keep the paper from loading up with dust.

Although it's usually beneficial, this coating can have an undesirable side effect if you'll apply a water-based finish to your project. The stearate may leave behind just enough oily residue to contaminate the finish and create adhesion problems.

STREAKERS NOT APPRECIATED WHILE BELT-SANDING

 I sometimes get streaks on my workpiece when I belt-sand. What causes that?

Here are four things you can check to avoid this problem:

- Make certain that your sanding belt isn't loaded with dust or that the abrasive is dull. Clean or replace the belt, if necessary.

- You may be pushing down too hard on the belt sander. You job is to guide the tool; it has enough weight to make the abrasive cut.

- Frequently stop your sanding to clear dust from the stock.

- If the workpiece contains glue lines, make certain that the adhesive has completely cured so it can't gum up the abrasive belt. Pitch or resin in the wood will also foul the belt, and these materials can become streaks.

WHY SANDPAPER WEARS OUT

 My sandpaper wears out really fast. What's the problem?

It could be a variety of problems, or even a combination of the following items:

Choosing "economy" abrasives that fracture too quickly or prematurely separate from the backing. Applying excessive pressure to the sander. Incorrect product selection — for example, using an abrasive that's suitable only for hand-sanding in a machine application. A sanding belt that is too stiff won't make proper contact with your stock.

TROUBLESHOOTING SANDING PROBLEMS

 Help me troubleshoot an abrasive that loads up too quickly and forces me to stop often to clean it. What are the possible problems?

Make certain that you're not using a closed-coat abrasive in an application that requires an open coat. Check the dust collection system, including all ports and hoses, for obstructions. Inadequate exhaust flow can quickly clog the abrasive. If your sander has a variable-speed control, try slowing it to match the rate of waste production with the pace of dust extraction. Check the moisture content of the wood — if the wood is too damp, it won't sand cleanly. Experiment with a coarser grit to be sure that you're not trying to make the abrasive remove more stock than it was engineered to handle.

SAND AWAY THOSE PESKY WHISKERS

 I've heard people talk about "raising the grain" as a final sanding step. How does that work?

After you've completed sanding with the final grit, thoroughly dust the workpiece, then wipe it with a barely damp cloth. This raises tiny "whiskers" of wood that you then remove with a quick and light hand-sanding. Don't overdo this step or you'll go past the "whisker shaving" stage and expose a fresh surface that will sprout new whiskers when the wood is dampened. This step is helpful before applying a water-based stain or finish because it helps ensure a smoother surface. The procedure has questionable merit when you're working with oil-based materials because they won't swell the wood as water does.

WHEN TO SAND AND FINISH SIMULTANEOUSLY

 The guy at the paint store was telling me about using sandpaper when applying a penetrating oil finish. I had never heard of that before. What does it accomplish?

This process knocks down any minute amount of grain raised by the application of the finish, and creates a fine slurry that helps fill the pores of the wood, enhancing the hand-rubbed look.

You'll need very fine waterproof silicon carbide abrasive, starting at 400 grit. Flood the surface with oil, and rub the surface with the paper to spread the finish and work it into the wood. If your energy level permits it, you can continue the sanding with progressively finer grits, all the way up to 1200 grit. But when the abrasive is that fine, you get nearly the same polishing effect with a soft cotton cloth.

FURNISHING A BURNISHING

 Is burnishing the wood always a bad thing?

On softwoods or those that are prone to accept stain in a blotchy manner, burnishing may work to your advantage. By sealing off the pores of the wood, the stain will penetrate less deeply, producing a lighter but more even appearance.

Garnet is a good abrasive to choose for a burnished effect because the grains don't fracture and produce new cutting surfaces. Although the abrasive wears out more quickly, it gives a smoother surface compared to aluminum oxide of the same grit. Sanding end grain with garnet paper will help it appear less dark after you apply stain or finish.

Taking Lacquer to Another Level

How do I polish a lacquer finish for a super high-gloss look?

Smoothing and polishing the finish removes part of the film's thickness, so make certain you've applied enough material so you won't accidentally go through it — it's a very discouraging feeling when that occurs.

Give the finish enough time to thoroughly shrink and cure because the harder the finish is, the smoother it will polish. Consult the finish manufacturer's specifications to discover the recommended curing time.

With mineral oil or mineral spirits as a lubricant, start with 600-grit waterproof silicon carbide paper and sand the piece, wiping away residue with a dry cloth to check your progress. Your goal is a uniformly matte surface with no shiny spots. Continue the smoothing with finer grits until you complete with 1200 grit.

Sprinkle some rottenstone on the surface, and begin polishing the finish with a balled-up soft cotton cloth. (If your hardware store doesn't have rottenstone, check at a professional paint store, or order it through a catalog.)

Some people start polishing with pumice, another powdered abrasive, but it's relatively coarse and can rapidly cut through a finish if you're not careful.

You can continue the process with the same lubricant, although some people like paraffin oil for rubbing a finish. You can work in circles, a figure-8 pattern, or in long strokes. Actually, it's best to vary among all these so your muscles don't tense up and boredom doesn't get the best of you. Switch to new areas of the cloth as the abrasive powder breaks down and stops cutting.

There's no need to press down — the weight of your arm provides enough pressure. As the gloss develops, reduce the pressure.

Browse your auto-parts store or at an automotive finishing supplier for abrasives that are even finer than rottenstone and have the ability to bring the surface up to a wet-look shine. Also refer to the procedure on page 291 in Chapter 14 for using a power buffer to speed the process of polishing a surface.

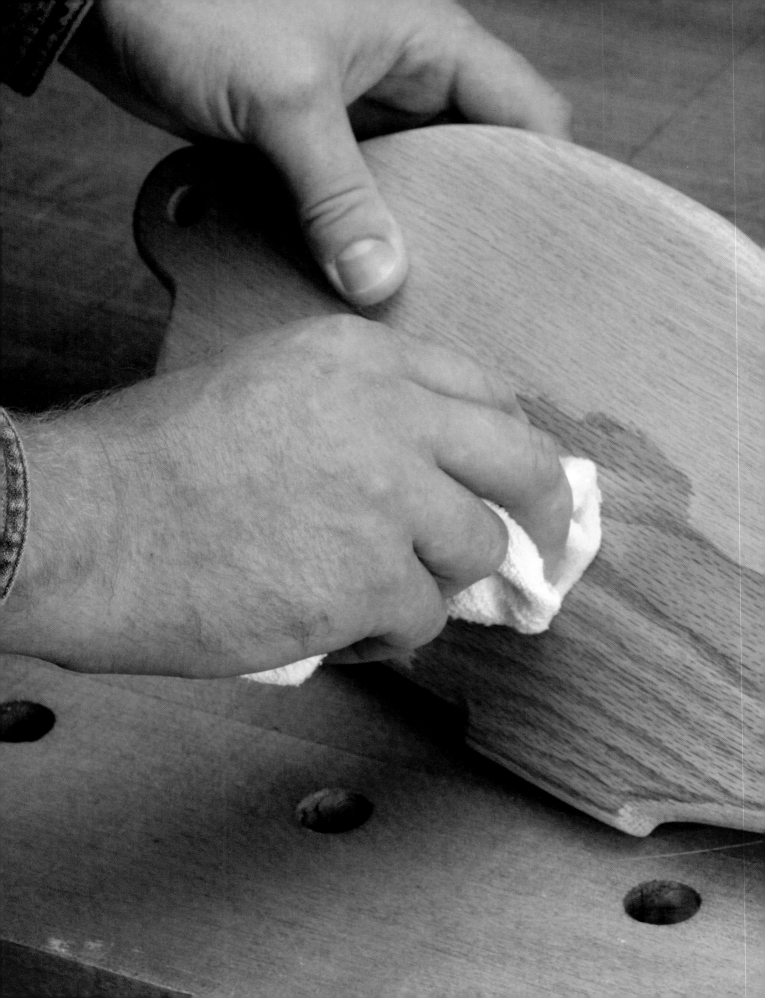

9
APPLYING
FINISH

THE INSIDE STORY ON TODAY'S FINISHES

 All of the advertisements for different types of woodworking finishes leave me confused. So let's get right to the heart of it: What's the best finish?

Some finishes are versatile and satisfy many needs. Others are true specialists, doing a job that common finishes can't handle. But there is no single universal finish that will do a great job in all situations. That goal is as elusive as a perpetual motion machine. A quick look at the principal types of finishes will acquaint you with some of their virtues and vices.

OIL FINISHES

When someone refers to an oil finish, it can mean a "pure" oil that contains no dryers, such as linseed oil, tung oil, or mineral oil (sometimes called butcher block oil). These finishes are not intended to build a surface film, nor could they really do that because they lack a chemical drying agent. Applying one of these finishes is quite easy: You simply brush a liberal amount onto the project, allow it to soak in as

recommended, then rub off the excess. Establishing the initial finish requires repeated applications — for example, one application a week for four to six weeks. While that may sound like a long finishing schedule, the fact of the matter is that you really never complete the finish. Pure oils require an additional application at least once a year.

OIL/VARNISH BLENDS

Another type of oil finish includes a small amount of varnish as a drying agent, so these finishes are sometimes referred to as oil/varnish blends. They are sometimes also called "penetrating oil" finishes, but don't confuse this with the type of penetrating oil that helps loosen rusty bolts. Penetrating oil finishes produce the "close to the wood" look of an oil finish but without the need for perpetual renewal. Interestingly, you can purchase tung oil as a "pure" oil or as a blend with the dryer added, so read labels carefully.

Application of an oil/varnish finish is similar to the "true" oils: brush on, let stand, wipe off. The difference is that this finish dries. Because it doesn't build a surface film, an oil/varnish blend cannot achieve a high gloss nor does it protect your wood from scratches. But if the wood does later get scratched, you can wipe on more oil at any time to conceal the damage. You'll find these finishes sold under names like Watco, Nordic Oil, and Danish Oil.

VARNISH

Varnish includes an extraordinary number of products — wipe-on versions ranging from thick gels to water-thin formulas, brush-on or aerosols formulations, water- or oil-based varieties, and even varnish mixed with stain that both color and protect the wood. Some varnishes withstand the fading effects of UV light, while others can be used outdoors in direct contact with elements. All varnishes stand up well to occasional spills and abrasions, but they are tough finishes to repair once they're damaged. Varnish offers the best all-around protection and ease of application for most woodworking projects.

LACQUER

Lacquer is such a quick-drying finish that it's usually applied with a spray gun or aerosol. You can purchase brushing lacquer or add retarder to standard lacquer if you prefer that application method. Lacquer can be polished to a high luster, but the process isn't easy for an amateur.

SHELLAC

Shellac is often overlooked, but it's another versatile fast-drying finish. It comes in dry flake form or premixed and ready for use. The flakes mix with denatured alcohol to form a liquid for brushing. Shellac can be applied under other finishes as a sealer or in multiple thin coats to build a protective film. You can purchase shellac in a range of colors from orange (actually amber) to bleached (blond).

If you buy premixed shellac rather than flakes, check the expiration date on the can. Both aerosol and flake forms have long shelf lives. One downside of shellac is that it can be easily damaged by alcohol, some strong household cleaners, and heat.

PLAY IT SAFE WITH FINISHES FOR FOOD ITEMS

 What's the best finish that's safe for food-contact items such as cutting boards and wood bowls? How about for toys that may go into a child's mouth?

The key consideration for utensils and toys is that the finish must be non-toxic when it's dry. You may be surprised to learn that virtually any wood finish — even those with nasty-smelling solvents as a vehicle — is safe after it's dry. For example, denatured alcohol is toxic in its liquid form when employed as a solvent for shellac. Once the alcohol evaporates, the dried shellac film that's left behind is non-toxic.

Some people skip a finish altogether on cutting boards, while others choose a non-drying oil, such as mineral oil. However, non-drying oils require frequent renewal, and you should beware of oils that could turn rancid. An oil-varnish blend offers increased durability without building a film that can be damaged.

Film-building finishes, such as a specialty salad bowl finish or shellac, are good choices. If you're a stickler for maintaining a like-new appearance, you'll need to renew these finishes occasionally.

Cleaning is another important consideration for cutting boards and wood bowls. Wash them promptly, towel-dry, and then allow to thoroughly air-dry before storage. Never let a board or bowl soak in water. Using a dishwasher is out of the question because of the prolonged wetting and extreme drying temperature. If you load a cutting board into a dishwasher, you'll probably unload kindling wood.

KITCHEN CABINETS REQUIRE SPECIAL ATTENTION

What's the best finish for kitchen and bath cabinets?

Kitches and baths are two of the most hostile environments in your home for wood to survive. There are wide swings in humidity and heat, contact with wet hands, scuffs and abrasions, grease and oil, as well as a wide range of strong cleaning chemicals. Some cabinet manufacturers combat these problems by applying extremely durable catalyzed finishes, but these exotic finishes often require elaborate safety precautions and specialized equipment to apply them that are well beyond the reach of home woodworkers and small-shop professionals. As a result, you essentially need to choose among three approaches: paint, clear film-building finishes, and clear oil/varnish finishes. Each has its own set of considerations.

A painted finish of oil- or water-based enamel is relatively easy to apply with a brush, roller, or spray. It's highly resistant to moisture and stains, cleans easily, and can be repaired or renewed by simply applying an additional coat. It may arguably be the best DIY finish for kitchen or bath cabinetry.

Film-building clear finishes include varnishes, oil- and water-based polyurethane, lacquer, and shellac. Each of these choices has a moderate to high level of hardness, and a corresponding resistance to abrasion. Polyurethane varieties offer the toughest film finish for general kitchen and bath use. Some finishes, such as gel varnish, apply easily with a rag, while the others require brush or spray application. Although most fresh spills will wipe easily from any of the finishes, harsh cleaners can damage some films. Allowing a spatter of water, milk, or cake mix to sit on the surface until it evaporates or hardens is a recipe for finish failure.

When you apply a film-building finish, you need to build enough thickness to minimize moisture absorption into the wood and damage from abrasion without making the finish overly thick. Some finishes, such as lacquer and shellac, are relatively easy to repair because a subsequent application dissolves into the surface of the previous coat. Other finishes, such as oil- and water-based varnishes, can be extremely difficult to repair.

An oil/varnish finish is easy to apply and renew. Although it has low resistance to abrasion, scratches rarely show. These finishes have fairly low resistance to moisture and stains.

LIGHTING AFFECTS STAIN MATCH

? *I do all my woodworking and finishing in a garage that's detached from the house. I custom-mix stain colors to get just the tone I want, and it looks great in my shop. But when I bring the project into the house, it's like the color changes. Are my eyes playing tricks on me, and how can I get consistent results?*

You're probably the victim of a change in color temperature between the lighting in your shop and in the house. An example from photography will explain what's going on.

Most film is manufactured to give good color rendition in daylight or with a flash that approximates the daylight spectrum. But if you use that film to take a picture illuminated by ordinary light bulbs, the photo will have a yellow or orange cast. That's because the light bulbs emit a different color of light than daylight. And if you take a picture under fluorescent lamps, the photo will probably have a greenish tint to it.

Unlike film, your eyes and brain unconsciously adjust to different lighting, even when it comes from mixed sources. From experience, your brain knows what color various objects are, and that's what you think you're seeing. But when you change the lighting — by moving the project to the house — your eyes may not register the same colors.

You'll get the results you want by judging the color of stain samples in your house, under the lighting conditions in which you'll view your project. Wipe some stain on a sample scrap of the same wood you are using for a project. Stain color will vary, depending on the wood species. For instance, "golden oak" stain will be lighter on fresh white pine than it will be on aged red oak. The color on the can is just a general indication of stain tone.

RIGHT EFFORT ELIMINATES RIPPLES IN FINISH

? *I'm trying to get a nice high gloss finish on a tabletop. Between coats of varnish, I rub down the finish with an abrasive pad to remove the tiny specks of dust that settle. Even though I remove these imperfections so the surface is smooth, it isn't flat. Viewed at an angle, it looks like my finish has tiny ripples in it. What's going on?*

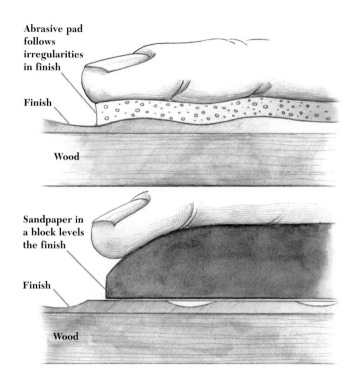

Abrasive pad follows irregularities in finish

Finish

Wood

Sandpaper in a block levels the finish

Finish

Wood

Rub with sandpaper, not an abrasive pad, to level a finish. The drawings give a highly magnified view of what's happening. The abrasive pad rides up the crests and down into the troughs of the wavy finish. As you've discovered, subsequent coats of finish then make the waves shiny.

When you level a finish, be sure to put sandpaper into a flat, stiff sanding block so you'll span the troughs as you cut down the crests.

THE SMART WAY TO WET-SAND

? *I've heard of wet-sanding a finish to get it super smooth. But if I sand all the way through the finish, won't the water swell the wood?*

You're absolutely right, and that's why you should choose mineral spirits or naphtha as your lubricant when wet-sanding. Even if you do accidentally sand through the finish, these solvents won't damage the wood.

When you buy mineral spirits, check the label to find a low-odor formula. But even then, you should do your wet-sanding in an well-ventilated location. If you need to apply another coat of finish after wet-sanding, be sure the mineral spirits has completely evaporated.

PUTTY IN YOUR HANDS

Despite what the labels say, I haven't found a wood putty yet that takes stain exactly like the wood itself. As a result, I can always clearly see where I countersunk every nail on door casings and window trim. How do I get results that really disappear?

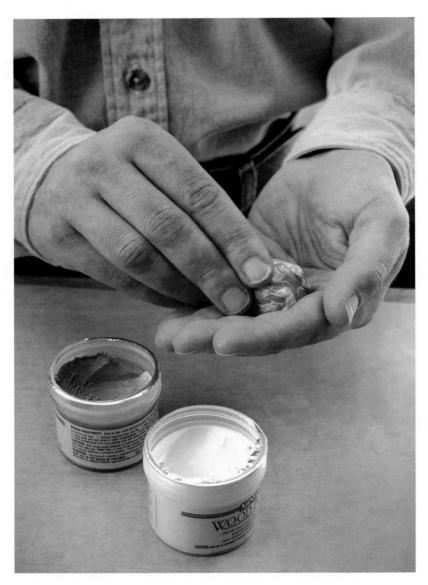

Unfortunately, you're making two common mistakes — you're applying the putty too soon, and you're using the wrong kind of putty.

After you've countersunk all the nails — no deeper than 1/32 in. is recommended — proceed with stain, sealer, and the first coat of finish. While you're at it, do these same steps on a small sample of matching wood (sanded and finished the same as your project) that you can take to the paint or hardware store.

While you're there, look for small jars of premixed color putty — it's available in white and a wide range of wood tones. Purchase a jar that's close to the darkest tone in your sample, and another that matches the lightest tone. When you get back to your shop, scoop out a small amount of each color, and knead them together. Don't overmix — leaving the putty a bit streaky makes it disappear better. Now scoop out a small ball each of the light and dark putties.

Hold those three balls in one hand, and you're ready to fill the nail holes with the other hand. With a little practice, you'll learn how to rub one of the balls over the wood with enough pressure to fill the hole with putty. You'll instantly be able to tell if you need to try a lighter or darker shade. If you do, don't worry about removing the first application because the second one will cover it. The finish that's already on the wood will help keep the putty from sticking anywhere but in the holes.

When you're satisfied with the results, apply the last coat of finish to the wood, and it will help permanently lock the putty in place.

PLANNING FOR WOOD'S MOVEMENT

 I enjoy woodworking as a year-round hobby. But the cabinet doors I've made in the summer always give me a problem. When the drier weather of winter arrives, the panel shrinks inside the frame, exposing unsightly raw wood along both door stiles. Of course, the effect is much worse with stained projects. How do I avoid this problem?

You have the diagnosis absolutely correct, and the cure is very easy. Simply stain and finish the panel before you assemble the door parts. Dividing the work like this also will simplify the finishing process. You'll speed through the panel finishing because all its surfaces are exposed.

When you finish the door frames, you'll be able to handle the doors by putting one hand on each side of the panel. Rig up a cardboard box like the one in the photo, and apply finish to the back side of the door without waiting for the front to dry. After you've done both sides of the door, transfer it to a drying support such as a gallon paint can, then move on to the next door.

THE DIFFERENCE IN MASKING TAPES

 The masking tape I bought a couple of years ago is giving me fits. Instead of pulling away cleanly from the roll, it splits down the middle. Is there an easy solution for this?

There's a very simple solution to this problem — throw away the tape. It's trash. When you go to buy the replacement, you'll see a variety of choices, so here's a quick buying guide.

You may be tempted to choose bargain-priced masking tape, but generally speaking, it's not a good value. The adhesive is often overly aggressive, and that will lead to the same problem you just experienced, or it may tend to leave a gummy residue on your project. Choosing a name-brand tape may be more expensive, but it's generally less frustrating to remove.

General-purpose masking tape has high adhesion, so it's a good choice for chores such as bundling together items or hanging plastic sheeting to non-sensitive surfaces. Painter's tape, sometimes called "painter's grade," has medium-high adhesion so it's less likely to damage surfaces. Some brands of painter's tape will survive up to three days of exposure to sunlight before leaving a gummy residue. You can apply painter's tape to previously painted or varnished surfaces such as window and door trim.

Clean-release tape, which often has a blue color, is a medium-adhesion tape that's well suited for painted walls and trim, glass, and metal. It is more resistant to deterioration by sunlight, and some brands will survive up to 14 days of exposure.

You'll also find masking tape specially designed for delicate surfaces, such as wallpaper, that could be damaged by more aggressive adhesives. Like clean-release tape, it's said to survive up to 14 days of sunlight.

If you spray lacquer on furniture, visit an automotive paint store to get a special masking tape that will survive exposure to lacquer thinner and other powerful solvents. This tape has high adhesion but a special solvent-less adhesive, so it won't dissolve and bond to the finish.

A Clean Paint Line With Your Baseboards

How do I get a clean edge when I mask off the baseboards before painting the walls? Sometimes, the paint seeps under the tape, and other times I get a jagged edge because the tape takes some of the paint with it when I rip it off.

Selecting the right tape is the first step, but you also need to make sure that it adheres continuously along the wood. To do that, firmly draw a plastic putty knife over the tape, burnishing it to the wood as shown in the top photo. Next, you need to realize that using masking tape doesn't give you a license to paint sloppily. Select an angled sash brush to apply paint up to the tape, but don't slosh all over it.

When the paint is dry, slice along the joint between the paint and the tape with a new blade in a crafts knife. This will cut through any paint that's stuck to both the wall and tape, giving you a paint line that's literally razor sharp. But even after you've taken that precaution, remove the tape carefully instead of ripping it so that you can handle any stubborn areas before they turn into a big problem.

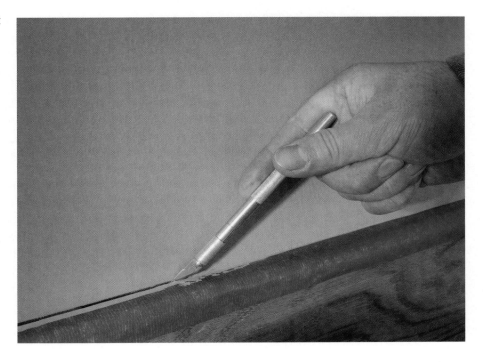

WAXED PAPER SHORTENS TRIM WORK

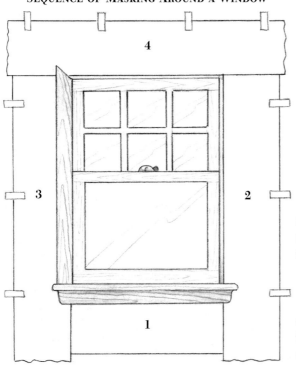

I want to stain and finish the trim around a wood-frame window after installation to make sure that all of the wood components blend together well. The difficulty I foresee is that I'll probably get stain or finish onto the walls, and when I touch up the paint, I'll probably get some on the wood. How do I avoid this problem?

If the walls need painting, do that first. After the paint dries, hang strips of waxed paper in the sequence shown in the drawing. Cut and attach your trim as usual, nailing it tightly to the wall. Stain the wood, and apply your finish. Even if some stain or finish gets on the paper, it won't flow onto the wall because of the way the strips overlap.

When the finish is dry, you should be able to remove the paper by yanking it sideways. This is a little bit like pulling a tablecloth and leaving the dishes in place. If the paper rips or refuses to let go, trim it along the wood with a sharp utility knife or single-edge razor blade.

POUR IT ON

Whenever I pour solvent or finish out of a flat quart can, it glugs and splashes, with part of it sometimes missing the container. How do I coordinate my pouring technique to catch all the solvent?

It's not a matter of coordination — it's how you're holding the can. Grip the can as shown in the photo, and you'll easily control the pour. When you hold it this way, air flows into the can to replace the fluid you've poured out, eliminating the gurgling and sloshing.

READ ALL ABOUT IT: NEWSPAPERS ARE DUST AGENTS

I sometimes paint the inside of cabinets but spray a clear finish on the exterior. Using tape and newspaper, I carefully mask off the interior, and I keep my finishing area as dust-free as possible. But when I spray the sealer, I often get tiny nibs of dust that settle on the finish. What's the source of the dust?

The newspaper is the likely culprit. The newsprint can release fibers as you handle it and also when compressed air stirs up the atmosphere in your finishing area. To solve the problem, take your leftover newspapers to the recycling center, then purchase a roll of masking paper. This special paper is far less likely to produce dust flecks.

Masking paper is sold in a wide range of widths, so if your hardware store doesn't have the size you want, go to a professional paint store or an automotive-finishing supply shop. For speedy application of the paper, consider purchasing a masking-paper machine that applies half the width of masking tape to the paper and leaves the other half free so you can adhere it to your project.

For occasional jobs, an inexpensive hand masker will probably meet both your needs and budget. But for bigger masking tasks, you can purchase larger models — even freestanding units that hold rolls in several sizes.

GLUE SQUEEZE-OUT

When I apply stain, I'm sometimes surprised by areas that don't accept stain because glue squeezed out and I didn't sand enough to get rid of the problem. Other times, the stain reveals cross-sanding scratches or small dings that weren't apparent in the raw wood. Is there some way I can preview the results I'll get before I apply the stain?

Slightly dampen a rag with naphtha, and rub it onto the wood to reveal any problem areas. Any unevenness or defects will be much more apparent when the surface is wet. But unlike water, naphtha evaporates quickly without raising the grain of the wood.

You'll find naphtha in the solvent aisle of your hardware or paint store. It's often sold as V.M.&P. naphtha, with the initials representing "Varnish Maker's and Painter's."

Naphtha also is an excellent general-purpose solvent to have around the shop for thinning oil-based finishes (check the finish's label to ensure compatibility) and for cleanup. In addition, it excels at removing gummy residue from price stickers.

STRAINING TO IMPROVE YOUR FINISH

When I opened my can of varnish, some flecks of dried finish dropped into the liquid. How do I fish them out?

Don't try to pick out the dried bits — filter them instead. Get a supply of disposable filter funnels at your paint store, and strain the finish before each use. Pour the liquid through the filter, depositing it in a clean container into which you'll dip your brush.

OUTDOOR FURNITURE REQUIRES SPECIAL PAINT CONSIDERATIONS

 I wanted to put a durable finish on a small table for our deck, so I brushed on some leftover latex house paint. But the table sometimes feels sticky, especially in hot weather. What went wrong — was the paint too old?

For outdoor furniture, choose enamel paint because it won't get tacky like house paint will. Select either oil- or water-based enamel because each gives virtually identical results when dry.

House paint is deliberately formulated to produce a film that will stretch when the wood expands. This helps eliminate cracking that can shorten the life span of a painted surface. But, as you discovered, it can produce a tacky feeling in hot weather. That's not a problem when the paint is on your house's exterior walls, but it produces a sticky situation when you apply it to chairs or tables.

To fix your table, find a good enamel at a paint store to apply over the existing finish.

BLUSHING FROM THE HUMIDITY

 Last summer, I couldn't work in the garden because it was raining, so I opened up the garage door to spray a coat of lacquer onto a small project. When I came back to apply to a second coat, the first coat was dry but had a murky, clouded look to it. What happened?

When you sprayed on the lacquer, humidity on the surface of the wood got trapped under the finish. So in a sense, it looks cloudy because it is a cloud. Professional painters call this a "blush."

To repair the problem, you can strip off the first coat by using lacquer thinner. Wait until a dry day and start finishing again.

As an alternative, you can add retarder to lacquer thinner to slow down its rate of evaporation, and spray the entire piece with the modified thinner. The thinner will dissolve into the finish. On a dry day, the trapped moisture may have enough time to escape into the atmosphere before the finish hardens again.

GRAIN DIRECTION

 When I'm sanding the finish between coats, do I have to follow the direction of the wood's grain?

When you're sanding just the finish, you can go in any direction you want. That's because the finish itself has no grain direction. You can go across the grain of the wood, diagonally, even in circles, and you won't introduce any problems. Just be careful not to sand through the finish layer. If the stain color underneath suddenly gets lighter, you've gone too far.

HEADBAND SAVES FINISH HEADACHES

 When I sprayed finish on a tabletop, I tipped the spray gun a bit too far, and several drips from a hole in the cup's cover landed on my fresh finish. I can't plug this hole because that would prevent the necessary siphoning action. What can I do to avoid this problem in the future?

One quick solution is to equip your spray gun with a bandanna made from a shop towel or other absorbent material. That way, if anything drips from the hole, the rag will soak it up before it can fall to the surface you're spraying.

Another good strategy is to limit the occasions when you have to tip your gun that far forward. In the example of your tabletop, prop it into a more upright position for easier spraying, then lower it immediately after spraying into a horizontal position to eliminate sags and runs in the finish.

FIVE-GALLON BUCKET SOLUTION

The top of my spray gun has a hook that I use for hanging it while I move the next item into position for spraying. Once I accidentally knocked it off the hook, and the cup came off when it hit the ground, spreading finish everywhere. It was a miserable cleanup job. How can I avoid this problem in the future?

Get a five-gallon plastic bucket, and put at least four inches of sand in the bottom so you can't accidentally kick over the container. Now you can hang your spray gun over the edge of the bucket. As the photo shows, you don't even have to disconnect the air hose.

If the cup does fall off, it will drop harmlessly into the bucket. And if you have a spill, you can throw sand on it immediately to absorb it.

Two Sides to Every Finishing Job

I read somewhere that I should apply a finish to the bottom of a solid-wood tabletop, but that seems like a waste of time to me. Why should I bother to finish the underside when no one will ever see it — just so chewing gum won't stick as easily?

Applying finish to both sides of your tabletop will help keep it flat, and here's why: One purpose behind every type of wood finish — whether it's clear or opaque — is to seal it from airborne humidity. The seal is not perfect, so there will always be some wood movement in response to changes in humidity. As you know, wood swells when it absorbs moisture and shrinks when it becomes drier.

If you apply finish to only one side of a panel, you're inviting trouble. As the drawings show, uneven absorption and loss of humidity sets the wood into motion. The unfinished lower side will move at a different rate from the top, and that will introduce cupping in humid weather and bowing during dry periods.

To keep the wood moving evenly, you should apply an equal number of coats to both the top and bottom of the tabletop.

END VIEW OF TABLETOPS FINISHED ONLY ON TOP AND EDGES

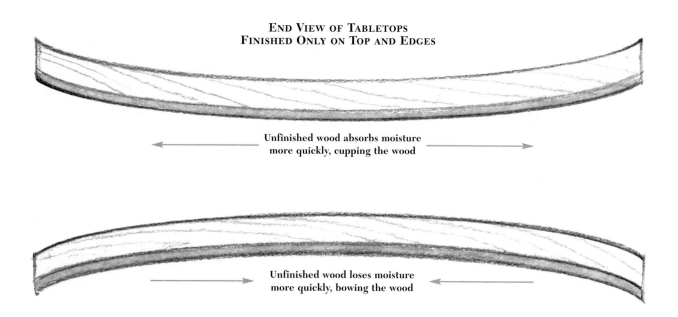

Unfinished wood absorbs moisture more quickly, cupping the wood

Unfinished wood loses moisture more quickly, bowing the wood

THE INSIDE STORY ON FINISHING DRAWERS

 My neighbor and I got into a discussion about whether the insides of drawers should be finished. He says "no," but I think he's just lazy. I say "yes," and he thinks I'm nuts for doing unnecessary work. Who's right?

The correct answer is — it all depends. At the very least, you should apply finish to the inside of the drawer front to keep the wood flat. If you're trying to make a living at furniture making, finishing the insides of drawers will add time and materials to the job without necessarily improving the quality of the product in the minds of your customers. In that case, give the sides, back, and bottom a thorough sanding, and ease the edges with a plane or sandpaper. Tell your client that many of the masterpieces of furniture have unfinished drawer interiors, and that you're following in that tradition.

If you get a client with deep pockets who thinks that drawers should be finished inside and out, agree heartily and take the money.

On a more practical note, kitchen drawers with a finish will be more resistant to spills than unfinished drawers, and a lingerie chest with finished drawers will be less likely to snag delicate clothing. Small-scale drawers, such as those in a jewelry box, deserve a finish to carry a high level of quality workmanship throughout the piece.

The key rule is that whatever finish you apply to one side of a board, you do exactly the same to the other side to prevent uneven wood movement.

OIL AND WATER: SPRAY GUNS' ENEMIES

I've had a compressor for years that powers my air nailer. But I finally bought a spray gun. I'm about half satisfied with my first attempt at spray finishing. I was able to get relatively even coverage, but the finish has a problem I never had with brush-on finishes — the whole surface has a random pattern of tiny dots that seem hazy. What happened?

The dots you see are tiny droplets of oil and water from the air supply that contaminated the finish. If you sprayed paint, you can apply another coat after solving the air problem. If you sprayed a clear finish, the only choice is living with it or completely removing it.

When you used a nail gun, your only concern was the quantity of air from the compressor. But when you spray finishes, you now also have to worry about the quality of the air. Here's a multi-step approach that will clear the air:

IN-LINE
EXTRACTOR

OIL AND WATER
EXTRACTOR

1   Drain your compressor regularly to remove oil and water. Leave the drain valve open when you're not using the compressor so the tank can dry.

2   From the compressor, run a length of hose or pipe that's at least 10 feet long to help cool the air. Elevate the line so any condensed moisture can drain back into the tank. At this point, install an oil and water extractor (also called a trap) that will pull the water and oil from the air (right, in photo). Securely fasten the extractor to a wall or other support in the upright position suggested by the manufacturer.

3   Buy a new air hose exclusively for spray finishing, and attach it at the outlet side of the extractor.

4   Buy an in-line oil and water extractor, and attach it between the end of the hose and your spray gun.

When you ask for extractors at your hardware store, you'll probably get a blank stare in return. Go to an automotive finishing supply store, and they'll have exactly what you need.

WAXING ON ABOUT PASTE WAX

 Should I wax my cabinets and furniture, and if so, what kind of wax should I choose? Any application tricks to make this an easier job?

A good quality paste wax adds another line of defense to your projects, protecting your finish from handling and the atmosphere. You can choose a clear wax or a tinted version that conceals minor imperfections in the wood as well as not leaving a white residue in corners.

Select a furniture wax or even an automotive wax, but beware of any product that bills itself as a "cleaner/wax." The cleaning component is an abrasive that's meant to remove surface oxidation from a finish. That might help an older piece of furniture with a dull, neglected finish, but you run the danger of getting a product that's too aggressive for furniture finishes. Test the wax in an inconspicuous spot.

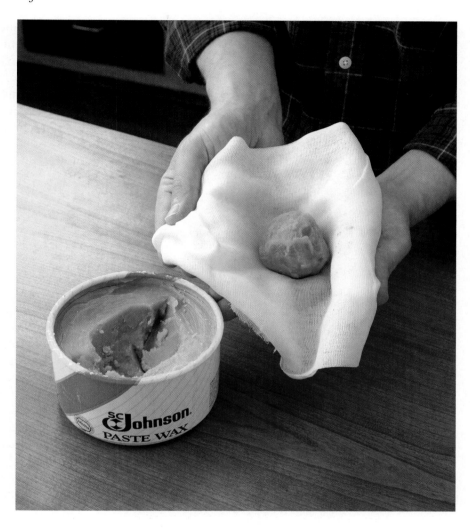

Many paste waxes are so hard that it's difficult to spread the thin even coat that's critical to success. Read the wax's label to see if it lists a recommended solvent. Transfer a lump of wax to a smaller covered container, and see if the addition of mineral spirits, naphtha, or another solvent makes it more workable.

To apply the wax, wrap a softened ball of it inside a piece of cheesecloth, and rub the wood vigorously to work the wax through the cloth. Apply a thin, even coat, then buff with a soft cloth and repeat.

SPARE THE FURNITURE POLISH

 As an option to waxing, what do you think of those products that you spray or wipe on for an instant shine?

While these products — including popular spray-on furniture polishes — offer quick application, the shine is often the result of an oily residue that will attract and hold dust. Similar products may contain silicone, another shiny film that doesn't dry. Silicone may cause extreme problems if you want to refinish a piece of furniture. Even a minute amount of silicone produces a problem called "fish eyes" — craters that repel the finish you're attempting to apply.

GOING NATURAL OR SYNTHETIC?

 I can never remember the rule of what finishes to apply with a natural bristle brush and which require synthetic. So maybe my best plan is to get synthetic bristle brushes and use them with both oil- and water-based finishes. Does that sound like a good idea?

If you know anyone whose hair gets frizzy on a humid day, it's easy to translate that knowledge into the rule of not using a brush made from natural hair with a water-based finish. The bristles swell when they absorb water, making the brush unmanageable.

Synthetic bristle brushes will work with either oil- or water-based finishes, but it's not a good idea to switch the same brush back and forth between the different types. That's because you run the risk of contaminating a finish with an incompatible solvent.

Although some synthetic brushes have excellent quality, not even the most advanced has topped Mother Nature. The best brushes for oil-based finishes are still made from natural bristle. Once you get past the sticker shock of a great brush, you'll enjoy the way it can flow on a finish and smooth it.

BRUSH WITH GREATNESS: AVOID STIFF BRISTLES

When I get a little way into a painting project, the paint starts drying halfway up the brush, right at the line that marks how far I've dipped into the paint. Pretty soon, the bristles start going in all directions and the brush is too stiff to flow on the paint. How can I avoid this problem?

This problem is caused because the bristles above the dip line are dry, and that hastens the set-up of the paint in the brush. Before you start painting, saturate the full length of the bristles with the solvent for the paint you're using. For example, if you're brushing an oil-based finish, soak the bristles with naphtha or mineral spirits. Brush the excess solvent onto a rag, partially dip the brush into the paint, and brush it out on a piece of scrap until you no longer have the paint overdiluted.

Now you can paint for an extended period before the undipped portion of the bristles start to dry.

During a long painting session with water-based paint, you may need to occasionally sprinkle the upper portion of the brush with water to prevent premature drying.

AVOIDING AIRBORNE DUST

 I carefully sand between coats of finish, and blow off the dust with compressed air, but I still get a lot of dust that settles into the wet finish. How can I cure this problem?

Unfortunately, your attempt to cure the dust problem made it worse. When you let loose with the compressed air, it blasts the dust off of the wood and makes it airborne. By the time you've laid down the wet finish, the dust is ready to settle onto it.

Both compressed air and a vacuum throw dust into the air. If you want to employ these methods, take your project outdoors, well away from your finishing area.

A more reliable dust removal technique is a tack cloth, available in the paint department of your hardware store or home center. A tack cloth is essentially a piece of cheesecloth treated with a varnish so it will grab and hold onto dust particles. To use the cloth, unfold it completely, then lightly crumple it, and wipe gently over your entire project. Between jobs, store the tack cloth in a zip-top plastic sandwich bag.

Naphtha will remove the stickiness from your hands, then wash them with soap and water. Don't use a tack cloth before applying a water-based finish. Substitute a lint-free cloth misted with just enough water to pick up the dust.

If you're finishing a small project, you can protect it from settling dust by putting it beneath a cover as shown in the photo. Wipe any dust from the cover before you put it in place.

UV Additives Improve Outdoor Finishes

 I'm going to build some patio furniture, and I can't decide between a clear finish, a semi-transparent stain, or paint. Which one will survive the longest?

Paint is the longest lasting choice because its high pigment content does the most efficient job of blocking ultraviolet (UV) rays from the sun. Just as your unprotected skin will shed dead cells after exposure to the sun, wood cells also suffer damage and will slough away from the lumber, taking the finish with them. When properly applied over a good quality primer, paint should last 7 to 10 years.

Products with less pigment, such as solid-color stain or semi-transparent stain, have a shorter life expectancy — three to seven years. Finishes without pigment, such as an oil finish or water-repellant preservative, may require you to renew them every year or two.

Exterior varnish, often called marine or spar varnish because of its use as a boat finish, has a short life span. It may last a year, perhaps even two under favorable conditions. But when subjected to intense sunlight, it may fail as quickly as six months. Some exterior varnishes include UV blockers to extend the life of the finish, but these additives also quickly degrade in sunlight.

When you buy your finish, you should check whether it contains a mildewcide. If it doesn't, ask your paint dealer for an anti-mildew additive that you can stir into the finish.

Regardless of the finish you choose, you'll extend its life span by keeping your patio furniture in the shade as much as possible.

ADDITIVES HELP
PAINT FLOW BETTER

 Every so often, I need to brush an oil-based painted finish onto wood. But the appearance of brush strokes always annoys me, especially when I want a nice high-gloss finish. I'm afraid that simply adding more thinner to the paint will leave too thin a coat of paint on the wood. What should I do?

You're absolutely right to be concerned about overthinning your paint. In addition to reducing the thickness of the film, you may compromise its adhesion. Instead of thinning, add a paint conditioner, such as Penetrol, manufactured by The Flood Company. (Please see Resources, page 314.)

Mix Penetrol with oil-based paint or varnish, and you'll find that your brush glides on the finish instead of dragging and pulling. The finish also has better flow-out, reducing the appearance of brush strokes. The amount of Penetrol you add depends on the type of finish you're using, as well as the application temperature, so experiment to get the feel of the product.

The same manufacturer also produces a product called Floetrol that mixes with waterborne finishes such as latex paint. The improved paint consistency makes a dramatic difference when you use a paint roller. You'll get rid of the sucking sound that a roller usually makes on a wall, and the improved paint flow reduces spatters and produces a smoother result.

PURCHASE STRATEGIES FOR SPRAY FINISHES

 I'm thinking about getting into spray finishing, but I'm confused about whether I should purchase a gun with a quart cup or get a pressure-feed system. Which one is better?

There are several variables in this decision, including the type of material you'll spray and the volume of finishing you'll do. A pressurized "paint pot" won't need to be filled as often as a quart cup, so it holds real appeal for production situations. It also relieves your wrist and arm from the strain of holding the weight of the finish.

On the other hand, cleaning the pot and pressure line is certainly more difficult than the smaller cup, so changing the material that you spray becomes a major production. For that reason, the pressure feed system is better suited to an assembly line type of operation where you're always doing the same job with the piece of equipment.

A siphon-feed cup system has no problem with thin materials like stains and many clear finishes, but some finishes are simply too thick for this setup. You may be able to avoid that problem with a gravity-feed cup, but you'll need to carefully research that before you commit to a system.

THE HARD FACTS ON ROCK PUTTY

 I've seen a product called "Water Putty," but I've never used it. Frankly, its low price makes me wonder whether it really works very well. What can it do?

Durham's Rock Hard Water Putty is an inexpensive material that's been around for a long time, and it does have a number of good applications around the shop and job site. You simply mix the powder with water to produce a quick-drying, sawdust-colored wood filler that works well under painted finishes.

Despite the product's name, the dried filler isn't rock hard — it actually sands quite easily. You'll also get some shrinkage, so it's a good idea to slightly overfill the voids so you can sand the putty flush with the wood's surface. Filling nail holes and voids in the edges of plywood are two applications for water putty. Prime and paint, and you'll get a smooth finish.

FILLED TO THE RIM? THERE'S AN ANSWER

 Whenever I pour finish out of a can, it fills up the rim. Cleaning it out is a tedious job, but if I don't do it, the lid sticks so tightly I can barely remove it the next time. How can I avoid this problem?

You can either punch holes in the rim so the finish will drip back into the can, or cover the rim with tape to keep the finish out in the first place. Both of these solutions are shown in the photo.

Poke a series of holes through the bottom of the rim's trough with a hammer and nail. If the finish doesn't readily drain, grab a larger-gauge nail to enlarge the holes. These holes don't affect the seal of the lid because it's designed to fit tightly against the sides of the rim and not the bottom.

Masking tape or duct tape seals the rim while you pour the finish into another container. You may need to apply several overlapping pieces of tape to cover enough of the rim so you can pour easily. Immediately after you've finished the pour, strip off the tape and discard it.

Shaking Out the Difference in Gloss and Semi-Gloss

Gloss

Semi-Gloss

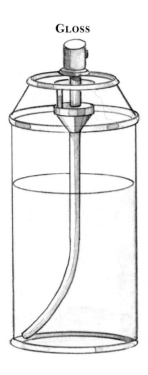
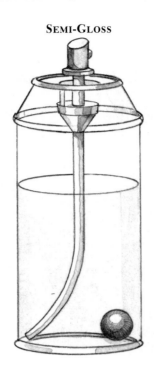

I spray both gloss and semi-gloss aerosol lacquer. But the design of the label is virtually identical, so I always have to study the can every time I pick one up. Is there an easy way to avoid using the wrong finish?

This is a neat little trick that will let you tell gloss from semi-gloss — even with your eyes closed. Simply pick up one of the cans and shake it before spraying. If you grabbed the semi-gloss, you'll hear the rattle of the agitator ball that mixes the solid shine-reduction additive with the liquid finish to suspend it before you spray. The can of gloss finish doesn't have that additive so it doesn't contain an agitator ball. If the can is silent when you shake it, the finish is gloss.

Touch Up Your Finish

I like to apply the stain and finish to door casings, window trim, and baseboards before installing them because it really saves my back from repeated stooping and reaching. But I'd like to find an easy way to minimize the raw look at the cut-lines. Even a tiny bit of raw pine at a mitered corner is distracting. Is there an effective cure that doesn't involve having an open can of stain in my way?

Minwax is one company that makes touch-up pens in colors that match its line of stains. The pen is like a felt tip marker, and a swipe along a cut end of wood will make it blend into its surroundings. Even if the color is not an exact match for your stain, it will certainly eliminate the high contrast of raw wood next to a stained surface.

THERE'S A SCIENCE TO LOADING A BRUSH

To avoid drips when I apply varnish, I have to wipe so much off the brush that it takes forever to complete the project. Of course, I run into the same problem when painting. How do I transfer more finish without making a mess?

LOADING A VARNISH BRUSH (CUTAWAY VIEW)

Dipping merely wets the outside of the bristles, so you're not really using the fluid-carrying capability of the brush. The secret is in knowing how to load the brush, and a container with straight instead of curved sides will give you better results. You'll employ one loading technique for varnish and a completely different approach for paint.

Take a gentle approach with varnish because you don't want to whip air into the liquid. The small bubbles produced by rough handling might not burst before the finish dries, and that would give your project a gritty feel. Dip about half the length of the bristles, and move the brush to the left side of the container. Gently push the side of the brush against the side of the container as you remove it, forcing varnish into the interior of brush. This technique is shown in the top drawing. Then move the brush to the right, wipe it against the container's side to remove excess varnish (step 2), and you're ready to apply finish.

To load a brush with paint (bottom illustration), dip half of the bristles' length, withdraw from the liquid, and slap the bristles against both sides of the container. For fine control, as when you're "cutting in" along a surface that won't be painted, purchase a paint container that has a wire across it. Load the brush as usual, then simply wipe one side of the bristles along the wire to remove excess paint.

Step 1

Step 2

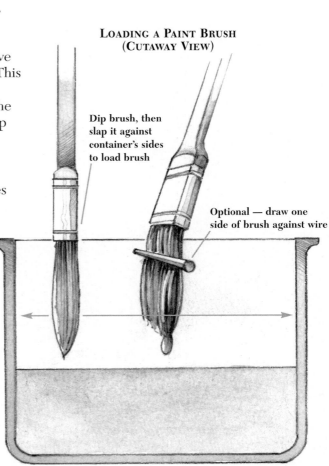

LOADING A PAINT BRUSH (CUTAWAY VIEW)

Dip brush, then slap it against container's sides to load brush

Optional — draw one side of brush against wire

10
JIGS AND
FIXTURES

CRADLE YOUR ROUND STOCK

What's the best way to hold round stock while drilling?

Take a look at the photos, and you'll see how easy it is to make a V-block that allows you to safely cradle round stock while you drill into it. Start with a piece of stock that's 2¾ in. square and 12 inches long. The exact size isn't critical, but it is important that the stock is straight.

Tilt your table saw blade to 45 degrees, and lock your rip fence ½ in. from the lower edge of the blade. It isn't necessary to make the angled cuts to full depth in one pass. By slowly raising the blade after each cut, you'll sneak up on the setting that will make the cuts meet perfectly.

But perfect cuts are more a matter of appearance than function. If you slightly overshoot the cuts it won't affect the accuracy of the jig.

Line the angled walls with 120-grit sandpaper to prevent the round stock from shifting as it's drilled.

Don't throw away the waste wedges from the V-block. Simply glue them to a plywood base, and you'll have a second V-block. Keep it as a backup, or give the second jig to a woodworking friend.

GET TO THE CENTER OF DRILLING ROUND STOCK

 When I use a V-block at the drill press, how do I make sure the bit is absolutely centered?

Purchase a centering tool — it's usually sold for precision positioning of router bits — and chuck it into your drill press chuck. Lower the tool, and adjust the position of the V-block so the tapered tip of the tool settles into the block's angle. Slide the drill press fence against the V-block, and clamp it securely.

Put the round stock into the V-block, and very gently press the tip of the centering tool into the wood. With your drill press turned OFF, push only hard enough to make a shallow dimple. This small mark will help prevent your bit from skating across the surface of the wood. Using a brad-point or Forstner bit will also help ensure accurate drilling.

Store the centering tool carefully to preserve its accuracy.

TO GLUE OR NOT TO GLUE

When I make jigs, should I glue and screw the joints, or do screws have enough strength on their own?

There's no question that a joint reinforced with both glue and screws will have superior strength, but there's another consideration that comes into play — the ability to replace parts of the jig that wear out or are damaged later. Large or complex jigs can require a considerable investment in time and materials, so the ability to unscrew and replace one damaged part is certainly better than junking the entire assembly.

Nifty Jig Tames Plastic Laminate

When I try to cut plastic laminate at my table saw, it slides under my rip fence and spoils the cut. How can I tame this thin material?

Create a channel to guide the laminate by ripping a table saw kerf ¼ in. deep located ¼ in. from the edge of a plywood auxiliary fence. As shown in the photo, you can rip a second groove in the opposite edge of the fence to double the life of the jig. When you clamp the plywood to your rip fence, take it easy on the clamping pressure to avoid damage to your fence.

The depth of the kerf serves another important purpose by automatically creating an offset that makes the laminate larger than the surface you'll cover. For example, if you're covering a panel that's 12 inches square, you simply measure that dimension from the face of the plywood fence to the edge of the blade. But when you insert the laminate into the guide groove and make your cut, the plastic emerges at 12¼ in., creating a ⅛-in. overlap at each edge. Mount the laminate on your project and trim off the overhang with a router and piloted flush-trim bit or a dedicated laminate-trimming bit.

Slick Spline Slots for Mitered Frames

I'd like to cut spline slots into a couple of assembled mitered frames, but I don't want to build a complicated jig. Is there an easy way to set up for this cut?

Attach some miter offcuts to each corner of the frame as shown in the photo, and you'll have the accuracy you need at the speed you want.

Double-faced cloth carpet tape does an excellent job of holding the scrap blocks to the frame. Hold the assembly firmly against your table saw's rip fence to ensure a vertical cut. If you're working with a large frame, you may want to boost stability by adding an auxiliary high face made of ¾-in. plywood to the rip fence.

THE STRAIGHT STORY ON FREEHAND DRILLING

 Whenever I need to drill holes freehand, I just can't seem to get them vertical. It makes me plumb crazy. What can I do?

Purchasing a guide for a portable drill is one answer, but if you have a drill press and some scrap lumber, you can make a guide in less than one minute.

To make a guide for a ¼-in. bit, for example, chuck a ¹⁷⁄₆₄ in. bit into your drill press, and bore a series of holes near the end of a 2x2 strip. (To keep friction to a minimum, always drill a guide hole at least ¹⁄₆₄ in. larger than the bit you'll be guiding.)

Crosscut the wood at least 10 in. long to give you enough leverage to hold onto the jig in case the bit gets snagged in the guide hole. Mark the bit size onto the jig with a permanent marker. You'll also grab the marker to cross out a hole after it becomes worn. You can add another bit size on the opposite end of the strip. If you select a thicker block, you can adapt this same concept to drill a series of holes that are vertical and an identically deep. Calibrate the jig by adjusting the length of the drill bit that projects from the chuck.

WIN-WIN WAYS WITH EURO HINGES

 I have a love-hate relationship with Euro hinges. I love the quick installation and easy adjustability, but hate the tedious setup to get the hole for the hinge cup positioned just right. How can I eliminate this nuisance?

The next time you make a successful setup at your drill press, fabricate a jig that will duplicate the offset and depth settings almost instantly the next time. Simply drill a hole in a scrap piece of door stock, and label it with the dimensions. You can even add the model number of the hinge, and that will eliminate looking up the installation specifications.

ZERO-CLEARANCE TABLE-SAW INSERT FOR ALMOST ZERO MONEY

I need to rip some narrow strips for a laminated assembly, but the throat of my table-saw blade insert sometimes catches the ends, and the kerf in the wood often wants to close up immediately behind the blade. How can I make the ripping of narrow pieces a safer and more dependable procedure?

A zero-clearance table saw insert with a built-in splitter will address both of the problems you've experienced. Although you can purchase an insert, it's easy and inexpensive to make your own. Even without the splitter, the insert helps prevent chip-out of plywood and plastic-covered sheet goods by providing better support to the edges of the cut.

Choose a blank of ½-in. plywood that's flat and slightly larger than your existing metal insert. Use cloth double-faced carpet tape to adhere the upside-down metal insert to your plywood blank, and band-saw to within ⅛ in. of its perimeter. Chuck a flush-cutting bit into your table-mounted router, and finish smoothing the edge.

If your existing insert has a metal pin projecting from its back end, you'll have to carefully steer the router bit around it, and finish that portion of the edge after separating the metal and plywood. You can omit the metal pin in your wood insert, or replicate the original by drilling a pilot hole for a finishing nail, partially driving it, and clipping the nail to the required projection with wire cutters.

On the bottom of your insert, drill countersunk pilot holes for #8 x ⅜-in. flathead screws. These screws serve as leveling feet to bring your insert flush with the saw table. Use your existing insert to help position these screws. You can also drill a ¾-in. finger hole in the insert — just like the original — to make it easy to lift out of the saw.

Fully lower your saw blade, place the wood insert into your saw, and level it to the table's surface by using the adjustment screws. Slide the table-saw's rip fence over the edge of the insert to hold it down during the next step. Turn on your saw, and slowly crank the blade upward through the insert. Raise it slightly more than the required cutting height, then lower it about a quarter turn of the crank to reduce noise and friction.

The zero-clearance insert is complete and ready to go to work. Adding the optional splitter involves only a few more steps. Remove the insert from the saw, and replace the stock one. Adjust your rip fence to make a cut that extends the kerf through the back end of the insert. After you make that cut, glue a ⅛ x 1½ x 3-in. piece of hardboard into the rear of the kerf. Sand chamfers at the leading edge of the splitter so it can do its job of keeping the kerf open behind the blade. NOTE: If you are using a thin-kerf blade in your table saw, cut the splitter stock to match the blade thickness — usually about ³⁄₃₂ inch.

While you're making the insert, consider making a batch of them to use as throatplates for your dado blade. Each time you set the blade for a new width, cut a new throatplate opening and label the cutting width for future use.

Best Jigs: Birch and Maple

What's the best material for jig construction?

For sheet material, birch plywood is a good choice for several reasons — it's widely available, reasonably priced, has smooth faces, and is dimensionally stable.

When you need solid wood, reach for maple or birch. Whether you need smooth-sliding runners or a surface that will stand up to a router bearing, these two woods meet the job's qualifications.

But even great choices in materials won't make up for poor storage. A jig that's stored on a damp floor or in a super-heated attic will show its discomfort by warping.

YOUR JIG WORK DESERVES A FINISHING TOUCH

Some woodworking articles I've read suggest putting a coat of finish onto a jig. Isn't that just a waste of time and materials?

If the jig is a single-use template that you'll discard at the end of the project, a finish doesn't make any sense. But if you're building a table-saw jig that you'll rely upon for years, a quick application of finish is a good idea. The finish will help seal the wood against dirt and also slow down the effects of moisture gain and loss, stabilizing the parts so that they will work smoothly.

For small jigs, a quick-drying aerosol finish, such as shellac or lacquer, is a good choice. To minimize cleanup and to make efficient use of your time, you can coat larger jigs when you're applying finish to a project. An oil finish will help prevent glue from sticking, so it's a good choice for fixtures that are used in glue-ups.

A JIG WORTH BUILDING IS WORTH PRESERVING

I just built a set of chairs, and I'd like to save the templates and jigs that I made in case I want to make another batch of chairs in the future. Any good ideas on keeping all these odd-shaped parts together?

One method uses stretch wrap that's sold in the shipping materials section of office supply stores. You also may find it at a well-stocked hardware store. You simply hold all of the parts tightly together, and then bind them with the wrap. To unwrap, slit the film with a sharp knife. There's no tape residue or other mess.

Another method involves bolts and wing nuts. Simply drill holes through the stacked parts, slide in a bolt, and spin on the nut. Of course, you need to make sure the hole will miss any critical locations.

Be sure you boldly label the package with a permanent marker so you won't have to unwrap all your templates to find the one you want.

STOP! A JIG WORTHY OF STOPPED DADOES

 When I rout dadoes, I'm always concerned that the router will stray away from the guide board and ruin the cut. In addition, it's a hassle to constantly figure the offset from the bit's centerline to know where to clamp the guide. Is there a jig that can solve these problems?

Check out the jig in the photo, and you'll see the solution to your concerns. With this jig, you can rout continuous or stopped dadoes. To make the jig, simply rip ¾-in. plywood into strips 4 in. wide, and then cut them to the required lengths. The only critical dimension is the distance between the rails, which should equal the diameter of your router's baseplate. To get an exact fit, place your router as a spacer between the rails when you screw them into position.

You can make the rails of the jig any length you want, and you'll find it convenient to make several jigs in varying lengths. The setup is much more manageable when the scale of the jig is appropriate to the parts.

One special feature of the jig is the clear acrylic center finder. This strip fits between the rails to accurately position the jig. With a scratch awl, scribe a centerline into the bottom face of the acrylic, and you'll position the jig quickly and accurately.

After you place the jig where you want it, securely clamp it to your stock. Remove the acrylic strip, and rout the dado.

GREAT JIG RUNNERS

Whenever I make jigs that ride in my table saw's miter gauge slot, I always run into trouble. Either the wood runner eventually shrinks down to a sloppy fit, or it swells and won't fit into the slot. How can I get a good fit regardless of the humidity?

Some woodworkers choose ultra high molecular weight (UHMW) plastic for jig glides because it's slippery but dimensionally stable. (You can find UHMW in many woodworking catalogs or stores.)

Unfortunately, it can also be a bit pricey, so here's a less expensive alternative you can adopt. It enables you to quickly adjust the fit of the runners with micrometer precision, and the adjustment is not merely an initial setup. If the runners ever change in width, you can easily alter the fit at any time.

When you rip the runners, orient the grain so it's quartersawn (with the tree's growth rings nearly vertical) as shown in the drawing. Quartersawn lumber changes very little in width during moisture cycles. Its change is primarily in thickness, but that doesn't affect the fit of the runner. Rip the runners about 1/16 in. narrower than the width of your table saw's miter gauge slot. The next step will fine-tune the fit.

Again referring to the drawing, drill each side of the runner with three countersunk pilot holes for #8 x 1/2-in. flathead screws. Center one, and position the others about 2 in. from each end. To prevent the screws from interfering with each other, slightly stagger the holes so that they aren't directly opposite each other.

To fit the runner into the slot, first drive all of the screws so the heads are flush with the surface on the runner. On one side of the runner, back out each screw an equal amount — one-quarter turn, for example. Slip the end of the runner into the slot, and back out the first screw until it just scrapes the wall of the slot. Repeat the adjustment for other screws until the runners slide freely but without extra play.

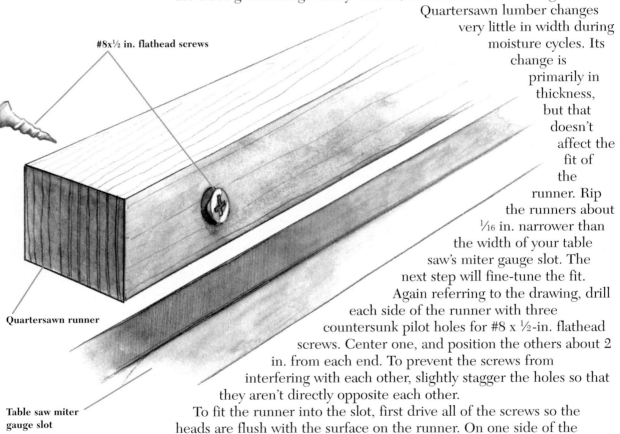

#8x½ in. flathead screws

Quartersawn runner

Table saw miter gauge slot

CROSSCUT SLED: JUST THE RIGHT SIZE

My miter gauge is good enough for small crosscutting jobs, but it tends to be wobbly when I need to deal with wide panels such as shelves and carcase parts. How can I boost my accuracy when making these cuts?

For accurate crosscuts in wide stock, make a crosscut sled to fit your table saw. You can modify the dimensions shown in the drawing to suit your saw or the material you need to cut. If you often crosscut long stock, you'll benefit from making the sled longer. However, a sled with reduced cutting capacity may still handle the jobs you need, and you'll find that the smaller size is easier to handle and more convenient to store.

Construction of the jig is a straightforward process, but you'll have to be careful when you attach the runners to the base so you'll get straight cuts. The following procedure will help ensure success.

Assemble the sled, but don't attach the runners yet. Make certain your table saw's rip fence is parallel to the miter gauge slot, and set it so you can cut the kerf centered along the sled's length.

After you make that cut, leave the rip fence in position and the sled on your table saw. Slip the runners under the base of the sled. By measurement, locate the centerlines of the runners, and drill pilot holes through the sled's base. Screw the runners in place and check for an easy sliding motion. Then turn the sled upside down, and reinforce the runners by driving additional screws through them into the sled base. Rub a little bit of paste wax onto the runners to reduce friction.

Don't forget to drill hanging holes though the base. Hang the sled on the wall to keep it out of your way.

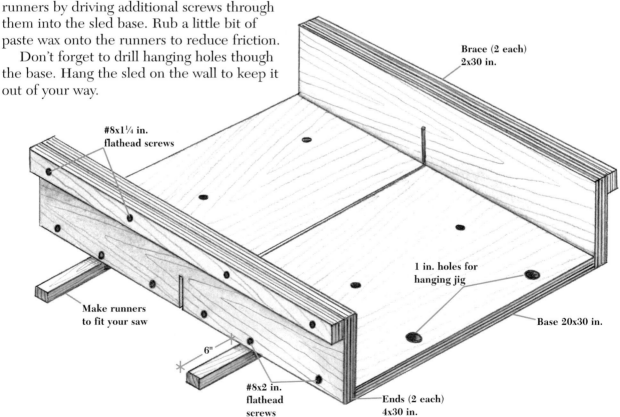

Brace (2 each) 2x30 in.

#8x1¼ in. flathead screws

1 in. holes for hanging jig

Make runners to fit your saw

Base 20x30 in.

6"

#8x2 in. flathead screws

Ends (2 each) 4x30 in.

BRACE YOURSELF: TRY METAL BRACING

I don't know how many different jigs I've made over the years for crosscutting and ripping sheets of plywood. They have all warped, twisted, bowed, bent, and sagged themselves into oblivion. How about a super-strong jig that will endure?

You may have already tried a variation of this jig, but the version shown in the photo literally has a backbone of steel. Purchase a piece of ¾-in. square steel tubing, clean it, and hacksaw to length.

Using your drill press, drill holes through the steel for the ¼-in. bolts that will hold the plywood base to the tubing. Make the first hole about 1½ in. from the end, and then at approximately 12-in. centers. Crosscut a 10-in.-wide piece of ½-in. plywood to the required length. Clamp the steel to the plywood, and use the holes through it as guides to drill through the plywood. Turn the plywood over, and drill countersinks to ensure that the flathead bolts won't scratch your stock. Complete the assembly with flat washers and nylon-insert locking nuts.

To complete the jig, register your circular saw's base firmly against the plywood and steel, and make a cut along the plywood. For the cut along the other side of the steel, hold the opposite side of your saw's base against the metal. This double cut permits you to use either side of the jig.

Bear in mind that the calibration is accurate only for the type of blade that you used for the initial cut. As long as you stick with identical blades you'll get accurate results, but switching to a different blade type may mean you'll have to replace the plywood base.

To put the guide to work, simply align the edge of the plywood with the cut-line on your workpiece, clamp, and cut.

ROUNDING THE CORNER ON TABLETOPS

 I'm making a batch of tables that will have corners with a 2-in. radius. How can I get consistent results with a minimum of sanding?

By making one accurate template from hardwood, you can quickly make rounded corners with a router and flush-trim bit. Take your time making the jig because any irregularities in it will be transferred to every corner of your tabletops.

Put your stack of tabletops face down on your workbench, and use the template and a pencil to draw the radius at each corner. Band-saw most of the waste, but keep your cut about ⅛ in. to the waste side of the line.

Drill shank clearance holes in the template, and screw it to the underside of a top at the first corner. Chuck a flush-trim bit into your router, and rout along the template to create a smooth line. With a solid wood top, rout from the end grain to the side grain for the smoothest results. After you've routed all the corners, complete the smoothing with sandpaper in a block.

If your template starts to show signs of wear, simply screw it to a length of hardwood, and let the template clone itself.

SORTING THROUGH JIGS AND FIXTURES

 Some people call a shop-made gadget a jig, and others call it a fixture. Is there really a difference?

Technically speaking, a fixture means that it holds something — fixes it in position. If the device and your workpiece are clamped together, call it a fixture. A jig, meanwhile, can refer to a fixture or to an accessory that's positioned or guided by hand. So all fixtures are jigs, but not all jigs are fixtures.

To most people, this is a distinction without a significant difference. Call all of them gizmos, and you'll be on the safe side.

PICTURE THIS: AWESOME FRAME CORNERS

The last time I made some picture frames, my miter saw gave me a real workout. I don't even know how many times I switched back and forth between right and left. Is there an easier way?

Make the sliding jig shown in the drawing, and you'll make mitered corners with impressive accuracy. One of the keys to the jig's exactness is that you cut left miters on one side of the jig and rights on the other. This creates complementary angles, so as long as the two fences are at 90 degrees to each other, the two cuts you make will always be a precise right angle.

Make all the jig's parts from ¾-in. plywood, and cut the base to any convenient size. After you've screwed the end to the base, follow the procedure described in the construction of the crosscut sled (page 213) to fasten the runners.

When you select the front-to-back placement of the angled fences on the base, make certain that you can position the widest stock you'll miter without banging its tip into the front end of the jig. Carefully position one of the fences at 45 degrees to the kerf in the base, and screw it in place. With a framing square, ensure that the second fence is precisely 90 degrees to the first fence. Attach 120-grit sandpaper to the fences so the pieces you're mitering can't slip.

To check that the fences are at an exact 90-degree angle, follow the procedure described for checking the angles of a mitered box. (page 105)

You can make sturdy but removable fence extensions by teaming plywood with aluminum angles. Cut biscuit slots into the ends of the fences and extensions, and glue a biscuit only into the extension.

When you prepare your frame stock, mark the inner edge of each piece with a length of tape as a reminder to always position that edge against one of the fences. This ensures that each corner is comprised of one right and one left cut.

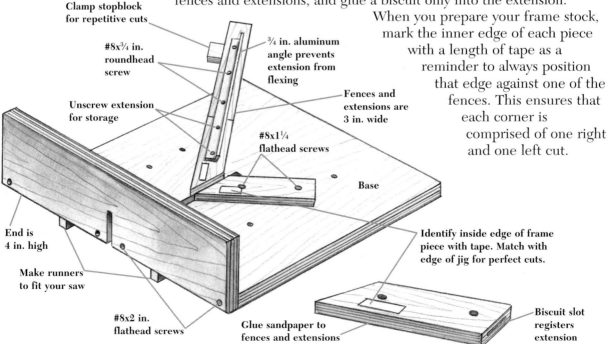

Clamp stopblock for repetitive cuts

#8x¾ in. roundhead screw

¾ in. aluminum angle prevents extension from flexing

Unscrew extension for storage

Fences and extensions are 3 in. wide

#8x1¼ flathead screws

Base

End is 4 in. high

Identify inside edge of frame piece with tape. Match with edge of jig for perfect cuts.

Make runners to fit your saw

#8x2 in. flathead screws

Glue sandpaper to fences and extensions

Biscuit slot registers extension

FAST AND STABLE SPLINE JIG

 I'm going to embark on a long production run of picture frames. How about a spline jig that's fast and stable?

The jig shown in the photo holds the frame securely, and it has a large enough footprint to make it a steady performer on your saw's table.

To make the jig, start with two pieces of ¾-in. plywood that are 7 x 20 in. Make the miter cuts in one piece, and attach these angled supports to the backboard with #8 x 1¼-in. flathead screws. Of course, keep all screws out of the saw blade's path.

Cut four 4 x 5 blocks from ¾-in. plywood, and screw them to the backboard/support assembly. To ensure that the jig will stand upright, make certain all bottom edges of the jig are flush.

To set up the jig, position the rip fence so the blade will slice into the jig at the desired location — halfway into the thickness of the supports is a good choice. Raise the table-saw's blade to the required height, and turn on the motor.

While holding the jig firmly against the rip fence, slide the jig forward until the top of the blade enters the rear support. You'll know you've reached this point when the cut in the rear support doesn't get any higher. Shut off the saw, and let the blade stop. Put a piece of masking tape on the saw's table at the forward end of the rear support block. This will show you how far forward you need to push the jig to make the cut.

To use the jig, clamp a frame into position, slide the jig forward, then pull it back. Always keep firm contact between the jig's backboard and the rip fence. If you're working with jumbo-size frames, add a higher auxiliary face to the rip fence for additional stability.

11
SHOP
ORGANIZERS

LOCK DOWN THOSE MOBILE CABINETS

 I put casters under a cabinet and mounted my miter saw on top, thinking that would be a handy way to move it out of the way when it's not needed. That part works fine. But when I cut with the saw, the cabinet has the annoying habit of scooting around no matter how hard I push down the locks on all four wheels. Can I have mobility when I want it and a solid lock when I need it?

What you need is a special type of caster that not only prevents wheel rotation but also locks down the swiveling motion. One toe lever activates and releases both mechanisms. You'll find these casters in many mail-order woodworking catalogs.

You also mentioned that you mounted four locking casters, but it's really an unnecessary expense to have all four wheels swivel. You'll get great results and save money by putting two swiveling casters on the front of the cabinet and two less-expensive rigid-plate casters at the rear. With this combination, you'll sacrifice a tiny bit of mobility (you won't be able to push the cabinet straight sideways), but you'll gain an impressive amount of stability.

WIRE SHELF PERFECT FOR YOUR BAND SAW

I'd like to store my band saw's rip fence and a few items on the metal stand under the saw, but how do I keep the shelf I would install from collecting sawdust?

Measure the shelf size you want, then go to the closet-organizing aisle at a home center and buy a piece of open-wire shelving that will let the sawdust fall through. While you're at the home center, also buy a few nylon electrical ties to attach the shelf to the stand without the hassle of drilling for bolts.

SHOP STRATEGY ORGANIZES HARDWARE BINS

 I've tried several different systems to keep my fasteners organized, but the variety of lengths, drive types, and sizes of boxes defies all of my attempts to bring some order out of the chaos. How can I simplify the storage?

Organize screws by length and bolts by diameter and thread, regardless of the drive or material. For example, put all your boxes of 1-in. screws into a single bin. That way, if you run out of 1-in. zinc-plated #6 slotted flatheads, you'll immediately see that you have some #8 stainless steel Phillips panheads that might substitute nicely.

Corral your bolts, nuts, and washers by diameter and thread. For example, one bin will have ¼-20 bolts in varying lengths, plus individual boxes of flat washers, lock washers, fender washers, standard hex nuts, and nylon-insert hex nuts. You can quickly pick out what you need.

There's a strange irony to the process of organizing things. Sometimes, trying to carry the organization out to a finer degree has the opposite effect — there are so many individual categories that you can't find anything. Don't make it any more complicated than it needs to be.

CORRAL YOUR TAPE WITH A CHAIN

 I've tried stacking them and hanging them, but rolls of tape keep rolling away. How do I get these round things to stay put?

Go to the counter where they make keys at your hardware store, and you'll probably be able to purchase beaded chain by the foot. Get about 18 inches of it, and buy a connector so you make a secure loop. String all of your rolls of tape onto the chain, and snap it shut for roll-proof storage that stays put on a shelf or hook. You don't even need to unchain the tape to tear off the length you need.

HAVE BUCKET AND TOOLS, WILL TRAVEL

Whenever I need to go to a relative's house for even a minor repair job, it seems that I always run into something unexpected, and a tool that's right near my workbench would have made the job go faster and easier. I can't lug around my entire shop, but being better prepared would sure help. Any suggestions?

Instead of packing up for each trip, stay packed all the time. Keep all your frequently used tools in a five-gallon bucket organizer near your bench, and you'll save steps in the shop and be ready at a moment's notice for repairs anywhere in your own home or at someone else's house.

Build a swiveling platform from a couple of pieces of ¾-in. plywood and a 6-in. lazy Susan bearing, and you can twirl the bucket to grab the right tool fast. Store the bucket on the swivel at the end of your workbench, and your most-used tools will never be more than a couple steps away.

The following tools store easily within the bucket, and won't yank your shoulder out of its socket when you lift it. Add or subtract from the list to suit the kinds of projects you handle on a regular basis.

Options for bucket contents: 16-oz. claw hammer; ¹⁄₁₆-in. nailset; small pry bar; 16-ft. tape measure; 6-ft. folding rule with brass rule extension; adjustable bevel; 12-in. combination square; scratch awl; center punch; safety glasses; plumb bob and nylon line; torpedo level; flashlight; hacksaw with frame; spare hacksaw blades with 16, 24, and 32 teeth per inch; 18-inch crosscut saw; dovetail saw; duct tape; electrical tape; masking tape; small bottle of woodworker's glue; small tube of construction adhesive (Liquid Nails is one brand); two C-clamps; long-nose locking pliers; 10-in. locking pliers; slip-joint pliers; 10-in adjustable wrench; tin snips; push drill with bits in handle; utility knife with spare blades; ¾-in. cold chisel; ½-in. wood chisel; block plane; package of tapered shims; interchangeable bit screw driver with small and large Phillips and slotted drives; electrician's wire stripper/wire cutter; neon electrical tester; round file; flat file; four-in-one file/rasp; rubber sanding block and a few strips of 80-, 120-, and 220-grit paper; putty knife; pencils; and an adapter for a grounded plug to an ungrounded socket. Get a pocket-sized plastic fishing-tackle box, and fill it with an assortment of brads, finishing and box nails, flathead and roundhead screws, and electrical wire connectors. This box is merely your job site backup of fasteners — just enough to avoid a trip back to the shop.

A Tip Borrowed from Auto Mechanics

 Whenever I'm assembling a project, only half the screws go into the wood; the other half get knocked onto the floor. I hate to be wasteful, but I got into woodworking for fun, not to spend my time sorting through floor sweepings. How can I fight gravity?

To conquer gravity, enlist the help of one of the other main forces of the universe: magnetism. Go to your local auto-supply store, and you can buy a stainless steel bowl that's fitted with a powerful magnet underneath it. Mechanics use it to store fasteners as they work on cars because steel parts won't fall out, even if you turn the bowl upside down.

The bowl will also do a great job in your shop by keeping screws or nails exactly where you want them. If you want to save a few dollars, team a surplus speaker magnet with a metal bowl you purchase or pilfer from the kitchen.

Expand Tool Storage to Your Doors

I like storing tools on pegboard, but the problem is that while my tool collection keeps growing, my wall space remains constant. How do I gain more hanging room in the same number of square feet?

Instead of installing pegboard horizontally, go vertically to create floor-to-ceiling storage. For convenience, you'll want to keep your most-used tools at elbow level, and seldom-used items down low or up high. For safety's sake, store heavy or sharp tools down low where they can't fall and injure you, your project or someone else. One other spot you may have overlooked is the back of the door that leads into your shop. Screw on a few spacers, then slap on a piece of perforated hardboard. Now you can go shopping for more tools!

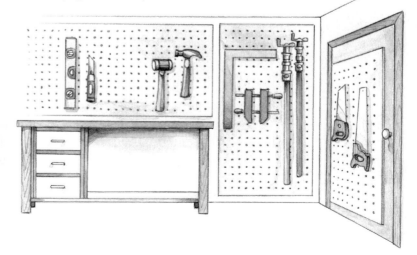

THRIFTY WAYS TO STORE ROUTER BITS

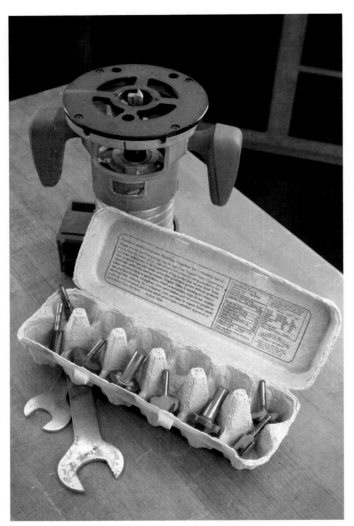

I've seen all kinds of fancy router bit holder projects in the magazines, but I don't want to spend all weekend making one. How about some quick and easy solutions? I'd especially like an easy way to carry router bits to a job site.

Woodworkers usually think of wood as the solution to a problem, but if you open up your thinking, you'll find a number of other materials that you can use. For example, get a piece of 1½-in.-thick rigid foam insulation (expanded polystyrene), and you can make a drawer-size router bit organizer in minutes. Drill holes for the router bits' shanks with a handheld drill.

An even quicker solution is a sheet of high density polyfoam (foam rubber). At a camera store, you can buy die-cut polyfoam sheets that photographers modify into custom-fitted equipment cases. But you can use the die-cut slits to insert router bits. It's a quick solution that you can reorganize at any time.

For a handy zero-cost bit case for your shop or the job site, grab an empty egg carton. To keep small bits from shifting around, you may need to add a thin sheet of polyfoam to the inner lid of the carton.

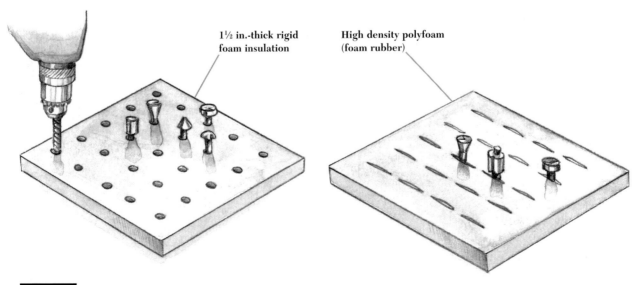

1½ in.-thick rigid foam insulation

High density polyfoam (foam rubber)

ELECTRIFYING ADDITIONS TO YOUR WORKBENCH

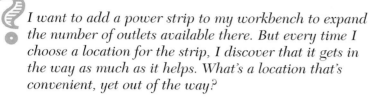

? *I want to add a power strip to my workbench to expand the number of outlets available there. But every time I choose a location for the strip, I discover that it gets in the way as much as it helps. What's a location that's convenient, yet out of the way?*

You're going to love this solution, because you get the power strip, plus a swing-arm lamp. Best of all, you can move them close to your work or scoot them out of the way. The drawing carries the concept.

A switch isn't absolutely necessary, but a pilot light that indicates when the power strip is energized is a real convenience, letting you know that you're plugging into a live outlet.

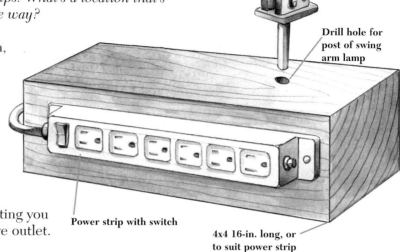

Drill hole for post of swing arm lamp

Power strip with switch

4x4 16-in. long, or to suit power strip

STORE YOUR SPADE BITS IN PVC

? *I have a number of spade bits that I store in their plastic factory sleeves to protect the cutting edges. But they have a habit of scattering all over my toolbox, so finding the one I need is like a game of hide and seek. Is there any way to keep them together?*

Make the easy spade-bit case shown in the drawing, and you'll have a nearly indestructible container. After you solvent-weld together the PVC components, give the assembly a few hours at room temperature for the bond to cure and the odor to dissipate before you load it up with bits.

You can change the scale of this idea to make all kinds of durable containers. For example, by increasing the diameter and length, you can make a level case that's stronger than the store-bought variety. Shove a little piece of foam rubber into the bottom of the case to prevent the level from rattling.

SPADE-BIT CASE

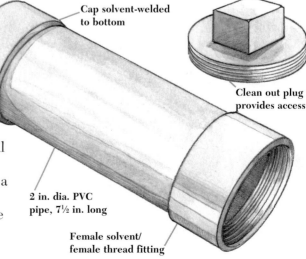

Cap solvent-welded to bottom

Clean out plug provides access

2 in. dia. PVC pipe, 7½ in. long

Female solvent/ female thread fitting

CAST YOUR EYES UP FOR THE OUTLET BOXES

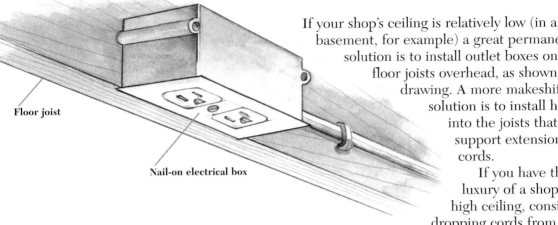

? *When I'm assembling a project in the middle of the shop, it seems that I have extension cords everywhere. Is there a way to get all this tangle off the floor?*

Floor joist

Nail-on electrical box

If your shop's ceiling is relatively low (in a basement, for example) a great permanent solution is to install outlet boxes onto the floor joists overhead, as shown in the drawing. A more makeshift solution is to install hooks into the joists that can support extension cords.

If you have the luxury of a shop with a high ceiling, consider dropping cords from the ceiling at convenient locations. Any way you attack this problem, you'll make your shop safer by reducing tripping hazards.

BOX UP YOUR SCRAPS BY SPECIES

? *I hate throwing away lumber, but the scraps are overtaking my shop. Even more maddening is the fact that I have a terrible time finding a usable piece of wood in my jumbled pile. How can I get organized?*

Line up some cardboard boxes — one for each wood species you use. That way, you won't have to sort through cherry off-cuts looking for a piece of oak. And when a box fills up — that's it! Further scraps go into a kindling box. As an alternative, donate its contents to a youth group, such as Boy or Girl Scouts, or a church-sponsored organization that has crafts activities.

Limiting packrat tendencies is a tough thing to do, but you have to set some limits. If you don't, you'll have to give up woodworking and call yourself a wood collector instead.

ARM'S LENGTH IDEA FOR PENCILS

 I'd like to keep a few pencils near all the stationary tools in my shop, but finding a place to store them has me stumped. Any suggestions?

Foam insulation (expanded polystyrene) and foam pipe insulation are both excellent for storing pencils and other sharp instruments, such as a striking knife, craft knife, scratch awl, or center punch. Cut a piece of foam insulation to any size you want, and attach it to a stationary tool with double-faced cloth carpet tape. To store your pencils and other tools, simply jab them into the foam. Even if you mount the block sideways, the foam will hold them snugly. Set a block on your workbench, and you'll always have sharp tools at hand.

Split the pipe insulation down its seam, and it will grip onto the edge of a tabletop, wall stud, or tool stand. Again, storage is jab-in easy.

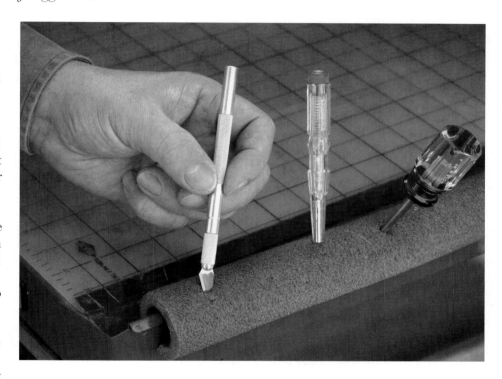

BABY YOUR FILES AND RASPS

I just invested in an expensive pattern-maker's rasp, and I'd like to keep it sharp for a long time. I don't want to toss it in with the other files and rasps clunking against each other in the drawer. What's a good way to protect my new investment?

Foam pipe insulation offers excellent cushioning, and it will gently hold on to the rasp for storage in the shop or transport to the job site. It's cheap enough that you can make protectors for all your files and rasps. If you allow them to strike against each other, the impact will dull both tools.

KEEP TRACK OF YOUR VACUUM TOOLS

Cleaning my shop is always a frustrating experience because I spend half my time trying to remember where I set down the vacuum's brush attachment or crevice tool. Is there an easy way to keep all of these accessories organized?

If you don't already have a muffler for your shop vacuum, buy one and stick it into the exhaust port. (Mufflers are made to fit most shop vacs.) The muffler creates a place to hang a small plastic bucket to store other vac accessories, such as filter bags, hearing protection earmuffs, and any other small items you want.

By the way, the muffler and earmuffs are a good idea in themselves, because a shop vacuum is typically the loudest tool in a home workshop.

PRESCRIPTION FOR DISPOSING OF UTILITY BLADES

 I learned a long time ago that trying to work with dull blades in a utility knife or craft knife causes me problems faster than it saves money. To safely dispose of the blades, I wrap a couple layers of tape around them before putting them in the trash. Is there a better way?

An empty plastic prescription medication container safely stores used blades, and it is small enough to fit into a pocket of your tool belt. Having a second container is a good way to carry a supply of new blades when you're involved in a big project that goes through blades quickly, such as hanging drywall.

You can also dispose of blades by cutting a slit into the lid of a plastic yogurt or cottage cheese container. Simply drop in the dull blades without going through the trouble of taping them.

HANDY APPROACH FOR DRILL GAUGE

 I like to keep my drill gauge and box of twist drill bits close together, but it seems they are always getting separated. I don't want to fool around with a rubber band every time I need to get out a drill bit, so what can I do?

Send your problem packing with the solution shown here. Get a self-adhesive packing list envelope at an office-supply store, and cut off one end before you stick it to the top of the drill bit box. Now you can simply slip in the drill gauge, and it will always be right at hand when you need it.

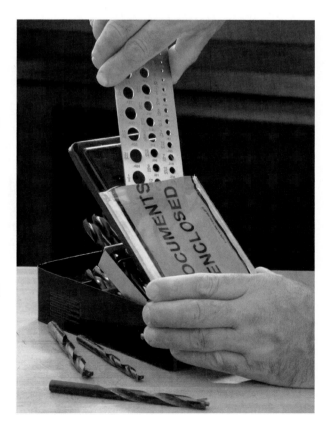

TAKE YOUR WORK TO NEW HEIGHTS

Whenever I do repair jobs around the house, I wish I had come from a taller family. Hauling in the six-foot stepladder is a nuisance because I only need about a 12-in. boost most of the time. What's a safe way to work taller?

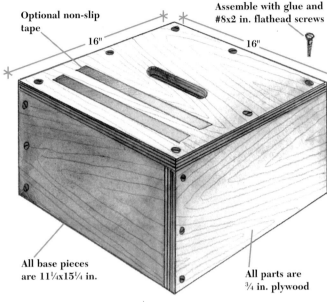

STEP BOX

Optional non-slip tape

Assemble with glue and #8x2 in. flathead screws

16"

16"

All base pieces are 11¼x15¼ in.

All parts are ¾ in. plywood

HANDLE DETAIL

6" to end of top

4"

Saw

Drill 1 in. holes

Make the box shown in the drawing, and you'll take your work to new heights. All the base pieces are identically sized, so the corners chase each other around the box. After you square up the base assembly, mark and cut the top.

Glue and screw the top to the base, and mark its centerline to position the handle cutout. Referring to the handle detail on the drawing, mark and drill a pair of 1-in. holes, and draw pencil lines connecting their rims. Use a jig saw to cut along the lines, creating the handle. Sand away any splinters on the top and bottom of the cutout. As an option, you can add non-slip tape to the top of the box.

At the job site, the box also makes a sturdy sawing platform. Tilt the box onto a side, then clamp a workpiece to it. Make a pair of the step boxes, and they will be twice as helpful. Put a sturdy walkboard between them to make a mini-scaffold.

HARDWARE LIST FOR YOUR WALLET

I got tired of forgetting to buy things at the hardware store, so I started keeping a list on a clipboard in the shop. But that doesn't do me any good when I stop at the hardware store on the way home. I can't keep lists everywhere, can I?

The best place to keep the list is in your wallet. If you forget the list, you can't buy anything anyway. Simply fold a 3 x 5-in. index card in half, and it's about the same size as a credit card. You'll have your list with you virtually all the time, so it eliminates the necessity of remembering. Add to the list whenever and wherever you think of a new item.

ORGANIZE THOSE OWNER'S MANUALS

I always save the owner's manual when I buy a new tool, because I'll probably need it some day to look up a replacement part number. I run across the manuals all the time, because they're scattered everywhere in the shop, but I can never locate the one I want without an extensive search. What's the best way to organize them — in the tool's case or in a central location?

You're going to have a central location for tools that don't have storage cases, so you might as well keep everything together in one place. Go to the office supply store, and buy a thick three-ring binder, some index dividers, and a supply of top-loading clear plastic sheet protectors that will handle 8½- x 11-in. paper.

As you put the manuals into their sheet protectors, separate them into categories that make sense to you. For example, you may create one group that includes your router plus all its accessories and attachments. When you've finished sorting, write up the index tabs, and load the sheets into the binder.

COMPUTERIZE YOUR CATALOG LIBRARY

 I must be on every woodworking mailing list because I get catalogs all the time. I like to save them for comparison shopping and ordering, but trying to tame them is a nightmare. Once, I set them up in alphabetical file folders, but if I forgot a company's name, I had to look in all the folders until I found it. Isn't there a better way?

You can set up a simple sorting program on your home computer that will let you quickly find a catalog — even if you remember only the type of products the company sells. Go to a spreadsheet program — Microsoft Excel is one — and set up three data columns: company name, products offered, and reference number.

Take any catalog from your stack, enter the data in the first two columns, put 1 in the third column, and use a permanent marker to write 1 on the cover of the catalog as well. You don't have to alphabetize the catalogs as you go, just assign each one the next number in the third column.

Get some hanging file folders, and insert the catalogs in numerical order. You can bunch several of them into a single folder. Go back to the program, sort it alphabetically by the first column, and print it. Now, sort by the information in the second column, and print it. On that list, all the lumber dealers will be together, turning supplies will be neatly grouped, and so on. Keep the lists near the file folders. When a new catalog arrives, simply look it up on the alphabetical list, write the number on the new version, and replace it in the file folder.

SOLVE A GRITTY PROBLEM

I haven't figured out a good way to organize my sandpaper inventory. I tried file folders, but when I accidentally knocked the stack of them off of a shelf, sheets went flying everywhere. Disks for my random-orbit sander are even worse — they roll right out of the folder. How can I smooth out this gritty problem?

The next time you're at the office-supply store, buy a couple of accordion folders. Get a large size for sandpaper sheets, and a smaller version (cancelled check size) for the disks. The cover and elastic strap on the folder keeps the contents secure, even if you drop it. The multiple pockets let you store a wide range of grits.

This storage system really pays dividends when you need to take sandpaper to a job site. The spill-proof folders are secure but easy to access.

CLAMP STASHES MAKE SENSE

Handscrew clamps and C-clamps take up a lot of storage space, and no matter where I put them, I'm always on the other side of the shop when I need one.

As a general rule of organization, you should always store something as close as possible to its point of use. For an item like clamps, that means creating a main storage depot but also stocking several satellite caches at frequently used spots.

If you do most of your assembly work at the workbench, stash most of the clamps there. Putting them on a stretcher under the workbench is a great strategy. But you always need a few clamps at the drill press to secure fences and jigs, so you may as well leave a few there permanently. A simple wood box on the drill-press base is a good place for the clamps and other frequently used accessories.

ELECTRIFYING SOLUTIONS FOR YOUR WORKBENCH

 I have a list of electrical problems I'd like to solve: I need an adjustable-height portable lamp, an outlet strip that I can use at the job site, and a place to store extension cords. And as long as I'm wishing, let's make this a quick and inexpensive solution.

Check out the lamp and power stand in the drawing, and you'll see a design that exceeds your specifications. The spacing between the cross-arms lets you position a clip-on lamp (or several of them) anywhere from floor level to about 6 ft. high. You can put the light right on the task, no matter where it is. The ability to fine-tune the position of the lamp is a big help when you want illumination that just glances off the surface — perfect for inspecting the coverage of finishes as you apply them.

The cleats at the ends of the cross-arms prevent large extension cords or even something as large as a coiled air hose from falling off. The inexpensive screw-in hooks are a great place to store shorter cords or hang up your tool belt.

Screw an outlet strip to the post to gain plenty of outlets, and you'll also eliminate bending to power up — a definite plus whether you're working in the shop or outdoors.

Construction of the stand is straightforward and easy. Skip the glue when you assemble the pieces, and rely strictly on the screws. This will make it much easier to replace a part that gets damaged.

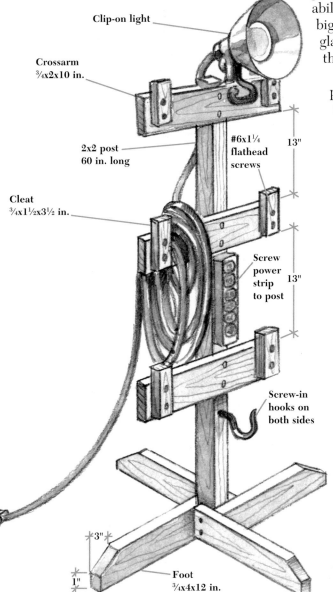

Clip-on light

Crossarm
¾x2x10 in.

2x2 post
60 in. long

#6x1¼
flathead
screws

13"

Cleat
¾x1½x3½ in.

Screw
power
strip
to post

13"

Screw-in
hooks on
both sides

3"

1"

Foot
¾x4x12 in.

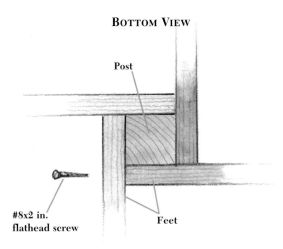

BOTTOM VIEW

Post

#8x2 in.
flathead screw

Feet

GLUE BUCKET HAS SEVERAL ADVANTAGES

 A leaky glue bottle created quite a mess. There are now a few sheets of sandpaper permanently stuck to the shelf, but I should consider myself lucky because it could have caused much more damage. How can I prevent this from happening again?

At the very least, you should move all your adhesives to a bottom shelf. That way, you can limit the damage instead of having glue cascade from shelf to shelf. An even better solution is putting all your glue containers into a small plastic bucket that also holds sticks for mixing epoxy and brushes for spreading glue. When you're ready to assemble a project, you can just grab the bucket and get to work.

Leaky containers of paint, finish, and other liquids also create quite a mess. Store them on cookie sheets that have a raised lip all around the perimeter, and you'll have a good containment setup. Buy new cookie sheets for the kitchen so you can use the hand-me-downs in your shop.

EXPAND YOUR TABLETOP SPACE

 It seems that my shop often shrinks in the middle of a project. My workbench has so many parts stacked on it that I run out of room to work. What can I do?

For a temporary increase in space, set up a banquet-type table that has folding legs. You can buy the legs and add your own top, or buy a ready-made unit. Do some quick arithmetic with the price of folding legs and lumber, and you might find that some ready-made tables are an excellent value. Stored with its legs folded, a four-foot or six-foot table leaned against the wall has a relatively small footprint.

A folding card table doesn't offer as much space, but you may already have one in the attic. Yet one more solution is a folding ironing board, but you'll have to be careful not to overload it. By the way, you can also use an adjustable-height ironing board as an outfeed table for the table saw, router table, or band saw.

SHOP INVENTORY MAKES SENSE

 I know I should make an inventory of everything in my shop for insurance purposes. I've heard too many stories about people who have a difficult time dealing with the insurance company after theft, fire, or other disaster. But I don't feel like spending a whole weekend writing down descriptions and serial numbers. Isn't there an easier way?

If you have access to a video camera, you can do a thorough inventory very quickly, and the only writing required will be the label on the tape. Recruiting a friend to help will make the process go even

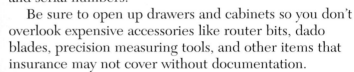 faster — one of you can concentrate on filming while the other one keeps up a narrative, reading off tool model and serial numbers.

Be sure to open up drawers and cabinets so you don't overlook expensive accessories like router bits, dado blades, precision measuring tools, and other items that insurance may not cover without documentation.

If you don't have a video setup, a still camera will also do a great job, although you may have to resort to writing down serial numbers.

Store the videotape or photos in your safe deposit box.

While you're at it, it would be a good idea to repeat the process in every room throughout your house. Of course, you hope you'll never need to resort to the inventory, but it's comforting to know that you had the foresight to take this step.

CUTLERY TRAY HAS A PLACE IN THE SHOP

 I haven't figured out a good way to store small screwdrivers. They would simply fall through the holes in the wire rack hanging on my pegboard that holds my other drivers. What can I use?

Buy a new plastic cutlery tray for the kitchen drawer, and take the old one into your shop. It's a convenient way to organize those drivers plus other small tools.

KITCHEN CABINETS FIND A HOME IN YOUR SHOP

 At the end of my kitchen remodeling project, my workshop will inherit the old cabinets. Are there any special considerations in converting them to their new role?

You should consider altering the height of the base cabinets, and make sure that you use extra care to fasten the wall cabinets securely.

Most base cabinets are designed to produce a finished countertop height of 36 in., and you may find that's too high for comfortable woodworking. As a general rule, an efficient workbench level is the same as the height of your wrist crease above the floor when you're standing comfortably.

Lowering the cabinets is usually a relatively easy task, thanks to the presence of the toekick in most cabinets. Simply make your cut line around the cabinet, and use a saw to perform the corrective surgery.

When you hang the upper cabinets, be sure to use screws that are both thick and long to maximize their pullout resistance and strength in shear. (Shear is the force across the diameter of the fastener.) Use #10 x 3-in. screws or larger. Also put a washer under the head of each screw to help distribute the bearing stress. Of course, every screw must hit a stud.

Having the cabinets is great, but if you have to fight to get at the contents, you're not maximizing their storage potential. Consider adding pullout shelves to the base cabinets so you can easily reach items stored in the back. Lazy Susan carousels are easy to build and make upper cabinets more efficient. Purchasing inexpensive door-mounted accessories made from plastic-covered wire is a good way to organize lightweight items.

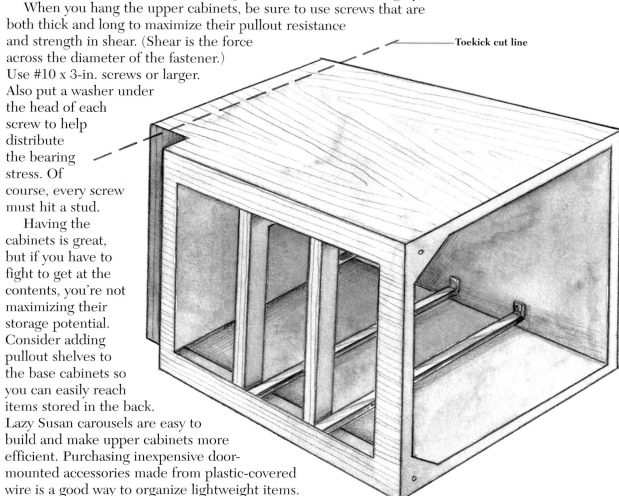

Toekick cut line

12
SHOP SAFETY

GET A HANDLE ON YOUR FILES

I've bought a lot of files in my life, but never a file handle. Aren't they just for sissies?

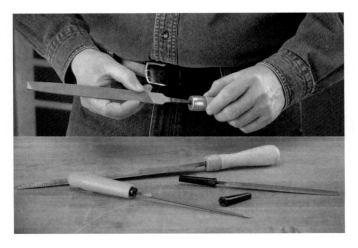

A file handle will help you do better work by improving your grip on the tool, but it's also important for avoiding an accident. If a file or rasp jams on your workpiece, the pointed tang of the tool can easily spear into the flesh of your forearm just above your palm. Unfortunately, that's the location of a major artery plus tendons and bundles of nerves.

Some file handles have threaded inserts that grip the tang. Or, choose a style with mechanical jaws that tighten when you turn a knob at the end of the handle. If you have a lathe, you can even turn your own handles. But whatever style you choose, don't file without a handle.

PROTECT YOUR TOOTSIES

The last time I bought work boots, the salesman asked about my hobbies as well as my everyday job. When I mentioned woodworking, he suggested that I get steel-toed shoes. Does he really think I'm going to get my foot up onto the saw table?

He was probably thinking much more of dropping and crushing hazards. For example, a sharp chisel that rolls off a workbench will slow down only slightly as it slices through the fabric of an athletic shoe. After it goes though the flesh, the first really hard surface it will encounter is bone.

Crushing accidents also are common, and many are somewhat self-inflicted by a strange instinctual reaction. When some people drop an object, their first impulse is to extend a foot to break the object's fall. Unfortunately, the breakage often involves the foot rather than the object. Your toes are also at risk if you have heavy machinery mounted on large casters — they'll roll as easily over your toes as they do over the floor.

HEAR THIS: WOODWORKERS NEED HEARING PROTECTION

 Do I really need to bother with hearing protection? I haven't noticed any damage so far.

A person with hearing loss is often the last one to notice it, and lost hearing is like wasted time — it's something you can't recover. All you can do at that point is hope to prevent further deterioration.

Hearing loss is not usually a distinct event when you suddenly realize that someone turned down the volume — it occurs gradually and unevenly across the sound spectrum. The progression of frequencies lost is like the loading order for lifeboats on a sinking ship — women and children first. The higher pitched sounds of those voices are usually the first to diminish in clarity. The loss of mid-range and deeper sounds comes later.

PLAY IT SAFE: KEEP THE SHOP LOCKED

 What's the best way to protect children from unauthorized access to tools, especially power equipment?

Early education and strict enforcement of firm rules is mandatory, but you also need to protect children from their own curiosity. Putting a lock on the shop door isn't a sign of mistrust; it's a way of showing that you care.

You might also consider shutting off the electrical breakers that control the lights and outlets in the shop area. If you have a separate breaker box for your shop, put a lock on its door.

DECIPHERING CODES FOR HEARING PROTECTION

What's the best kind of hearing protection?

Some methods of hearing protection have a higher noise reduction rating (NRR) than others, but the best kind of hearing protection is the one you'll actually wear. In the following examples of three representative types of products, the NRR numbers reflect items from one supplier. You may find examples from other sources that vary.

It's an interesting progression among the products. The easier it is to wear, the larger and more expensive it is. Ironically, the smallest and cheapest style offers the best protection.

The easiest type to put on is the earmuff style, with a NRR of 20. If possible, try on a set before you buy to ensure that it is comfortable. After a few years, you may notice that the rubber ear cushions aren't as resilient as before and don't seal as well to your head. It's a sign that you need a new pair. The position of the headband also influences the NRR, with the overhead position usually yielding the greatest sound protection. Placing the band behind your head or under your chin diminishes the protection.

Band-style hearing protectors require more effort because you need to insert the tapered rubber or foam tips into your ear, not simply place them in your outer ear like a stethoscope. Of course, you need to follow the manufacturer's wearing recommendation to achieve maximum protection. A typical NRR is 23.

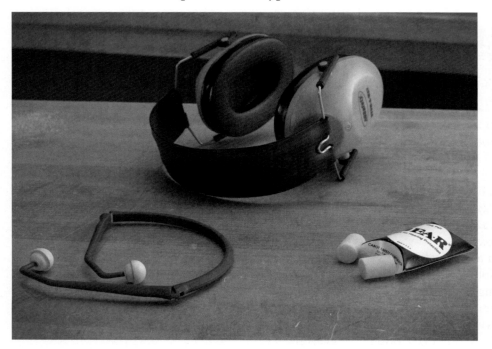

Foam ear plugs are very inexpensive but highly effective, with a NRR of 29. Again, follow the manufacturer's suggestions to properly place the plugs into your ear canal.

Hearing damage results from both intensity and duration, so if you're getting into a long session of extremely noisy machine operation, you can even consider teaming earplugs with earmuffs.

LISTEN TO WHAT THE EXPERTS SAY ABOUT HEARING PROTECTION

 I'm not so sure that I need hearing protection. After all, I'm no cream puff.

Even if you're a real tough guy, there's no such thing as immunity from hearing loss. It's like saying you don't need to wear safety glasses because you think you have tough eyeballs.

While it's true that some people can tolerate more noise before they find it annoying, it doesn't mean they have stronger auditory (hearing) nerves than the next person. Everybody's auditory nerves are extremely delicate, and those nerves will sustain permanent impairment when exposed to unfavorable conditions.

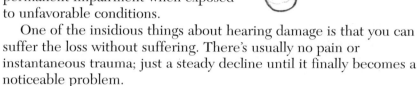

One of the insidious things about hearing damage is that you can suffer the loss without suffering. There's usually no pain or instantaneous trauma; just a steady decline until it finally becomes a noticeable problem.

WORK BREAKS PREVENT ACCIDENTS

Are there any overall guidelines that will help prevent shop accidents?

Several studies have shown that a high percentage of accidents occur when the worker is rushing to accomplish "just one more thing" before quitting for that session. A lack of focus combined with a desire to work more quickly form a dangerous combination.

Lapses in attention are also due to monotony or general fatigue. If you're a hobbyist, remember that woodworking is supposed to be relaxing and enjoyable, so take a break until you regain your concentration. If you're a professional, realize that a short break is a shrewd business investment because it can help prevent a long period of downtime resulting from an accident.

VACUUMS KICK UP
A LOT OF NOISE

What are the loudest machines in a typical home workshop?

You'll probably be surprised to discover that the noisiest tool in most shops is the vacuum. Even when it's equipped with a muffler (an inexpensive add-on, see page 228), it's a tremendous source of nerve-damaging noise.

The shop vacuum's impact is increased by the fact that you may have it turned on at the same time that you're operating other tools. For example, many people attach a vac hose to their sander, router, drill press, or other equipment, literally amplifying the noise problem.

Routers are usually the second loudest tool — unless you own a huge router and a wimpy vac. But a router's ability to cause damage is increased by the fact that you may have your head quite close to the tool

while it's running. That's significant because of the inverse square law.

In case you were absent from physics class that day, the inverse square law states that the intensity of sound or light changes by 1 over the square of the distance factor from the source. For example, if you double the length from the source (a distance factor of 2), the sound goes down by ½x2, or ¼. Double the distance, one-fourth the sound. Of course, the math works in the opposite direction: When you cut the distance from a sound source in half, the noise is four times greater, increasing the danger of hearing loss.

Reflection is another property of physics that affects sound in your shop. You don't hear the sound source just one time, but each time it bouncing off the floor, walls, ceilings, and every other surface in your shop. Like a high-energy billiard ball rebounding off the rails, the noise keeps bouncing around. A smooth hard surface like a concrete floor can reflect sound more efficiently than a mirror reflects light.

TABLE SAW BLADE GUARDS ARE WORTH KEEPING

When I bought my table saw, the first thing I did was toss the blade guard into the corner of the shop. But after my cousin nearly lost a finger on his saw, I'm starting to reconsider. But doesn't it take a lot of time to constantly put on the guard and take it off?

You may have noticed that a lot of guys who are too macho to use blade guards often have colorful nicknames like Lefty or Stumpy. Until medical science figures out a way that people can regenerate limbs the way that starfish do, blade guards will continue to be a good idea.

Time yourself putting on a blade guard, and you'll be surprised that this so-called time-consuming process actually involves only a few seconds. Compare that to your cousin's recovery time, and you'll discover you can remove and replace thousands of guards in less time than you can recover from the loss of a finger.

SURGE CONCERNS? JUST UNPLUG

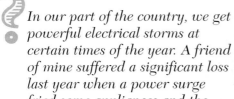

In our part of the country, we get powerful electrical storms at certain times of the year. A friend of mine suffered a significant loss last year when a power surge fried some appliances and the circuit board in his speed-controlled scroll saw. How do I protect my tools from this hazard?

Unplug them. You can purchase high-tech surge protection devices, but it's really an unnecessary expense when protection that's even more certain is so easy and absolutely free.

GFCI IS WELL WORTH THE INVESTMENT

 I'm getting ready to set up my woodworking shop, and I was about to order the ground-fault breakers, but now I've heard about arc-fault breakers. Do I want them instead?

Stick with the ground-fault circuit interrupters (GFCIs) because they are designed to provide protection from shock hazards. You can purchase GFCI breakers or you can protect several outlets by wiring them to a single GFCI outlet following the procedure packaged with the device. Of course, all wiring must be done in compliance with local building and electrical codes. If you don't know what you're doing, hire a pro to do the wiring. Whether you use GFCI breakers or outlets, test the equipment once a month to ensure proper operation.

The arc-fault circuit interrupter (AFCI) is engineered to prevent fires by opening the circuit when it detects arcing that can occur at loose connections — a result of damaged insulation and other causes. Initially, it sounds like a good idea for the shop until you look further.

According to a technical representative at a major manufacturer of both devices, many motors in the woodworking shop use brushes, and these tools could cause a significant number of false readings, leading to nuisance tripping.

As of this writing, AFCI installation is mandatory only in bedrooms of new homes.

FLAMING HOT TIPS FOR BUYING FIRE EXTINGUISHERS

 Maybe I should get a fire extinguisher for my shop, but the kid at the discount store barely knew where they were located. So I didn't even bother to ask for advice on which one to buy. After reading the labels, I left the store confused and empty-handed. What do I want to buy?

A fire safety supplier suggested a 10-lb. ABC extinguisher for a home woodworking shop. The fire suppressant is a dry powder that's delivered by pressure. The recommended unit has a rechargeable metal cylinder as well as all-metal head components.

So-called economy units may cost more in the long run because they cannot be recharged. Plus, the plastic handles are known to break. Accidentally dropping the extinguisher and breaking off the handle can happen anytime — or just when you need it the most.

Fire extinguisher prices can vary considerably, depending on the competitiveness of that industry in your local area. It pays to call several companies to compare prices.

At least once a year, you should verify that the seal on the release pin is intact. Also read the gauge to ensure that the unit isn't under- or over-pressurized. A safety supplier can perform an annual check-up for about the cost of a fast food lunch. After six years, again take the unit in to the supplier for a more thorough

evaluation. And six years after that, the unit is due for an overhaul to ensure that it will work when you need it.

If you run a professional woodworking shop, your operation will be subject to local regulations.

BREATHING EASY

 Sometimes I need breathing protection when I'm sanding wood, and also when I'm spraying finish. Do I want a dust mask or a respirator?

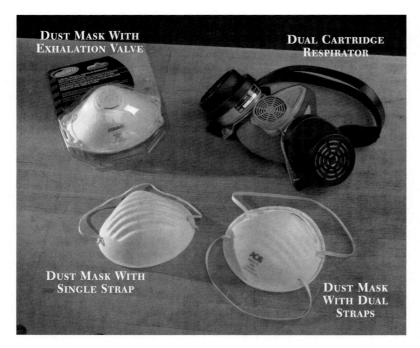

DUST MASK WITH EXHALATION VALVE

DUAL CARTRIDGE RESPIRATOR

DUST MASK WITH SINGLE STRAP

DUST MASK WITH DUAL STRAPS

You actually need both. But you can't simply grab the first product you see and figure that it will work. Both dust masks and respirators are engineered to meet specific requirements based on the size of the particle or type of molecule you need to block.

Concerning particulates, the bigger the piece is, the less harm it is likely do. You're probably not going to inhale a curl from a hand plane, but you can easily breathe in fine sanding dust. The smaller the particle size, the deeper it can go into your lungs, and the more difficulty your body will have dealing with it.

For example, the asbestos fibers that cause health problems for so many people can't even be seen with the naked eye — they are the size of bacteria.

The low-end dust mask with the single non-adjustable strap doesn't block anything smaller than pollen, so it's not much good in the workshop. The lower right dust mask in the photo has two adjustable straps for better fit and improved comfort. It also seals better to your face and blocks smaller particles. Some masks have an exhalation valve that permits easier breathing and reduces moisture buildup.

You'll see three categories of products that look like dust masks: N is not resistant to oil particles in the air; R is resistant; and P stands for oil-proof. The prefix is followed by a number representing the percentage of particles blocked. For general wood sanding in a home shop, a mask with an N-95 rating should be sufficient.

For protection against sprayed finishes, you'll need a dual-cartridge respirator to block particles as well as odors. Make certain that the elements are matched with the type of material you'll spray.

To extend the life of a dust mask or respirator, follow the manufacturer's guidelines for cleaning and storage.

By the way, no dust mask or respirator will give its rated performance if you have a beard.

For further details, contact the National Institute for Occupational Safety and Health, the certifying agency for masks, respirators, and many other products. Manufacturers and distributors of dust masks and respirators also can help you match the protection to the job. (Please see Resources, page 314.)

RAG STRATEGY FOR WOODWORKERS

 I often read the warning in woodworking magazines: "Be sure to dispose of finish-soaked rags in a safe manner." But they never say what the hazard is, or how to prevent it. So what should I do?

The danger is spontaneous combustion, which can result when cloths or paper towels soaked with finish or solvents are wadded. The chemical residue can generate so much heat as it cures or flashes off that it can literally burst into flames. Boiled linseed oil has this nasty habit, among others.

To kill the problem, you can hang the rags. But to be even more certain, you can drown them first, and then hang them.

Hang the rags with clothespins outdoors on a line, or loosely drape them so plenty of air can circulate around. To drown a rag, rinse it by hand in running water until the solvent odor disappears, then hang it up to dry. After the rags are dry, you can toss them into the trash.

MINIMIZE SOLVENTS TO REDUCE FIRE HAZARD

 I've accumulated quite a number of cans of solvents and finishes. I'm wondering how to safely store them. All together, I guess they could be quite a fire hazard.

You can safely store water-based finishes and latex paints indoors to protect them from freezing. But all finishes and solvents that are potentially inflammable deserve special handling.

The first step is to reduce your inventory by getting rid of gummy finishes or solvents stored in rusty cans. Contact your city or county government for information on hazardous waste disposal. In the future, buy smaller quantities to reduce both waste and hazards.

The safest way to store solvents indoors is in a metal cabinet that's specially designed for that purpose and includes a vent to the outdoors to get rid of any potentially dangerous vapors. The next best storage choice is a detached garage, shed, or outbuilding. Losing one of those buildings to fire would be sad, but having your house burn could be tragic.

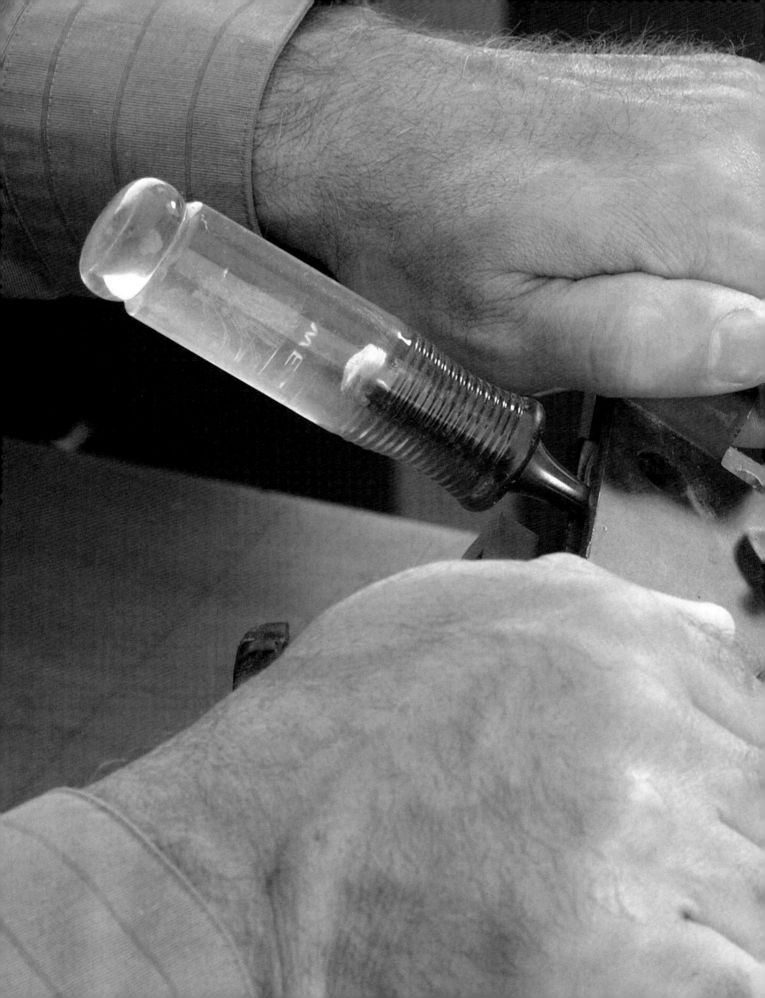

13

SHARPENING AND MAINTENANCE

CHOOSE EXTENSION CORDS CAREFULLY

 When I was building my deck, I gave my new circular saw quite a workout. Halfway through the job, the motor burned out. When I took it back to the store to complain, the salesman asked me what size extension cord I was using. Does that really make a difference, or was he just covering up for shoddy power tools?

Having an extension cord that delivers adequate power is one of the most important steps in making sure your power tools perform properly and don't burn out. In order to meet the tool's amperage requirement (found on the motor's nameplate), you need to match the required length with the correct wire gauge, as shown on the chart below.

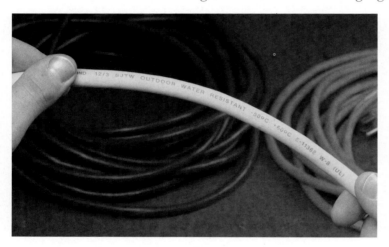

Wire gauge is a counter-intuitive measurement — the larger the gauge number, the smaller the diameter of the wire. For example, 16-gauge wire is smaller than 12 gauge. The measurement follows a system called American Wire Gauge (AWG), and the number is usually printed right onto the wire's outer insulation (called the jacket). For example, AWG 12-3 is a cord with 12-gauge conductors (wires), and the number 3 indicates that there are three wires: hot, neutral, and ground.

The chart shows you that a cord should increase in gauge as it grows in length or amperage requirement, and there are two reasons for that. First, just as a larger pipe delivers more water, a larger wire carries more power. Second, increased length introduces voltage drop, a decrease in the amount of energy at the plug.

The moral of the story is to use the shortest extension cord you can, and to choose a large enough gauge to satisfy your tool's appetite for electrical power. When in doubt, choose the next larger gauge.

TOOL'S AMPERAGE RATING

Cord length	Up to 2 amps	2-5 amps	5-7 amps	7-10 amps	10-12 amps	12-15 amps
25 ft.	16 ga.	16 ga.	16 ga.	16 ga.	14 ga.	14 ga.
50 ft.	16 ga.	16 ga.	16 ga.	14 ga.	14 ga.	12 ga.
100 ft.	16 ga.	16 ga.	14 ga.	12 ga.	12 ga.	NR
150 ft.	16 ga.	14 ga.	12 ga.	12 ga.	NR	NR
200 ft.	14 ga.	14 ga.	12 ga.	10 ga.	NR	NR

NR = not recommended because of voltage drop

AVOID HOT TIMES WITH EXTENSION CORDS

 I keep my long extension cord tightly coiled on a plastic gizmo, and I pull out only enough of the ends to plug in and reach the job. Hot idea, huh?

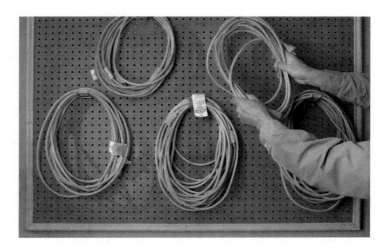

Unfortunately, that setup can generate significant amounts of heat that can damage the insulation. To promote heat dissipation, it's best to keep an extension cord loosely looped instead of closely coiled.

You should also make it a habit to occasionally check your tool's power cord and extension cord during a work session. If either one feels warm to the touch, you may be using an undersized extension cord or have an inadequate power source. Unplug from the power source until you trace the source of the trouble.

NOT ALL LIGHT BULBS ARE CREATED EQUAL

I'm constantly replacing the bulb in the task lamps mounted on my scroll saw and band saw. It's annoying and expensive. How can I extend the life of the bulbs?

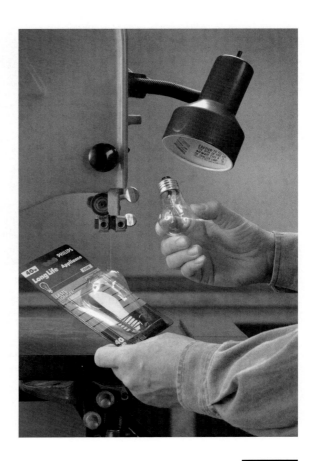

Instead of using ordinary lamps, try appliance bulbs — these are built tough to withstand the rigors of life inside a refrigerator or stove. Another choice is rough-service bulbs, engineered to endure harsh environments and vibration. Both choices are more expensive than generic light bulbs, but you may discover that their longevity warrants the expense.

CLEAN MOTOR EQUALS LONGER LIFE

I just had to buy a new motor for my table saw and was amazed at how expensive it was. Now I'm wondering how I can coax a little more life out of the other motors in my shop.

Motors in woodworking machines operate in a dusty environment, and that can lead to overheating and other problems. If dust can get inside the motor, clean it with a shop vacuum or with a stream of compressed air. Don't go overboard on the air pressure, because that could drive dust further into the motor or dislodge wiring.

Even if you have a totally enclosed motor, you can't ignore it. A thick coating of sawdust can lower the motor's ability to dissipate heat, and that could lead to premature failure.

If a motor begins to act erratically, take it in for service immediately. Prompt attention could spell the difference between an affordable repair and expensive replacement. In addition, a motor problem could become a shock or a fire hazard.

You Gotta Sharpen the Entire Dado Set

 A couple of my dado chippers got a nick from an embedded nail, so I went to the sharpening shop. The guy at the counter said they only sharpen entire dado sets, not individual cutters. Are they trying to gouge me?

Sharpening a circular blade will decrease the diameter slightly. That's no big deal for an ordinary saw blade, but it can become a problem when it's part of a set. If the shop sharpened only the damaged blades, they wouldn't slice as deeply as the other cutters.

While it might seem wasteful to grind blades that aren't dull, it's more aggravating to struggle with dadoes that aren't precise. All the cutting tips need to be ground evenly with the lowest tip.

TLC for Your Band-Saw Blades

I've heard that you're supposed to back off the tension on a band-saw blade at the end of the day. Why? What's the big deal?

There are at least three good reasons to release the tension on your band-saw blade. First, the tension on the blade compresses part of the rubber tires, producing flattened areas that can lead to poor blade tracking and uneven running. Second, leaving the blade under tension for an extended period compromises its ability to recover (spring back) from the stress. As a result, the blade requires more and more tension, leading to premature failure. Third, the tension is not merely on the blade — it also affects the bearings, wheels, and even the frame of the saw.

With those principles in mind, you'll see that it's also a good idea to back off the tension on a bow saw, hacksaw, coping saw, scroll saw, and even the lockdown mechanism on your table saw's rip fence. If you let the metal relax, it will perform better and give longer service.

IS MY SQUARE REALLY SQUARE?

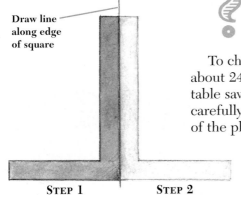

Draw line along edge of square

STEP 1   **STEP 2**

How do I check if my framing square is actually square? And if it isn't square, is there anything I can do to fix it?

To check your square, you'll need a piece of scrap plywood that's about 24 x 36 in. The longer edge should be ripped straight with your table saw. Place the square as shown in Step 1 of the drawing, carefully aligning the shorter leg of the square with the straight edge of the plywood. Using a fine mechanical pencil, draw a line on the plywood along the long leg of the square. (The long leg of a framing square is sometimes called the body, and the shorter leg the tongue.)

Flop the square over to the Step 2 position indicated by the dashed line, again aligning the short leg with the plywood. Slide the square toward the line until either the tip or corner of the square touches the line. If both points touch the line at the same time, your tool is square. If one end touches before the other, refer to drawings 3-A and 3-B to interpret the results. The difference you see is double the adjustment you'll make. In 3-A, the square is less than 90 degrees, so you need to open the angle to correct it. Drawing 3-B shows a square that's past the right angle, so it needs to be closed.

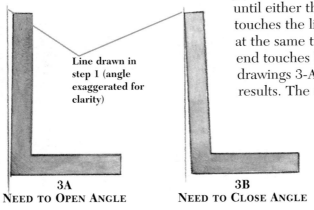

Line drawn in step 1 (angle exaggerated for clarity)

3A
NEED TO OPEN ANGLE

3B
NEED TO CLOSE ANGLE

STEP 4

Center punch

Corner of square

Strike center punch here to close angle

Strike center punch here to open angle

Midpoint

To adjust the square, lay it flat on your workbench as shown in the Step 4 drawing, and draw a pencil line from the outside corner to the inside corner. Measure to find the centerpoint of that line. To close the angle of the square, use a hammer to strike a center punch at a position along the half of the line closest to the outer corner. The closer you strike to the outer corner, and the harder you hit the punch, the more the square will move.

To check your results, begin again at Step 1. You can put the center punch back into a dimple you've already made or create a new one. Repeat the steps until the square is aligned.

DO YOUR LEVEL BEST

How do I check if my level is on the level? Can I fix it if it's not correct?

Put your level on a plywood platform atop your workbench, and level the platform using tapered wood shims as shown in the photo. Rotate the level end for end, and check the bubble again. If the bubble is perfectly centered in both positions, the tool is true. Any error indicates a problem; usually it's a bubble vial that's been knocked out of position or the frame is twisted or bowed.

A damaged frame means it's time to buy a new level. If the vial assembly is glued to the frame, replacement is again the most practical route. The only exception is if you own an expensive specialty level with replaceable vials that screw into the frame. Or return a quality level to the factory for repair.

HOLLOW GROUND: A GOOD THING FOR YOUR CHISELS

What's the advantage of a hollow-ground edge?

A hollow-ground edge lowers metal-to-wood friction by reducing the contact area, and it also speeds sharpening because you need to remove less metal to renew the edge between grindings.

As you can see in the Step 1 drawing, the rim of a grinding wheel scoops out a hollow on the end of a chisel — hence the name hollow ground. Check your progress carefully, and stop grinding before you get to a wire edge. At that point, there's not enough metal left to conduct away the heat generated by grinding, so you risk ruining the temper of the blade.

When you move the blade to the sharpening stone as shown in Step 2, you can see that the blade touches at only the ends of the arc, so you don't need to remove metal along the entire face of the bevel. The flat areas grow wider with each subsequent sharpening until the hollow finally disappears, signaling that it's time to grind again.

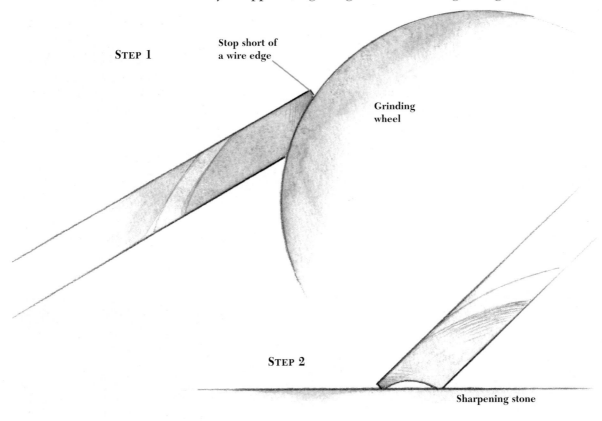

STEP 1

Stop short of
a wire edge

Grinding
wheel

STEP 2

Sharpening stone

Finished edge

PAY ATTENTION TO THE BACK OF CHISELS TOO

I've seen articles on sharpening that carry on about the importance of flattening the back of chisels and plane blades. Is this really necessary?

It's a critically important, but an often-overlooked step. The sharpness of an edge occurs at the intersection of two surfaces — the angled bevel and the back. If the bevel is rounded over, the chisel won't be sharp. Likewise, if the bevel meets a back that's wavy or uneven, you'll compromise sharpness.

The initial flattening of the back may take some time because of the large surface area involved. Start with a fairly coarse sharpening stone, and keep working with the blade until its back is covered with a uniform pattern of scratch marks from that stone's grit.

Take the blade through finer grades of stones to further smooth and polish the back.

FLAT SHARPENING STONES MAKE YOUR DAY

My bench oilstone has developed a hollow in it from sharpening narrow tools. I have a water stone with the same problem. How do I flatten them?

Get a piece of ¼-in.-thick plate glass and some 90x powdered silicon carbide grit, available through woodworking catalogs and specialty stores. Sprinkle some grit onto the glass, add oil, and work your oilstone over the surface until you've restored a flat face.

You can employ this same technique to flatten the metal sole of a plane. To flatten your water stone, substitute water for the oil.

SHORTENING SHARPENING TIME

 When I work at a sharpening stone, it seems to take forever. How can I get to a keen edge quicker?

The surface of your stone may be glazed — its pores filled with metallic particles. To check for this condition, wipe the surface of the stone dry and examine it with a glancing light. If it has a metallic gleam, you'll need to lap its surface. Follow the technique for resurfacing a gouged stone (see page 259).

You're probably using too fine a stone, not enough pressure, or both. When you're doing the initial sharpening, you want a stone that cuts quickly to raise the wire edge in a minimum amount of time. A finer stone will eventually produce the same result, but it will take much longer.

If you use a sharpening jig to hold the blade at the correct angle on the stone, put downward finger pressure on the back of the blade directly above the bevel. Push down hard, and you'll finish sooner.

KEEP YOUR STONES IN A DUNK TANK

 I know that if I store my water stones immersed in water, they will be ready to use. But when I put them into a plastic bucket, how do I keep them from banging into each other and chipping?

Buy some inexpensive plastic drinking glasses — the tall ones made for iced tea are the best — fill them with water, and put them in the water bucket. That way, the glasses may bump each other, but the stones will remain safely separated.

BELIEVE IN THE VALUE OF SHARPENING

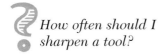 *How often should I sharpen a tool?*

Although some woodworkers consider sharpening an occasional ritual, you'll get better results if you touch up a tool's edge as soon as it shows the first hint of dulling. A minute or two at your sharpening station will restore an edge, so you should never put away a tool that's dull.

If you wait until the edge is chipped and rounded over, the job will require many more steps and take a great deal longer. If you try to work with dull tools, the quality of your work goes down and the energy required goes up.

GIVE YOUR CHISEL THE THUMB TEST

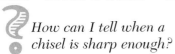 *How can I tell when a chisel is sharp enough?*

Test the blade by resting its edge on your thumbnail as shown in the photo. Push the blade slowly and gently forward as you simultaneously lift the handle. If the tip of the bevel catches on your thumbnail at a shallow angle, the blade is sharp. If you must raise the handle high, the blade is not as sharp.

You can also make a test cut into the end of a softwood board. If you can cut a chamfer that's glassy smooth, the chisel is ready for work. If the cut is ragged, go back to the stone. You may be surprised, but softwood is better than hardwood for this test because it takes an extremely sharp edge to make a clean slice in softwood.

A SHORT COURSE ON SHARPENING

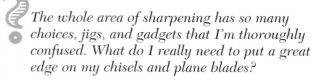

The whole area of sharpening has so many choices, jigs, and gadgets that I'm thoroughly confused. What do I really need to put a great edge on my chisels and plane blades?

It's easy to get confused if you try to solve too many problems at one time, so splitting the sharpening process into four steps will help you divide and conquer the essential skills. If you need to upgrade your sharpening equipment, you can zero in on the items you need most.

GRINDING

1 Grinding removes nicks from the blade and establishes the tool's bevel angle. You can grind with a wheel that's run dry or wet. If you opt for a dry grinding setup, be certain that you choose a wheel recommended for woodworking tools. Keep the speed to 1800 rpm or less, and apply a light touch when grinding to avoid overheating the steel. A water-cooled system virtually eliminates the possibility of ruining a tool's temper, but it will cut more slowly. The key grinding accessory is a tool rest. Another is a shopmade or purchased fixture that grips the blade and allows it to slide along the tool rest.

2 Sharpening is the process of putting a working edge onto the blade. You can accomplish this with an oilstone, a water stone, or with fine abrasive sheets adhered to a glass plate. To sharpen freehand, grip the blade at the required angle, then lock your hands and elbows to hold that setting against the stone. Move only at the shoulders to guide the blade over the full surface of the stone. You can also choose among a wide variety of sharpening guides to maintain the angle. You've sharpened enough when you raise a wire edge along the full length of the blade. Test for the wire edge by lightly stroking your thumb from the body of the tool to its end. Begin to remove the wire edge by turning the blade over and stroking it lightly a half-dozen times

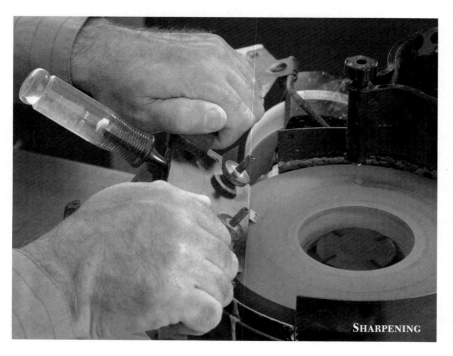

SHARPENING

on the stone. Alternate six light strokes between the bevel and back until the wire edge disappears. Although you could probably put the tool to work at this point, the next two steps are quick but make a big difference in a blade's performance.

3 **Polishing** employs a finer grit to reduce the size of the scratches on the bevel and back of the tool. You have the same choices as when sharpening — oilstone, water stone, or abrasive sheets. When the bevel loses its scratched look and begins to gleam, you've polished enough for general-use tools. To further refine the edge, you can run through a succession of increasingly finer abrasives.

POLISHING

4 **Stropping** is an easy finishing step that gives you a brilliant edge. Although you can purchase a power buff or strop, you can postpone that purchase by using a discarded leather belt. Lay the belt flat on your sharpening bench, and rub honing oil onto a 6-in. length of the rough inner side of the belt. Rub a bar of jeweler's rouge or other buffing compound into the oil to dissolve a small amount of this fine abrasive. With firm pressure, rub the bevel by pulling it along the belt. After only a half-dozen strokes, the edge should have a mirror gleam. Turn the belt over, and charge a length of the smooth side with oil and compound. A few strokes later, you've completed a great edge.

STROPPING

TWO BEVELS ARE BETTER THAN ONE

Is a secondary bevel a good idea? Doesn't it change the cutting angle of the plane iron or chisel?

Establishing a secondary bevel allows you to sharpen and touch up an edge quicker because you're not removing metal from the entire face of the main bevel. As long as you keep the secondary bevel (sometimes called a microbevel) small, you're not going to make a significant change in the tool's cutting angle.

A common mistake is making the secondary bevel too large. A microbevel as small as $\frac{1}{128}$ in. will do the job. To form the secondary bevel, slightly increase the sharpening angle after you've completed the main bevel.

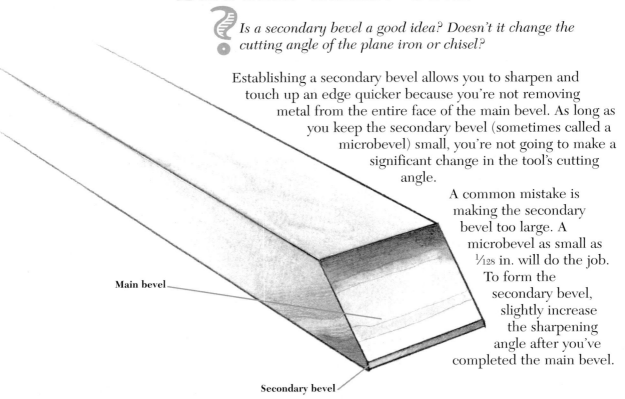

Main bevel

Secondary bevel

A 10-CENT TIP FOR YOUR POCKET KNIFE

How do I put a razor-sharp edge on my pocketknife?

There aren't any practical jigs that will hold your pocketknife at the correct angle to the stone, so this is a freehand operation. To get an idea of the shallow bevel angle that you'll form on both sides of the blade, lay a dime on the sharpening stone and rest the blade on it as shown in the drawing. Aim for an equal number of strokes on each side of the blade.

Grip the knife, and lock your wrist at this angle as you draw the blade back and forth along the stone. Count any convenient number of strokes, then switch your attention to the other side of the blade.

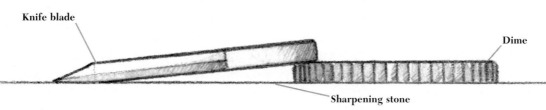

Knife blade

Dime

Sharpening stone

SANDPAPER: YOUR SHARPENING ALLY

 *What kind of sandpaper is suitable for sharpening tools?*

Mounting sandpaper to a ¼-in. plate glass sheet is a fast and economical way to sharpen and polish edges. You can adhere the abrasive to the glass with a glue stick or spray adhesive, but sandpaper with a pressure-sensitive adhesive (PSA) backing is faster and neater.

When used dry, virtually any type of sandpaper will give you satisfactory results. But when you want to refine the edge by using a lubricant on the paper, choose a waterproof silicon carbide sheet. Many hardware stores have silicon carbide paper that starts at 220 grit and progresses to 600 grit. An auto paint supply store will often have grits down to 1200.

But for a high polish on the tool's edge, you can purchase micro-abrasive sheets that reach 2500 grit. Sold through some woodworking catalogs, these Mylar-backed abrasives can be used flat, but they have the added virtue of not cracking when bent. This enables you to adhere it to a length of dowel, creating a tool to remove the wire edge from the inside curve of a gouge.

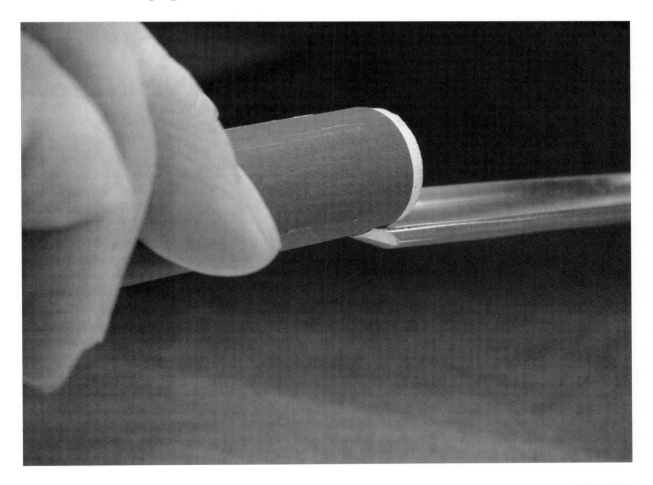

SYNTHETIC VS. TRADITIONAL WATER STONES

 What grits of water stones or oilstones should I buy?

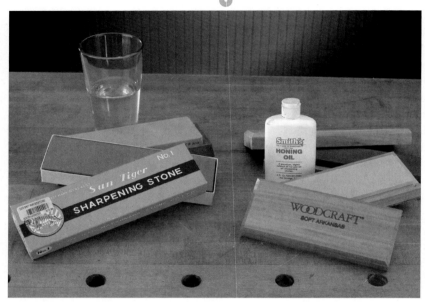

The grits of synthetic oilstones and water stones are not exactly equivalent, and somewhat surprisingly, the finer-grit water stones cut faster. If you want to try water stones, buy a combination 1000x/4000x stone, or separate 800x and 4000x stones. A combination oilstone often has 90x on one side and 600x on the other.

You can supplement either system with abrasive sheets. If you commit totally to one system or the other, you can purchase additional stones as your budget permits.

BABY (OIL) YOUR STONES

I'm always astonished by the high price of honing oils. Are there less expensive substitutes?

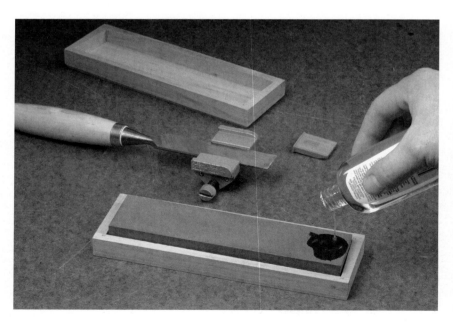

Instead of buying oil at the hardware store, go the drugstore. Look for generic brands of mineral oil or baby oil, and you'll save a lot of money and still get great results. After all, the purpose of the oil is uncomplicated — it merely keeps metal filings in suspension so they don't clog the pores of the stone.

Avoid thick-bodied oils like the type you put into your car or truck. They are so heavy that you'll struggle to keep the blade moving smoothly over the stone.

A DIAMOND IS A WOODWORKER'S BEST FRIEND

 The idea of a diamond sharpening stone intrigues me because it seems that it would never wear out. Are all of the diamond stones and rods the same, or do I need some buying advice?

Just as industrial diamonds are different from those used for jewelry, several other types of diamond crystals are suited for sharpening tools. The two basic types are monocrystalline and polycrystalline.

As you can see in the drawing, the monocrystalline type is a relatively large individual crystal bonded to the steel substrate. Monocrystalline diamonds have increased durability and are therefore more expensive than polycrystallines. The polycrystalline crystals are comprised of a number of small monocrystallines. During use, the polycrystallines can fracture and wear down to a less aggressive cutting surface.

Diamond stones and hones give you excellent service, but no manufacturer claims that they are absolutely indestructible. One significant advantage of diamond stones is they remain flat and won't suffer from the troughs that wear into oilstones or water stones with repeated use.

You'll usually employ water as the lubricant on a diamond stone, but for quick touch-ups you can skip the water. This is a real plus for jobsite sharpening.

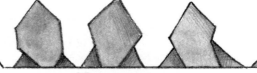

MONOCRYSTALLINE

POLYCRYSTALLINE

A BRIEF LESSON ON ACR PHILLIPS BITS

How can I extend the life of driver bit inserts? These little Phillips drivers aren't expensive, but I hate the way that a worn bit can chew up a screw head.

You might try buying a different brand of driver bit to see if you can get a better quality, or try the Phillips ACR (anti-camout rib) style that's designed to stay more securely in the slot. As an alternative to Phillips, try square drive screws. Those drivers seat more securely into the drive recess than the Phillips pattern does.

Ultimately, here's the best solution: As soon as a driver tip shows any signs of wear, toss it into the trash. There's no need to tolerate a problem when the solution is so inexpensive.

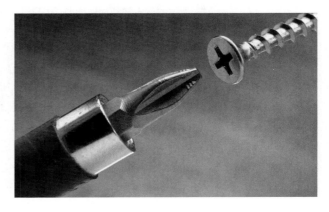

THE BURR FACTS ABOUT CABINET SCRAPERS

 How do I sharpen a cabinet scraper? Whenever I try it, I always round over the edge.

In theory, sharpening a hand cabinet scraper is easy — you merely file and hone a square edge on a piece of steel, and then raise a burr. But putting that theory into perfect practice requires either years of experience or a few tricks. Here's a short course:

STEP 1

Cut ¼ in. chamfers along 2x2 guide

Cabinet scraper

File

1 Grab a length of 2x2 lumber with sides that are square to each other. With your table saw or plane, run ¼-in. chamfers along each edge. (The chamfers reduce interference with the edge of the scraper.) Referring to the Step 1 drawing, lay the 2x2 guide atop a file on your workbench, and work the scraper back and forth until the edge is straight and square. If the guide tips to the side because you're using a narrow file, place a second file or spacer next to the file to support the guide. Repeat for the other long edge of the scraper. As an optional step, you can even sharpen the ends of the scraper — very useful if you need to get into tight areas.

2 Move the scraper and the guide to your bench stone, as shown in Step 2, to refine and polish the edge. Every few strokes, move the guide and scraper to a new location so you don't wear a groove into the stone. Then remove the wire edges from the scraper by laying it flat on the stone. Alternate between Steps 2 and 3 until you remove the wire edges to produce a perfectly square profile along both edges of the scraper.

3 Let the scraper overhang the edge of your workbench, as shown in Step 4, and rub a drop of oil along the first edge that you'll form. For the burnisher, you can purchase a special tool or simply use any smooth piece of steel that's harder than the scraper — the round shank of a high-quality Phillips screwdriver works well.

STEP 2

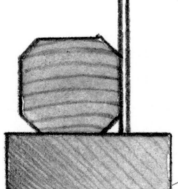

Bench stone

STEP 3

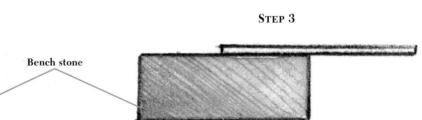

268

4 Hold the screwdriver about 5 degrees off vertical, and draw it along the edge of the scraper to raise the burr. If you filed and honed the edge square, it will take only a few light strokes to raise the burr. Check for an even burr along the entire edge by gently rubbing your thumb from the center of the scraper over the edge. Raise a burr along both sides of both edges, giving you a total of four cutting edges. If you can't raise a burr, the edge isn't square, so you'll have to repeat the filing and honing steps.

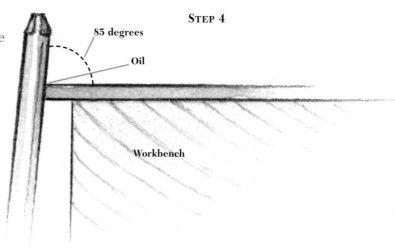

STEP 4

85 degrees

Oil

Workbench

5 To put the scraper to work, lightly flex it with your thumbs, and push it along the wood, tilting it slightly forward until the burr catches. With a sharp scraper, you'll produce tiny shavings of wood while holding the scraper at a high angle

STEP 5

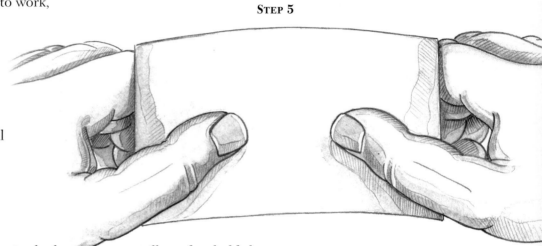

of about 75 degrees. As the burr wears, you'll need to hold the scraper at a progressively shallower angle. You can also use the scraper on a pull stroke. When you start producing dust instead of shavings, it's time to resharpen.

6 Fortunately, you don't have to repeat the filing and honing each time. As shown in Step 6, lay the scraper flat on your workbench so it's fully supported. Put a drop of oil on the face of the scraper, and rub with your burnisher to fold down the burr. Work back and forth along the edge, and also pull the burnisher toward you. Repeat Step 4 to form the burr again.

STEP 6

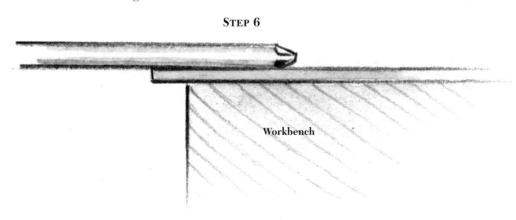

Workbench

Don't Get Hung Up on Plane Shavings

When I use my bench plane, I get shavings caught between the back side of the blade and the chip breaker. How do I eliminate this problem?

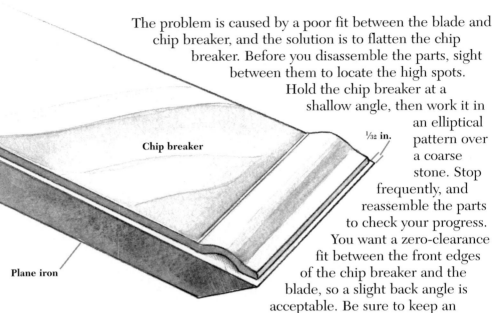

Chip breaker

¹⁄₃₂ in.

Plane iron

The problem is caused by a poor fit between the blade and chip breaker, and the solution is to flatten the chip breaker. Before you disassemble the parts, sight between them to locate the high spots. Hold the chip breaker at a shallow angle, then work it in an elliptical pattern over a coarse stone. Stop frequently, and reassemble the parts to check your progress. You want a zero-clearance fit between the front edges of the chip breaker and the blade, so a slight back angle is acceptable. Be sure to keep an absolutely minimal line — about ¹⁄₃₂ in. — between the front of the chip breaker and the tip of the blade's bevel.

Monthly Maintenance Extends Battery Life

Is there anything I can do to keep my drill and other battery-powered tools operating at peak efficiency?

In addition to following the manufacturer's recommendations on battery charging, you can clean the battery contacts to ensure efficient power transfer. If the contacts are accessible, rub them with an ordinary pencil eraser every month to remove oxidation. A few strokes will do the job. Just blow away the eraser crumbs.

GLOVED TREATMENT FOR SHARPENING TASKS

One of the many things I hate about sharpening is the way the metal particles and grit work into my hands, making them look dirty for days. How do I avoid this problem?

Disposable latex or plastic gloves are an inexpensive and effective solution, but you can also consider a pair of thin leather gloves. The looser and thicker the gloves you choose, the more they decrease the sensitivity of your touch. If you use a honing guide, that sensitivity is less important than if you're trying to establish the angle of the blade on the stone by feel.

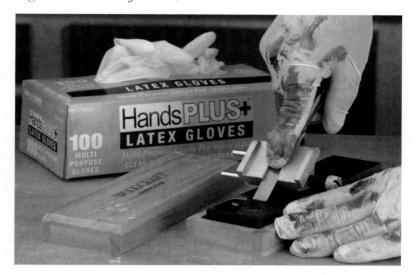

DEFINING SWARF

I read a catalog description for sharpening stones that referred to "swarf." Wasn't he the tall alien in the original Star Trek TV series? Seriously, what is it?

Swarf is the metallic powder that was formerly your chisel's blade — the tiny bits floating in the lubricant on your bench stone. When you use a dry grinder, swarf becomes airborne — an excellent reason to wear breathing protection during that task.

A QUICK LESSON ON SHARPENING SPADE BITS

 Can I sharpen spade drill bits myself? They're too expensive to throw away after I hit an embedded nail, and I sure can't hold up my project waiting on a sharpening shop.

A quick reality check: For precision woodworking, select a brad-point or Forstner bit. Spade bits are more of a rough carpentry tool. That said, spade bits are easy to sharpen with a low-tech approach that you can even do right on the job site.

Simply clamp the bit into a vise with the tip pointing upward. Take a look at the factory-ground bevel, and try to rest a fine file on the bevel at that same angle. Take a light stroke, and see if you're cutting along the full face of the bevel or if the file is tipped too far backward or forward.

Make the correction, and take another light stroke.

When you've zeroed in the angle, take enough strokes to remove any chips from the bevel and to raise a wire edge on the far side of the bit. Repeat the filing process on the opposite bevel, and then lightly stroke the file flat on each face of the bit to remove the wire edge.

GRINDING CAN SALVAGE STRAIGHT-DRIVE SCREWDRIVERS

 I make rustic-style furniture, and I think Phillips or square-drive screws would look out of place. However, my straight-slot screwdrivers are chewed up and a real pain to use. Can I grind a new tip onto them?

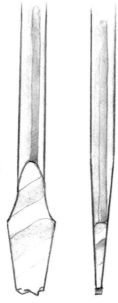
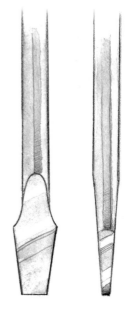

Filing will be more controlled than grinding, and it's an easy way to square up the tips of your screwdrivers. Strictly speaking, this is considered dressing a screwdriver rather than sharpening, but no matter what you call it, it works.

As you file, have sample screws on hand so you can custom-fit the width and thickness of the screwdriver's tip to completely fill the slot.

After you've lavished this attention onto the screwdrivers, you'll be rewarded with better results with less effort. Be sure to reserve these tools for driving screws. They are not designed to function as a lid lifter, chisel, pry bar, paint stick, or tent peg.

SALVAGE ROUTER BITS WITH OVEN CLEANER

 How can I get the built-up gunk off of my router bits? That stuff has already caused several burned cuts.

Before you put away a router bit, scrub it with a brass-bristled utility brush that's the size and shape of a toothbrush. These bristles are tough enough to scrub away pitch and gum, but the brass is softer than the cutting edge, so you won't damage it. For severe cases of residue buildup, use oven cleaner or whatever solvent you use to clean your table-saw blades.

14
REPAIRING WOOD AND FURNITURE

SLEUTHING OUT OLD FINISHES

How can I determine the original finish on a piece of old furniture?

A simple process with three different solvents will help you with your chemical detective work. Of course, you'll want to perform these tests in a hidden area, such as the bottom surface of a tabletop or beneath a chair rung.

Test 1: Moisten the tip of a cotton swab with denatured alcohol, and rub it in a tiny circle — about the size of a dime or smaller. If the surface turns gummy when you check it with your finger, the finish is probably shellac. If there's no result, move on to the next test.

Test 2: This time, moisten the cotton swab with turpentine, and rub another small circle. A softened surface indicates a varnish finish. No reaction? Move to the next step.

Test 3: Moisten the cotton swab with lacquer thinner and rub as before. A dissolved finish indicates that the original is probably lacquer.

IMPROVING FIT FOR LIDS AND BOXES

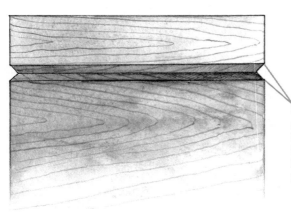

Chamfer edges of base and lid to disguise a less-than-perfect fit

I made a small box with a lift-off lid, but the fit between the base and lid is not absolutely perfect, and it's distracting. How do I make it look better?

Run a chamfer along the base and lid where they meet, as shown in the drawing. The chamfers create a slight visual separation that disguises any misalignment, and the shadow lines enhance the concealment.

AFTER YOU'VE FINISHED, DOCUMENT

 I'd like to think that the furniture I build is going to be around long after I'm gone, so I want to document the type of finish I apply so that someone in the future will be able to repair it with a minimum of fuss. Where should I write down that information so it won't get lost?

A notebook or a piece of paper can be separated from the furniture, so your best choice is to write the information directly onto the wood itself.

The back of an unfinished drawer is a good location, or choose the rear surface of a plywood-backed carcase if that part of the furniture is not meant to be seen. Neatly print the information in pencil, and protect it with a coat of aerosol shellac. You may be surprised to learn that a note written in pencil has better longevity than ink. That's because ink can change chemically over a period of years but a pencil uses inert graphite that's not going to alter.

But you may have to resort to a permanent marker (Sanford's Sharpie is one brand) if you decide to do your writing after applying the finish. The bottom of a tabletop or the underside of a chair seat is a typical location that works well for writing.

As long as you're in the writing mood, don't forget to sign your name to your furniture. If your signature isn't penmanship-perfect, consider a printed translation beneath the scrawl.

PLYWOOD SHORES UP RICKETY CHAIR SEATS

 I'm restoring a set of dining room chairs, and the slip seats consist of frames that have half-lap corner joints. Unfortunately, several of the frames are split, and the others have sagging webbing. Of course the seats aren't simple squares, so I'm really stumped on how to duplicate them.

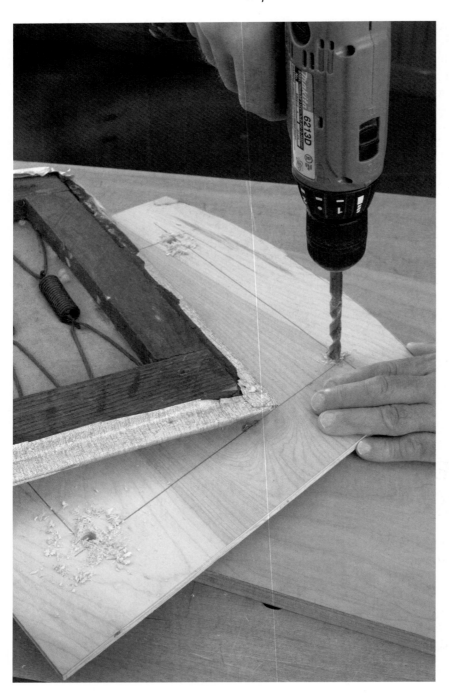

The joinery of the frames will never be seen by anyone but the upholsterer, so this is an appropriate place to take a timesaving shortcut. Make the frames from a good quality hardwood plywood such as birch, and you'll completely eliminate the need for joinery.

Choose plywood that matches the maximum thickness of the original frame, and carefully duplicate its perimeter. Drill holes in each corner of the waste section in the center so your jig saw will be able to make the turns, as shown in the photo.

Pay careful attention to all the shaping subtleties of the original frame. For example, there may be a rabbet along the lower perimeter of the frame, and the top edges may be rounded to improve comfort.

Unless you're experienced in upholstery, you'll probably get better results by taking the frames to a professional for replacement of the seat webbing, padding, and fabric.

FLOSS FOR REPAIRS

Sometimes I'll bump an edge and raise a sizable splinter of wood that's still attached at one end. It would make an invisible repair if I could glue it down, but I can't figure how to get glue into the tiny opening.

Go to the drugstore — or raid your own medicine chest — for dental floss. Although it's made for removing debris from the tight spaces between your teeth, floss can work in the opposite fashion by depositing glue into the split wood. This technique works great on either raw wood or furniture that's already finished.

A wishbone-shaped dental floss tool, as shown in the photo, makes the gluing an easy task. At the drugstore, you can purchase a bag of these disposable tools that are already loaded with floss. You also could buy a reusable tool that you load with floss. If you purchase the floss separately, buy the unwaxed variety.

After you've worked the glue in the crack, press the wood down firmly, and wipe away any excess glue. Apply a piece of tape over the repair until the glue dries.

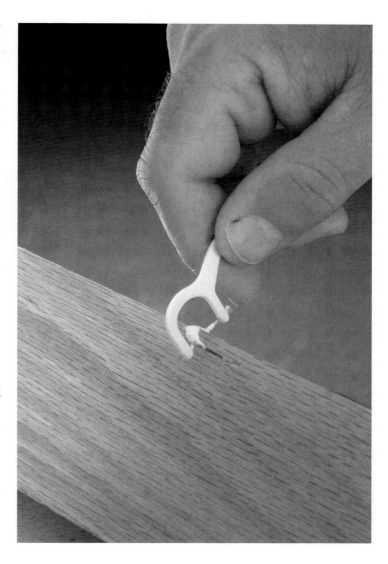

THE LIGHTER SIDE OF FINISH REPAIRS

When I'm concealing a scratch, do I want to go lighter or darker than the surrounding wood?

Lighter is almost always better. For a successful repair, you don't have to achieve an absolutely perfect color and tone match. You simply need to reduce the contrast between the scratch and the surrounding wood to the point where the damage is no longer easy to notice.

HINGE REPAIRS GO BEYOND MATCHES

 The original position for a hinge was off slightly, so I plugged the holes in the oak face frame with wooden kitchen matches that I dipped in glue and jammed into the holes. But when I tried to drill the new pilot holes and drive the screws, I still couldn't get the hinge exactly where I wanted it. Did I do something wrong?

The theory behind what you did was excellent, but you would have had better results by plugging the holes with oak instead of with the matches. The pilot bit and the screws followed the path of lower resistance offered by the softwood plug instead of going where you wanted.

A softwood plug is adequate for filling a stripped screw hole if you're replacing the fastener in the same location. Otherwise, fill the hole with a strip that matches the density of the surrounding wood.

STEP BACK FROM YOUR FINISH REPAIRS

 How can I judge when I'm finished with a spot repair or scratch filling?

You know where the damage is, so it's going to be hard to completely fool yourself. And you certainly can't pass judgment when you're staring right at that one spot. Try taking a step or two back from your work, look away from the furniture, then slowly look back at the entire piece, not that one area. If it clearly jumps back into view when you're trying to look elsewhere, you have more work to do. Another technique that will help your judgment is to squint slightly, throwing your eyes out of focus. If the repair isn't obvious, it will pass inspection by most people.

TRY THE VERSATILITY OF POWDERS

? *I've seen touch-up powders advertised as a refinishing product. How do these work?*

These powders are pigments ground to an extremely fine texture. By mixing powders in varying amounts with padding lacquer (see page 289), you can achieve either a relatively opaque color for painting in grain or a thin glaze to blend the tone of a repaired area with the rest of a piece.

OLD GLUE HAS JUST GOTTA GO

? *After I soften glue and get old joints apart, do I need to remove all the old glue?*

Absolutely. Glue is designed to adhere to freshly machined wood, not crust and gunk. Enlist the solvents that softened the glue, and also recruit every scraper and brass-bristled brush you can find.

If you need to build up the joints, glue pieces of veneer to a rectangular tenon or adhere a plane shaving to a round tenon on a chair rung.

WOOD CONDITIONERS REDUCE BLOTCHING

 I built a small cabinet from pine, and I want to darken the wood. I've been experimenting with various stains on pieces of scrap wood, and have been disappointed with the blotchy results. What causes the blotching, and how do I achieve a more even tone?

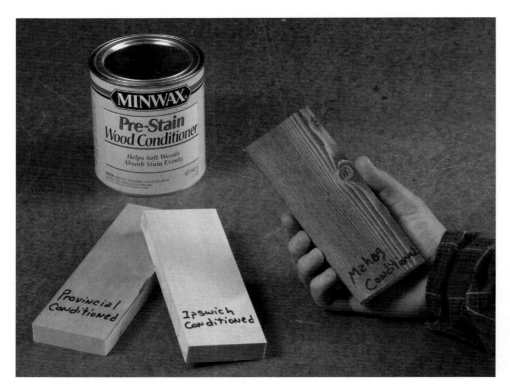

You were wise to do your color tests on scraps of the same wood as your project, and also fortunate that you discovered the blotching before committing the stain to the wood. It's easy to minimize blotching before you stain, but the only cure after staining is a large pile of sandpaper.

Because wood is a natural material that's produced over a long period of time, some portions are softer and more porous. As a result, these irregularly shaped areas soak up more pigment from an oil-based stain and appear as an unsightly blotch. Softwoods like pine are particularly susceptible to blotching, but it also occurs with some hardwoods — cherry is one example.

One way of minimizing blotches is to prepare the wood with a product that saturates the wood, particularly the soft areas, so they will absorb color at approximately the same rate as the harder portions. This type of product is called a wood conditioner. Minwax Pre-Stain Wood Conditioner is one brand that performs well under oil-based stains. To use the conditioner, brush or wipe on a generous amount, let it stand on the surface for 5 to 15 minutes, reapplying to areas that appear dry. When the time is up, wipe off the excess with soft cloths. Apply the stain within two hours, and you'll get more even results.

Of course, you should repeat your color experiments on wood that's received the conditioner treatment because you'll get a lighter tone than when you applied the stain to the bare wood samples.

HIDE YOUR ROUTER MISHAPS

When I was building on a solid-wood tabletop, I set my plunge router down on it, thinking that the bit had retracted past the baseplate. Unfortunately, the mechanism had jammed, and I accidentally drilled a ¼-in. hole near the center of the top. I can't patch my pride, but can I at least fix the wood?

Putting a patch into an unfinished piece of wood is easier than you may think, and with a little care, the repair will be barely noticeable.

With a Forstner bit in your drill press or in a portable drill guide, drill a hole so you can insert a tapered plug, as shown in the photo. You'll get the best results by cutting your own plugs from a scrap of the same wood as the tabletop.

When you shop for a plug cutter, make sure that it cuts tapered — not straight — sides. Before you cut the plugs at your drill press, mark the grain direction on the stock so you'll be able to match the plug's grain with the top. Cut a number of plugs to give yourself a choice of color and figure.

If you purchase factory-made tapered plugs, get a jumbo bag so you can search for one that will give you the best match.

Wipe the rim of the hole with some glue, match grain direction, and firmly tap in the plug with a hammer. Scrape away any excess glue with the tip of a toothpick. After the glue dries, trim the plug with a flush-cut saw, and sand the tabletop to final smoothness.

MISSING A DRAWER?
REPLACE THEM ALL

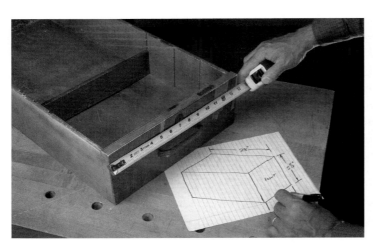

?
My mother got a great buy on a used china cabinet, but the bargain price was based on the fact that it was missing one of its three drawers. The other two drawers have a routed design that I can't figure out how to precisely duplicate. How can I make the third drawer match the other two?

The best way out of this dilemma is to adjust your thinking: It will be far easier for you to make three new drawers instead of attempting to make a single new one to match the two old ones.

You'll be working with identical materials for the trio of drawers, so even if they don't perfectly match the carcase, they will coordinate extremely well with each other, disguising any potential problem.

FRESHEN UP
YOUR CEDAR

?
I installed tongue-and-groove cedar inside a storage closet a couple of years ago, but now it's lost the aroma. How do I get that new closet smell again? By the way, my smart-aleck nephew claims that cedar doesn't have anything to do with preventing moth damage. Please tell me that he's not right.

The most important news first. Tell your nephew that scientific studies have confirmed what Grandma knew all along: moths don't like the aroma of cedar. As a result, they shun cedar locations as a place to lay eggs that turn into fiber-eating larvae.

To renew the cedar aroma, load up your random-orbit sander with medium paper (100- to 150-grit), and give all the walls a quick sanding. By exposing fresh wood, you'll encourage the natural aromatic oils to migrate to the surface.

PIN REMOVAL HINGES ON A GOOD PLAN

I need to do something with the squeaky doors in my house. When I tried to knock out a hinge pin with a hammer and screwdriver, I put a big gash into the casing but still didn't budge the pin. Is there a way to do this without messing up all my door frames?

Check if the bottom knuckle of the hinge provides access where you can insert a spare hinge pin to drive out the one that's stuck. You can purchase an individual hinge pin at many hardware stores. Work simultaneously on all the hinges to break them all loose before removing a single pin. Doing that would transfer strain to the remaining pins, making them even more difficult to remove.

If you can't get at the pins from the bottom, make yourself a hinge pin extraction tool by filing an arc into the end of an old screwdriver, as shown in the photo. After you force the tool under the head of the pin, tap your hammer upward to motivate it. If the tool slips, it will move through air instead of striking wood.

After you remove the hinge pins, consider whether you want to replace or refurbish the hardware. As a minimal restoration, scrub the pin with an abrasive pad until it's bright, and clean up the contact surfaces of the knuckles in the same way. Apply a coat of paste wax to the pin and knuckle contact points, and re-assemble. For a complete overhaul, take the hardware off the door and casing, and strip the hinges with paint remover. Avoid oiling hinges — even a single stray drop mixed with finely powdered metal is a devilishly difficult stain to remove from carpeting.

GIVE STUBBORN SCREWS THE HOT AND COLD TREATMENT

 I'm restoring an old chair, and there are several screws that just won't budge. How can I back out these frozen screws?

Appropriately enough, heat is a good cure for a frozen screw. As you know, metal expands when it's heated, and contracts when it cools, facts that will help loosen a stubborn screw.

Get a pistol-grip soldering gun that has a good power rating — 100 watts or more — and put as much of its tip as possible in flat contact with the head of the screw to maximize heat transfer. Carefully watch the surrounding wood for any evidence of charring. This part of the operation expands the screw's diameter, pushing it against the wood. As the screw cools, it shrinks to its original size, but the wood remains in its pushed-out position, creating (hopefully) enough clearance for withdrawal.

You can shrink the screw even further by applying an aerosol cooling spray available at electronics supply stores like Radio Shack. (This product is designed to find thermal defects in components and printed circuits, and it leaves no residue.) Don't bother trying to use ice to cool the screw. As the ice melts, the water will expand the wood, defeating your efforts.

Make certain the tip of your screwdriver precisely fits the screw's slot so you can apply maximum torque. If necessary, re-grind the tip. A screwdriver with a square shank will allow you to easily fit an adjustable wrench to improve your leverage. If you have a screwdriver with a round shank, reach for your locking-grip pliers. You can improve the friction between the screw slot and driver with a drop of a substance marketed for this purpose (Screw Grab is one trade name) or you can substitute valve-grinding compound from an auto-parts store.

DAMAGE CONTROL WITH CRAYONS

? *I've seen markers and wax crayons that are sold for furniture touch-up. How do I use them, and how big a repair can they handle?*

Keep your expectations modest for both of these products. The wax crayons are designed to fill in a nail hole or make a scratch less noticeable. The markers also are good scratch concealers, and they can quickly restore color to a small damaged area. For example, if you're leveling a coat of finish and accidentally sand through to bare wood, a few swipes with a marker will put you back on course.

You'll find a few colors of touch-up crayons at your local hardware or paint store or a much wider spectrum of colors through mail-order suppliers. And if you were wondering about purchasing crayons at the toy store, those are also pigmented wax, so they are a virtual identical product. Besides, it's a real boost to finally get the box of 64 colors you didn't have as a kid.

When you apply either product, hold it in one hand and a soft cloth in the other. The cloth will buff the wax, making it blend better with the sheen of the surrounding wood. Stroke a marker over the wood, and immediately follow it with a swipe of the cloth to remove the excess.

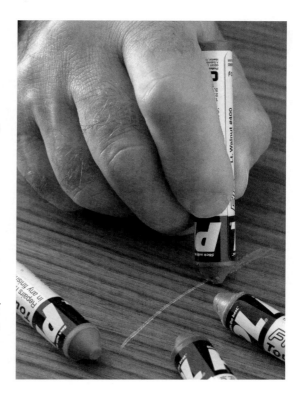

ONE-DROP REPAIRS TO FINISH

 How do I fix a pinhead-size chip in a finish? The underlying wood is completely undamaged.

Deposit a drop of finish into the recess with the tip of a toothpick. The surface tension of the liquid may hold the drop in a small mound, but don't try to smooth it. As the solvent evaporates, the level will lower, and you may even have a slight crater. If that happens, repeat the application with a smaller drop.

Give the finish a week or so to completely cure, then wet-sand with 600-grit paper abrasive in a block to level the finish. Move up the grit progression to 1200, and polish the repair and surrounding area to blend with the rest of the furniture.

GRIND A NEW NAIL-PULLER

I'm working on the restoration of an oak rocking chair, and somebody had driven small-headed nails to pin the joints. How do I remove these nails, and then how do I deal with the black mineral streaks caused by the steel's reaction with the wood?

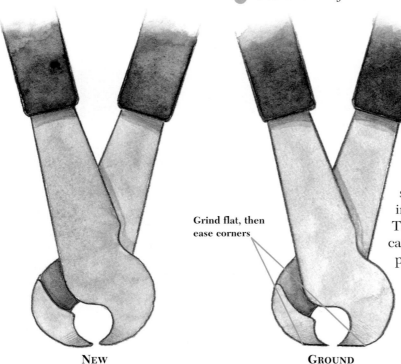

Grind flat, then ease corners

NEW   GROUND

Buy a pair of end-cutting pliers, and grind the end as shown in the drawing so you can work the jaws under the head of the nail. Grind straight across, then ease the corners into a smooth curve with the jaws. That way, after you grip the nail, you can extract it by rolling the jaws of the pliers as shown in the photo

These end-cutting pliers are under 6 in. long because they're designed for precision electronics work. At that scale, they are much easier to maneuver than similarly designed nail pincers intended for rough carpentry work.

After you've yanked the nails, you can deal with the mineral streaks by purchasing oxalic acid at your hardware or paint store. This product is usually packaged as wood bleach. Following label directions and all safety precautions, mix up a small batch of the solution, and apply it with a small brush or cotton swab to the discolored area. Neutralize and rinse the area thoroughly, again following the manufacturer's instructions. Give the area a day or two to dry thoroughly before moving ahead to other refinishing chores.

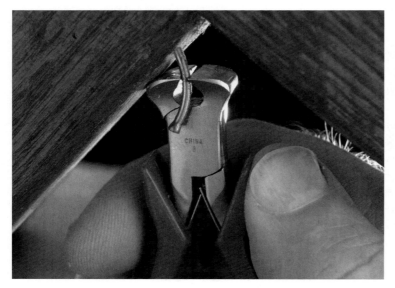

By the way, those nails may have been originally installed at the factory to pin the joints to free up the clamps for the next chair. If you want to do authentic restoration, you can drive a similar nail, but a couple of extra steps will avoid a rerun of the damage. Apply finish to the chair before driving the nail, and even give the nail itself a coat of finish to minimize wood-to-metal contact. To make the nail easier to remove for the next restorer, snip its shank so it's only ¼ in. long.

DISASSEMBLING A CHAIR FOR RESTORATION

How do I take apart the wobbly joints of an old piece of furniture so I can repair it?

Cover your workbench with a carpet remnant, and grab a dead-blow mallet. Its shot-filled head will deliver more joint-separating energy than a rubber mallet. Label the joints by writing matching letters on strips of masking tape applied to the project, and tap firmly to pop apart the joints. A clamp that can reverse to act as a spreader is another good tool.

Avoid the temptation to twist on a chair rung because you could split it apart, adding another chore to the restoration process.

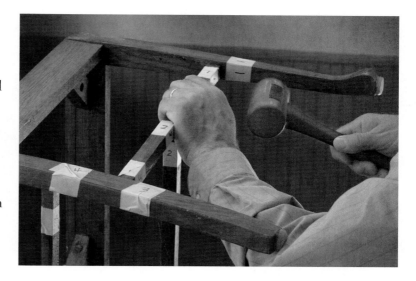

If a joint doesn't come apart, and it's not wobbly, leave it alone. Don't let your determination override your common sense. But if you insist on taking it apart anyway, soften the glue to loosen its grip on the parts (see page 290).

PADDING LACQUER NOT A LACQUER AFTER ALL

What is padding lacquer, and how do I use it?

The name of this product is somewhat misleading because it's actually a shellac-based product that's low in solids and therefore high in solvent.

Padding lacquer is a good medium for the application of toning or blending powders. Apply it with a fine brush or a pad. If you choose the pad route, keep it in constant motion to avoid marks where you begin or end a series of strokes.

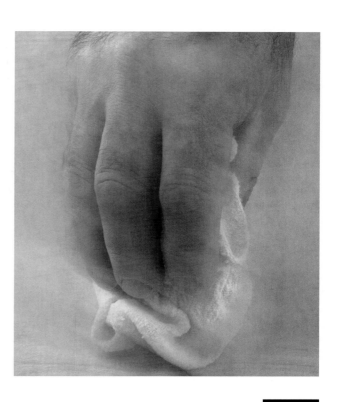

THE SOFTER SIDE OF GLUE

How can I soften glue to ease joint disassembly?

You'll first need to discover what kind of glue was originally used to assemble the piece or employed for later repairs. If the furniture was made before World War II, hide glue was the likely adhesive.

When you try any of the following disassembly methods, don't use a deadblow mallet or hammer on the joint. This time, exert steady pressure by hand or with a clamp to pull apart the joint.

You'll be able to identify hide glue with a few easy tests. Excess glue squeezed out of the joints will probably be dark brown or black. Do a scratch and sniff test to see if you can detect the musky aroma of hide glue. Finally, wet the glue with warm water and wait a few minutes. If it feels sticky, it's hide glue, and that means that you can use warm water and patience to soften the glue. For faster results, work denatured alcohol into the joints to crystallize the glue.

If the piece was assembled with white glue, the residue will be clear or white. Dampen the glue with water and see if it turns milky white. This is a more difficult bond to break, but hot vinegar and patience are a successful combination. If you want one more method of persuasion, warm the joint with a heat gun, but be careful not to scorch the wood. Also remember that wood is an excellent insulator, so it will take time for the heat to penetrate to the glue line.

Yellow glue will have, not surprisingly, yellow residue, and it's even more resistant to disassembly than white glue. Leave it alone, if you can, but resort to hotter vinegar and even more patience. A heat gun is even more effective than with white glue — the joint can lose up to half of its strength when heated to 150 degrees. Again, apply steady pressure to separate the joint.

POWER-BUFFER SAVES ELBOW GREASE

 I have a large tabletop that I'd like to polish with a buffer to save time. What are the techniques and material to use?

First of all, make sure you have a buffer, not a sander or a grinder with a buffing head. The relatively low speed of the buffer prevents the abrasives from overheating the finish and literally scorching it. If you don't want to invest in a buffer right away, rent one from a rental center.

Before you start polishing, apply masking tape to the ends and edges of the table so you don't accidentally go through the finish at these highly vulnerable areas.

Take a trip to an automotive finishing supply store, and buy a high-quality lamb's wool buff and power-buffing compound. You may be surprised by the coarseness of this compound, but the relatively light pressure exerted by the machine offsets its texture. If you used the machine-buffing compound for hand-polishing, the increased pressure would quickly eat through the finish.

If you don't already have a waterproof apron, get one. Compound ejected by the wheel can quickly ruin your clothes.

Read the directions on the compound's can to discover whether you need to dilute it. Before each application onto the tabletop, stir or shake the container to make certain the abrasive is suspended.

When you use the buffer, tilt it so that only about one-third of its surface makes contact with the tabletop, and always be conscious of the direction of the head's rotation. You want to make certain the buff sweeps off the edge, not into it.

You'll probably want to buy a finer texture of compound for a second round of machine-polishing. Your dealer can supply a succession of compounds with increasingly finer abrasives for machine- and hand-buffing.

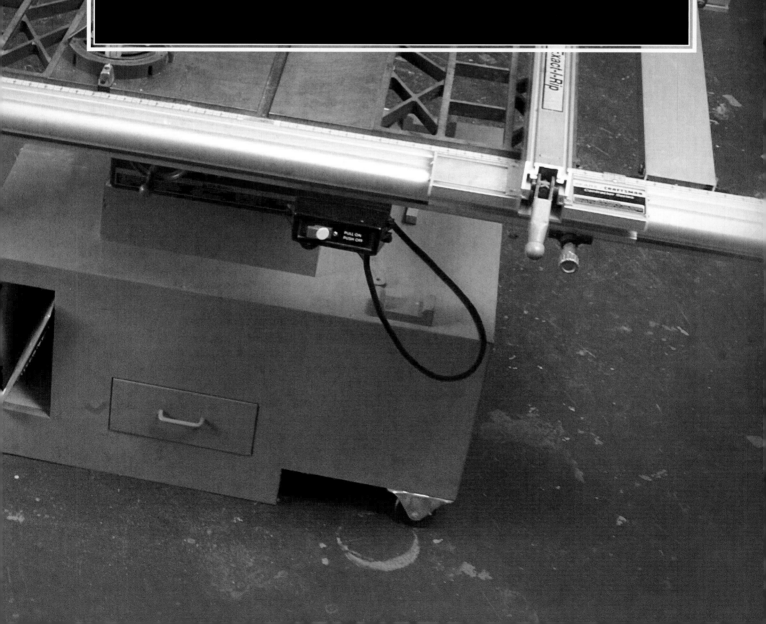

15
MACHINE
SETUP

SEVEN STEPS TO TABLE-SAW PERFECTION

 Whenever I make adjustments on my table saw, it seems that one setting throws off another. So I keep going back and forth endlessly. Is there a right sequence of steps to set up the table saw for maximum accuracy?

Follow this step-by-step procedure, and you'll minimize the backtracking:

STEP 4

1 Remove as much backlash (play in the adjustment) as possible in the tilt and elevation adjustments of your saw. Refer to your owner's manual for specific advice on doing that.

2 Level the throat plate insert to the saw table, positioning it just below the surface of the table so your stock doesn't hang up on its edge. Many inserts have setscrews that you drive or withdraw as needed. If your plate lacks this feature, you may have to resort to filing the contact points to lower the insert or adding strips of tape to raise it.

3 Square the blade to the table. For initial setup, crank the blade as high as it will go, and use an accurate square. To achieve perfection, use the 2x4 method described on page 62. Set the stop and your gauge pointer to make it easy to return to square after tilting the blade.

4 Take the sideways play out of your miter-gauge bar. To do that, use a hammer and pin punch to form dimples along both sides of the bar as shown in the photo. The metal that's expanded to form the crater rim of the dimple has the effect of making the bar wider. Stagger the marks from one side of the bar to the other, spacing them every few inches along the bar's length.

5 As you work, frequently check the bar's fit in the slot in which you'll run it more often.

6 Set the head of your miter gauge at a right angle to its bar by using an accurate square.

7 Set the blade parallel to the miter-gauge slot. To check whether an adjustment is needed, clamp a length of ¼-in.dowel to your miter gauge so that its end just touches one tooth of the blade as shown in the photo. With the saw unplugged, rotate the drive belt by hand to move that tooth to the rear of the slot, and check that the dowel contacts with the same amount of pressure. If the setting isn't perfect, slightly loosen the bolts that hold the saw's trunnion assembly, and tap it with a wood block from the rear to rotate it. Check with the dowel in both positions again. You'll probably have to repeat this process several times, and make certain that the process of tightening the bolts doesn't affect the alignment.

STEP 7

8 Align the rip fence by using the dowel and miter-gauge setup. Lower the blade to get it out of the way, and pull the miter gauge toward you until its rear is just resting on the saw table. Slide the rip fence until it just touches the tip of the dowel, and lock it in place. Slide the miter gauge forward to the far end of the table. In this position, slip the thickness of a dollar bill between the tip of the dowel and the fence. Adjust the fence if necessary. You want this clearance so the saw kerf won't be pinched closed as you cut.

Dado Shims Jump-Start Accuracy

Cutting dadoes is always a frustrating experience because I can't get a perfect fit with my dado set — it's always a little too tight or way too loose. How do I get an in-between size that's just right?

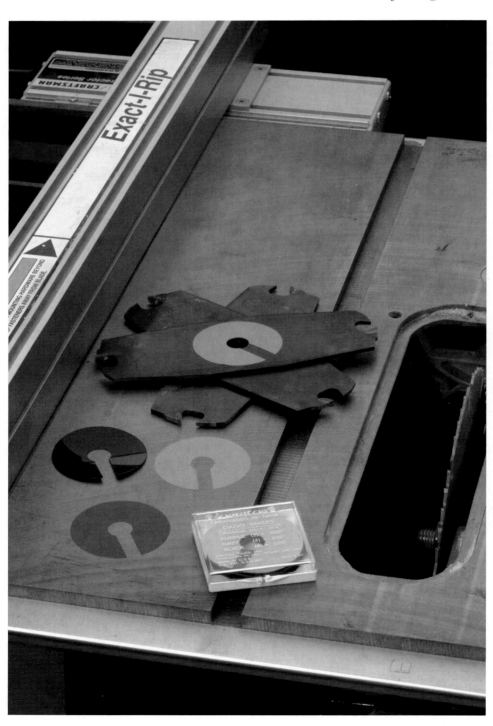

Place dado shims between the chippers to get an exact fit. Although you could make your own shims, a purchased set is inexpensive and highly accurate. A typical set has color-coded plastic shims in four sizes: .002, .005, .010, and .020 in. thick. You get several of each size, so you combine a number of shims with your cutters to get a tailored fit.

When you get the exact size that you want, write down how many of each shim size you added with the cutters to make the dado. Then, the next time you work with that material, you can set up the cutters with absolute perfection the first time.

WOBBLE DADOES ARE A POOR SUBSTITUTE FOR ACCURACY

Which kind of dado blade is better — the wobble type or the stacked set?

The biggest disadvantage of the wobble dado blade is the fact that it wobbles. Its asymmetrical construction sets up vibrations in your table saw that compromise its accuracy. In addition, the design cannot produce a perfectly flat-bottomed cut at all widths.

For example, a single-blade wobble dado that's engineered to produce a flat cut at ½ in. wide will give you a peaked cut at ¼ in. wide and a cupped bottom at ¾ in., as shown in the drawing. A twin-blade wobble dado blade runs smoother, but it is still incapable of flat-bottomed dadoes at all widths.

As a result, glued joints produced by wobble cutters have less than optimum strength, and the exposed ends of grooves and dadoes may show an unsightly gap.

The stacked dado set, though more expensive, is capable of a flat cut throughout its width range. The outer cutters on some sets may produce a scribe mark ("ear") or two that's visible in an end view.

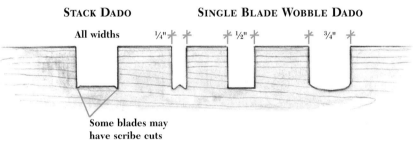

STACK DADO   **SINGLE BLADE WOBBLE DADO**

All widths   ¼"   ½"   ¾"

Some blades may have scribe cuts

PUT A CLAMP — OR TWO — ON YOUR DRILL-PRESS OPERATIONS

Adjusting the fence on my drill press always turns into a real juggling act because the scrap board protecting the table starts sliding around as well. How can I keep so many things from moving at once?

Assign two more clamps to this task, and you'll simplify the adjustment. First, clamp a generously sized piece of ¾-in. plywood to the drill press table to serve as the base. Clamp the fence to the base. If you want, cap the base with a sacrificial piece of scrap plywood to take the wear and abuse. Simply slide it against the fence, and you're ready to drill.

UNDERSTANDING TABLE SAW DIFFERENCES

 In table saws, what's the difference between a cabinet saw and a contractor's saw?

There are a number of differences between the two types, but the principal structural difference is the attachment of the saw's carriage and trunnion. (These parts support the saw's arbor assembly, the attachment shaft for the blade.)

In a cabinetmaker's saw (background), these parts are bolted to the saw's frame or shell. Meanwhile, the saw's table itself is fastened independently to the frame. If you have a strong friend, you can unbolt the table and remove it to gain access to the saw's running gear.

The contractor's saw (foreground) features a different construction method — the carriage and trunnion assembly bolt directly to the underside of the table. The table is again fastened to a frame, but it's like a mini-skirt compared to the floor-length design of the cabinet saw. As a result, a contractor's saw is usually mounted on a set of steel legs to raise it to working height.

The cabinetmaker's saw is designed and built as a stationary workhorse capable of industrial output, so you'll see heavy-duty construction that's usually teamed with a large horsepower 220 to 240-volt motor. The 10-in. blade is a common size, but you'll also find saws capable of handling 12-in. blades. It's a heavyweight contender with an impressive price tag. By the way, when some people refer to this saw type, they call it a cabinetmaker's saw because it works at that trade. Other people call it a cabinet saw because its base is a metal cabinet.

The contractor's saw is relatively portable for jobsite applications, but it's also right at home in many amateur workshops. It usually has a 110- to 120-volt motor teamed with a 10-in. blade.

PACK ON POUNDS FOR LATHE STABILITY

 When I start my lathe with an unbalanced bowl blank mounted, there's so much vibration that the lathe's stand shakes and the entire tool wants to start walking across the shop. What can I do to make this initial part of bowl turning less exciting?

A lathe is one tool where heavier is definitely better, so part of the solution is to pack on the pounds. If your lathe has an open metal base, put a heavy plank between the stretchers, and add as many sandbags as you can. When it comes to dampening vibration, sand is better than solid weight. Sand that's packed in a tube is convenient, inexpensive, and is less likely to tear than paper or plastic bags.

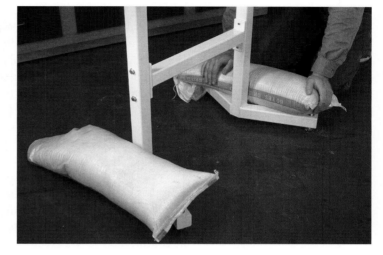

You may also want to trim the blank more carefully to further reduce the problem. An unbalanced load accelerates wear on bearings, so run your lathe at the lowest speed possible until you've removed enough stock so that it runs smoothly.

AVOID MELTING MOMENTS WHILE CUTTING PLASTIC

 I wanted to scroll-saw some Christmas ornaments from plastic, but the cut fused closed right behind the blade. How do I cut plastic?

You'll get better results by choosing a coarser blade and sandwiching the plastic between sheets of thin plywood.

As you've already discovered, choosing too fine a blade will generate so much heat that it will melt the chips to the edges of the cut instead of ejecting them. Leaving the protective paper sheet on the plastic also promotes smooth cutting; rubbing the blade with paraffin wax works for some scroll-saw enthusiasts.

GET YOUR SAW RUNNING SMOOTHLY

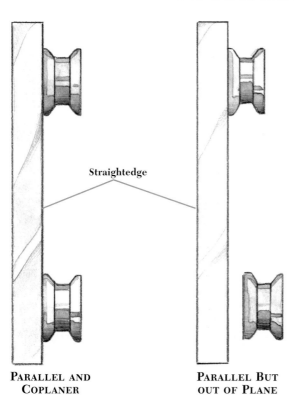

PARALLEL AND COPLANER

PARALLEL BUT OUT OF PLANE

Straightedge

I've set up my contractor's table saw as carefully as I can, but I notice that the motor hanging on the back of the saw bounces around, and that vibrates the entire saw. How can I make it run smoother?

The drive belt and the pulleys are the likely suspects. Unplug the saw, and lift up on the motor's plate to remove the belt. But before you go any further, it's wise to confirm that the problem is not in the motor itself. Plug in the saw, and switch on the motor. It should run quietly and smoothly. If not, remove the pulley and try one more time. Unplug the saw again.

With a straightedge, check whether the arbor pulley is parallel and coplanar (in the same plane) with the motor's pulley, as shown in the drawing. Any misalignment will reduce power transmission, introduce vibration, and accelerate belt wear.

Also examine the belt itself. During long idle periods, the belt can begin to take a set, conforming itself to the curvature of the pulleys. When you turn on the saw, these humped portions of the belt can introduce a hop to the belt's path as each hump enters and exits a pulley. After an extended running period, the belt may or may not smooth out its running.

If the belt shows any signs of wear, or if you simply want a belt that is more resistant to taking a set, consider a linked drive belt, such as the one made by Fenner Drives. (Please see Resources, page 314.) This type of belt also is available through woodworking catalogs. You can customize the length of the belt by simply twisting together or removing the interlocking links. By the way, it's a handy way to replace a captive belt, such as the kind used in some lathe heads and grinding setups.

If you also want to upgrade the pulleys, you can replace the stock stamped units with pulleys that are machined and balanced to minimize vibration. Several woodworking catalogs offer a kit that includes a linked drive belt plus a set of pulleys to fit popular contractor's saws.

SEVEN STEPS TO BAND-SAW PERFECTION

 There are so many different adjustments on the band saw that I hardly know where to begin. What's the best sequence?

Here's the step-by-easy-step approach:

1 Track the blade so it runs true on the wheels. With the saw unplugged, put just enough tension on the blade so it doesn't slip on the tires. Back off all the blade guides and the blade support bearings. Open the top door of the saw, and slowly turn the wheel by hand, being careful that you don't pinch your fingers in the spokes. The blade should run in the center of the tire. Adjust the tracking mechanism, if necessary, then lock the adjustment in place. Close the door, and turn on the saw to verify that the blade runs true.

2 Tension the band-saw blade. You can refer to the scale built into the saw (if yours has one) or employ the more accurate fluttering blade method detailed on page 302.

3 Use a square to set the table square to the blade.

4 Set the upper blade guide assembly at approximately the cutting height you need, and move the blade guide assembly so the blocks are approximately 1/16 in. behind the gullets of the saw teeth. Wrap a dollar bill around the blade, push the guide blocks against the bill, and tighten them.

5 You'll notice that tightening the setscrew on the left tends to push that block toward the blade, while tightening the one on the right moves it away from the blade. You'll have to compensate for this effect to get the blocks an equal distance from the blade. Turn on the saw to make sure that neither block scrapes the side of the blade. Repeat the process for the lower blade guides.

6 Advance the upper support bearing so that it is about 1/16 in. behind the back of the blade. Turn on the saw to make sure it doesn't touch the blade. Repeat for the lower guard.

7 To verify that the table is square to the blade, use the 2x4 method described on page 62.

STEP 3

GAUGING BAND-SAW TENSION

 How do I know when I have enough tension on a band-saw blade?

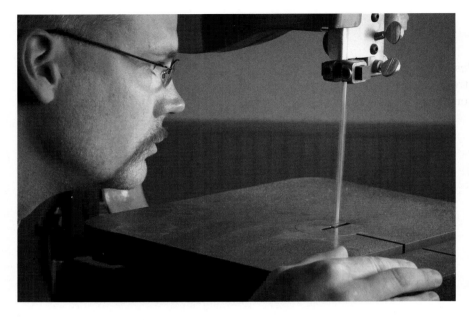

One current trend in woodworking makes the mistake of advocating an extreme amount of tension on a band-saw blade. This practice has no real benefit but quite a number of unfortunate consequences. You decrease the blade's life, wear out the tires and bearings more quickly, and you can even bend the frame of your saw.

Instead of going to extremes, follow this procedure to achieve just enough tension. Install the new blade, raise the upper blade guide assembly about 6 in. above the table, and back off the upper and lower blade guides as far as possible. Put just enough tension on the blade so you can set the tracking.

Turn on the saw, and as you look straight at the blade, you'll see it flutter from side to side.

Slowly add tension to the running blade, and you'll see the flutter decrease and then disappear as the blade begins to run true. Add one-quarter turn more tension, and you have the right setting.

DON'T BOTHER RADIUSING BAND-SAW BLADES

I've heard of people who take a sharpening stone to the back edge of a band-saw blade. What's that about?

The theory is that converting each of the square back edges of the blade to a slight radius will enable you to negotiate a tighter turn with the blade. While that's technically true, it makes such a microscopic difference that calling it infinitely small is being generous. Don't bother.

If you need to make a tighter turn, the only practical approach is to get a narrower blade.

TAKE THE FUZZ OUT OF CUTS

 Whenever I cut shapes with my scroll saw, I'm always annoyed by the fuzzy edges on the bottom of the piece. This problem seems to be worse when I cut plywood. Is there any way to avoid this difficulty?

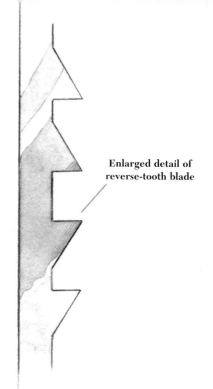

Enlarged detail of reverse-tooth blade

Ordinary scroll-saw blades cause this problem because they cut only on the downstroke, leaving a fuzzy edge where the blade exits. The cure is a scroll-saw blade that has a reverse tooth pattern at the bottom, as shown in the drawing.

With that design, the upstroke of the blade cuts into the bottom of the stock to produce a smooth cut. Olson Saw Company is one source for this style of reverse-tooth blade. (Please see Resource section, page 314.)

REMEMBER YOUR BAND-SAW SETTINGS

 How can I take the tension off a band-saw blade, but then easily return to the same setting for the next work session?

Relaxing tension from the blade between work sessions is a great idea because it extends the life of the blade and the band-saw's components.

Simply back off the adjustment knob an identical number of full turns (four, for example), and place a sign on the band saw's table to remind you to add the working tension to the blade.

Simply write "Add 4 turns" on a piece of scrap plywood, and place it on the saw's table.

If your adjustment knob has prongs, identify one with paint or tape to make it easier to count the turns.

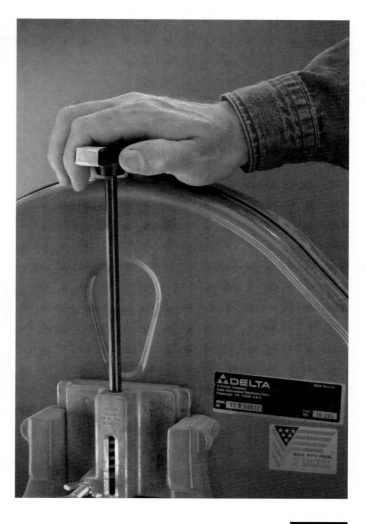

MAKE YOUR NEXT MOVE EASIER

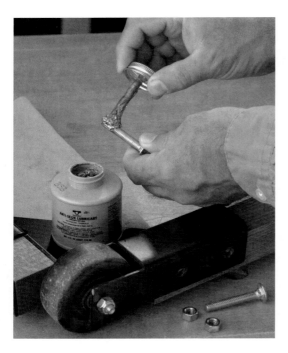

I had to disassemble most of my machine bases to move the equipment from the basement shop of one house into the basement of another. The high humidity in the first location made the bolts start to corrode, so I had a tough time breaking them loose. How do I avoid that same problem this time?

Go to the auto-parts store, and buy a container of anti-seize lubricant. To coat the threads, you can dip the bolts into the pasty material or brush it on. Wipe up the excess with a rag after assembly. The next time you move, you won't have to struggle with disassembly.

LOCK ON THOSE ROUTER BEARINGS

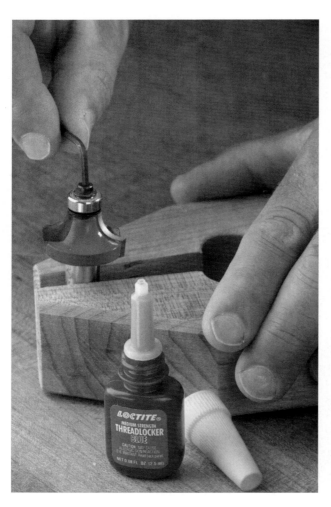

I had to take the bearing off the end of a router bit to replace it, and I want to make sure that the nut won't work itself loose. If it drops into a bit traveling at 25,000 rpm, I can foresee several things happening, and none of them are good. How do I make sure that it stays put?

You need a tread-locking compound, and Loctite Corporation makes two kinds for you to consider. You'll find both types at most automotive parts stores.

The company's 243 Threadlocker is a liquid that you apply to both parts before assembly. It cures to full strength in only a few hours, and you can later disassemble with hand tools.

There's also Loctite 290, a liquid that wicks its way down the threads of parts that are already assembled. It also produces a much stronger bond, requiring localized heating and hand tools for disassembly.

SLIPPING ROUTER BITS DESERVE ATTENTION

 My router bits sometimes slip, and simply applying more force to the collet isn't the answer. What's going on?

If the slippage occurs with only one bit, carefully examine its shank to make certain there's no corrosion or irregularity on the shank that would prevent it from accepting a tight grip. Remove corrosion with an abrasive pad, and polish away any tiny ridges or bumps with emery paper.

Also inspect the inside of the collet. If there's any corrosion, remove it with a narrow strip cut from an abrasive pad.

If those solutions don't work, you'll probably need to purchase a replacement collet for your router.

BRASS WIRE BRUSH PREVENTS THAT BURNING SENSATION

 When I run small-diameter bits in either my drill press or portable drill, the flutes get packed with wood chips. If I don't remove the material, the bit overheats. But if I try picking it out with my fingers, I get burned. Any easy way around this problem?

Keep your cool by using a small steel or brass-bristled brush that's about the size and shape of a toothbrush. To make certain that you always know where it is, drill a hole through its handle and tether it with a string to the drill press column. That way, you'll be able to easily pull it into reach when needed. And when you're finished with it, simply give it a toss but it won't be lost.

16
RESOURCES

Common Nails, Bright or Galvanized

Size	Length (in.)	Gauge	Head size (in.)	Approx no./lb
3d	$1^{1}/_{4}$	14	$^{13}/_{64}$	514
4d	$1^{1}/_{2}$	$12^{1}/_{2}$	$^{1}/_{4}$	292
6d	2	$11^{1}/_{2}$	$^{17}/_{64}$	168
7d	$2^{1}/_{4}$	$11^{1}/_{2}$	$^{17}/_{64}$	149
8d	$2^{1}/_{2}$	$10^{1}/_{4}$	$^{9}/_{32}$	91
10d	3	9	$^{5}/_{16}$	68
12d	$3^{1}/_{4}$	9	$^{5}/_{16}$	63
16d	$3^{1}/_{2}$	8	$^{11}/_{32}$	44

Box Nails, Bright or Galvanized

Size	Length (in.)	Gauge	Head size (in.)	Approx no./lb
3d	$1^{1}/_{4}$	$14^{1}/_{2}$	$^{7}/_{32}$	592
4d	$1^{1}/_{2}$	14	$^{7}/_{32}$	473
5d	$1^{3}/_{4}$	14	$^{7}/_{32}$	406
6d	2	$12^{1}/_{2}$	$^{17}/_{64}$	232
7d	$2^{1}/_{4}$	$12^{1}/_{2}$	$^{17}/_{64}$	203
8d	$2^{1}/_{2}$	$11^{1}/_{2}$	$^{19}/_{64}$	140
10d	3	$10^{1}/_{2}$	$^{5}/_{16}$	96
12d	$3^{1}/_{4}$	$10^{1}/_{2}$	$^{5}/_{16}$	84
16d	$3^{1}/_{2}$	10	$^{11}/_{32}$	71

Finish Nails, Bright or Galvanized

Size	Length (in.)	Gauge	Head gauge	Approx no./lb
3d	$1^{1}/_{4}$	$15^{1}/_{2}$	$12^{1}/_{2}$	792
4d	$1^{1}/_{2}$	15	12	584
5d	$1^{3}/_{4}$	15	12	500
6d	2	13	10	272
8d	$2^{1}/_{2}$	$12^{1}/_{2}$	$9^{1}/_{2}$	182
10d	3	$11^{1}/_{2}$	$8^{1}/_{2}$	121
16d	$3^{1}/_{2}$	11	8	88

Drilling Chart for Wood Screws

(All dimensions in inches)

Gauge	2	3	4	5	6	7	8	9	10	12	14
Head size	$^{11}/_{64}$	$^{13}/_{64}$	$^{15}/_{64}$	$^{1}/_{4}$	$^{9}/_{32}$	$^{5}/_{16}$	$^{11}/_{32}$	$^{23}/_{64}$	$^{25}/_{64}$	$^{7}/_{16}$	$^{1}/_{2}$
Shank hole	$^{3}/_{32}$	$^{7}/_{64}$	$^{7}/_{64}$	$^{1}/_{8}$	$^{9}/_{64}$	$^{5}/_{32}$	$^{5}/_{32}$	$^{11}/_{64}$	$^{3}/_{16}$	$^{7}/_{32}$	$^{1}/_{4}$
Pilot hole*	$^{1}/_{16}$	$^{1}/_{16}$	$^{5}/_{64}$	$^{5}/_{64}$	$^{3}/_{32}$	$^{7}/_{64}$	$^{7}/_{64}$	$^{1}/_{8}$	$^{1}/_{8}$	$^{9}/_{64}$	$^{5}/_{32}$
Phillips drive	#1	#1	#1	#2	#2	#2	#2	#2	#2	#3	#3
Square drive	#0	#0	#0	#1	#1	#1	#2	#2	#2	#3	#3

* For increased holding power in softwoods, pilot hole sizes may be decreased by 1/64 in.

GRADING SYSTEMS FOR COATED ABRASIVES

(For a discussion of these Systems, see Chapter 8, page 149)

FEPA (P-grade)	CAMI	JIS	Trizact	3M Micron	Average Particle Size in Inches	Micron Scale
P2000	1000	2000	—		.00042	9.5
P1500	800	1500	—	9	.00051	12.3
P1200	—	1000	A16	15	.00060	15.3
—	600	—	—		.00062	16.0
P1000	—	600	—		.00071	18.3
—	500	—	—		.00077	19.7
—	—	—	A20	20	.00079	20.0
P800	—	—	A25		.00085	21.8
—	400	500	A30		.00092	23.6
—	—	—	—		.00098	25.0
P600	—	—	A35		.00100	25.8
—	360	—	—		.00112	28.8
—	—	—	—		.00118	30.0
P500	—	400	A40	30	.00118	30.2
P400	—	—	A45		.00137	35.0
—	320	—	—		.00140	36.0
P360	—	360	—	40	.00158	40.5
P320	—	—	A60		.00180	46.2
P280	—	280	A65	50	.00204	52.5
P240	—	—	A80		.00228	58.5
P220	—	240	A90		.00254	65.0
—	220	—	70		.00257	66.0
P180	180	A100	80		.00304	78.0
—	150	A130	90		.00363	93.0
P150	—	—	100		.00378	97.0
—	120	—	120		.00452	116.0
P120	—	—	A160		.00495	127.0
—	100	—	—		.00550	141.0
P100	—	—	A200		.00608	156.0
—	80	—	—		.00749	192.0
P80	—	—	—		.00768	197.0
P60	—	—	—		.01014	260.0
—	60	—	—		.01045	268.0
P50	—	—	—		.01271	326.0
—	50	—	—		.01369	351.0
P40	—	—	—		.01601	412.0
—	40	—	—		.01669	428.0
P36	—	—	—		.02044	524.0
—	36	—	—		.02087	535.0
P30	—	—	—		.02426	622.0
—	30	—	—		.02488	638.0
—	24	—	—		.02789	715.0
P24	—	—	—		.02886	740.0

DRILL SIZE CHART

This chart displays an extensive listing of drill sizes that includes fractional inch, millimeter, wire gauge (numbered sizes), letter sizes, and decimal inch. The numbered and lettered sizes are sometimes considered more appropriate to metalworking but are used in woodworking as well. Pen turners, for example, frequently use letter-sized drills to prepare blanks.

Inch	Mm.	Wire Gauge	Decimals Of an Inch	Inch	Mm.	Wire Gauge	Decimals Of an Inch
		80	.0135	3/64			.0469
		79	.0145		1.2		.0472
1/64			.0156		1.25		.0492
		.4	.0157		1.3		.0512
		78	.0160			55	.0520
		77	.0180		1.35		.0531
	.5		.0197			54	.0550
		76	.0200		1.4		.0551
		75	.0210		1.45		.0571
	.55		.0217		1.5		.0591
		74	.0225			53	.0595
	.6		.0236		1.55		.0610
		73	.0240	1/16			.0625
		72	.0250		1.6		.0630
	.65		.0256			52	.0635
		71	.0260		1.65		.0650
	.7		.0276		1.7		.0669
		70	.0280			51	.0670
		69	.0293		1.75		.0689
	.75		.0295			50	.0700
		68	.0310		1.8		.0709
1/32			.0313		1.85		.0728
	.8		.0315			49	.0730
		67	.0320		1.9		.0748
		66	.0330			48	.0760
	.85		.0335		1.95		.0768
		65	.0350	5/64			.0781
	.9		.0354			47	.0785
		64	.0360		2		.0787
		63	.0370		2.05		.0807
	.95		.0374			46	.0810
		62	.0380			45	.0820
		61	.0390		2.1		.0827
	1		.0394		2.15		.0846
		60	.0400			45	.0860
		59	.0410		2.2		.0866
	1.05		.0413		2.25		.0886
		58	.0420			43	.0890
		57	.0430		2.3		.0906
	1.1		.0433		2.35		.0925
	1.15		.0453			42	.0935
		56	.0465	3/32			.0938

Inch	Mm.	Wire Gauge	Decimals Of an Inch
	2.4		.0945
		41	.0960
	2.45		.0966
		40	.0980
	2.5		.0984
		39	.0995
		38	.1015
	2.6		.1024
		37	.1040
	2.7		.1063
		36	.1065
	2.75		.1083
7/64			.1094
		35	.1100
	2.8		.1102
		34	.1110
		33	.1130
	2.9		.1142
		32	.1160
	3		.1181
		31	.1200
	3.1		.1220
1/8			.1250
	3.2		.1260
	3.25		.1280
		30	.1285
	3.3		.1299
	3.4		.1339
		29	.1360
	3.5		.1378
		28	.1405
9/64			.1406
	3.6		.1417
		27	.1440
	3.7		.1457
		26	.1470
	3.75		.1476
		25	.1495
	3.8		.1496
		24	.1520
	3.9		.1535
		23	.1540
5/32			.1563
		22	.1570
	4		.1575
		21	.1590

Inch	Mm.	Wire Gauge	Decimals Of an Inch
		20	.1610
	4.1		.1614
	4.2		.1654
		19	.1660
	4.25		.1673
	4.3		.1693
		18	.1695
11/64			.1719
		17	.1730
	4.4		.1732
		16	.1770
	4.5		.1772
		15	.1800
	4.6		.1811
		14	.1820
		13	.1850
	4.7		.1850
	4.75		.1870
3/16			.1875
	4.8		.1890
		12	.1890
		11	.1910
	4.9		.1929
		10	.1935
		9	.1960
	5		.1969
		8	.1990
	5.1		.2008
		7	.2010
13/64			.2031
		6	.2040
	5.2		.2047
		5	.2055
	5.25		.2067
	5.3		.2087
		4	.2090
	5.4		.2126
		3	.2130
	5.5		.2165
7/32			.2188
	5.6		.2205
		2	.2210
	5.7		.2244
	5.75		.2264
		1	.2280
	5.8		.2283

Inch	Mm.	Letter Sizes	Decimals Of an Inch
	5.9		.2323
		A	.2340
15/64			.2344
	6		.2362
		B	.2380
	6.1		.2402
		C	.2420
	6.2		.2441
		D	.2460
	6.25		.2461
	6.3		.2480
1/4		E	.2500
	6.4		.2520
	6.5		.2559
		F	.2570
	6.6		.2598
		G	.2610
	6.7		.2638
17/64			.2656
	6.75		.2657
		H	.2660
	6.8		.2677
	6.9		.2717
		I	.2720
	7		.2756
		J	.2770
	7.1		.2795
		K	.2810
9/32			.2812
	7.2		.2835
	7.25		.2854
	7.3		.2874
		L	.2900
	7.4		.2913
		M	.2950
	7.5		.2953
19/64			.2969
	7.6		.2992
		N	.3020
	7.7		.3031
	7.75		.3051
	7.8		.3071
	7.9		.3110
5/16			.3125
	8		.3150
		O	.3160
	8.1		.3189
	8.2		.3228
		P	.3230
	8.25		.3248
	8.3		.3268

Inch	Mm.	Letter Sizes	Decimals Of an Inch
21/64			.3281
	8.4		.3307
		Q	.3320
	8.5		.3346
	8.6		.3386
		R	.3390
	8.7		.3425
11/32			.3438
	8.75		.3345
	8.8		.3465
		S	.3480
	8.9		.3504
	9		.3543
		T	.3580
	9.1		.3583
23/64			.3594
	9.2		.3622
	9.25		.3642
	9.3		.3661
		U	.3680
	9.4		.3701
	9.5		.3740
3/8			.3750
		V	.3770
	9.6		.3780
	9.7		.3819
	9.75		.3839
	9.8		.3858
		W	.3860
	9.9		.3898
25/64			.3906
	10		.3937
		X	.3970
		Y	.4040
13/32			.4063
		Z	.4130
	10.5		.4134
27/64			.4219
	11		.4331
7/16			.4375
	11.5		.4528
29/64			.4531
15/32			.4688
	12		.4724
31/64			.4844
	12.5		.4921
1/2			.5000
	13		.5118
33/64			.5156
17/32			.5313
	13.5		.5315

Inch	Mm.	Decimals Of an Inch
35/64		.5469
	14	.5512
9/16		.5625
	14.5	.5709
37/64		.5781
	15	.5906
19/32		.5938
39/64		.6094
	15.5	.6102
5/8		.6250
	16	.6299
41/64		.6406
	16.5	.6496
21/32		.6563
	17	.6693
43/64		.6719
11/16		.6875
	17.5	.6890
45/64		.7031
	18	.7087
23/32		.7188
	18.5	.7283
47/64		.7344
	19	.7480
3/4		.7500
49/64		.7656
	19.5	.7677
25/32		.7812
	20	.7874
51/64		.7969
	20.5	.8071
13/16		.8125
	21	.8268
53/64		.8281
27/32		.8438
	21.5	.8465
55/64		.8594
	22	.8661
7/8		.8750
	22.5	.8858
57/64		.8906
	23	.9055
29/32		.9063
59/64		.9219
	23.5	.9252
15/16		.9375
	24	.9449
61/64		.9531
	24.5	.9646
31/32		.9688
	25	.9843
63/64		.9844

Inch	Mm.	Decimals Of an Inch
1		1.0000
	25.5	1.0039
1 1/64		1.0156
	26	1.0236
1 1/32		1.0313
	26.5	1.0433
1 3/64		1.0469
1 1/16		1.0625
	27	1.0630
1 5/64		1.0781
	27.5	1.0827
1 3/32		1.0938
	28	1.1024
1 7/64		1.1094
	28.5	1.1220
1 1/8		1.1250
1 9/64		1.1406
	29	1.1417
1 5/32		1.1562
	29.5	1.1614
1 11/64		1.1719
	30	1.1811
1 3/16		1.1875
	30.5	1.2008
1 13/64		1.2031
1 7/32		1.2188
	31	1.2205
1 15/64		1.2344
	31.5	1.2402
1 1/4		1.2500
	32	1.2598
1 17/64		1.2656
	32.5	1.2795
1 9/32		1.2813
1 19/64		1.2969
	33	1.2992
1 5/16		1.3125
	33.5	1.3189
1 21/64		1.3281
	34	1.3386
1 11/32		1.3438
	34.5	1.3583
1 23/64		1.3594
1 3/8		1.3750
	35	1.3780
1 25/64		1.3906
	35.5	1.3976
1 13/32		1.4063
	36	1.4173
1 27/64		1.4219
	36.5	1.4370

RESOURCES

BROOKS MANUFACTURING CO., INC.
2120 Pacific Street
Bellingham, WA 98229
Phone: 360-733-1700
Fax: 360-734-6668
Web Site: www.brooksmfg.com
Distributor of Plasti-Tak Adhesive.

FENNER DRIVES
311 W. Stiegel Street
Manheim, PA 17545
Toll Free: 800-243-3374
Phone: 717-665-2421
Fax: 717-665-2649
Manufacturer of link V-belts.

THE FLOOD COMPANY
P.O. Box 399
Hudson, OH 44263
Toll Free: 800-321-3444
Web Site: www.floodco.com
Manufacturer of wood finishes and additives, including Floetrol and
Penetrol.

GRIFFIN MANUFACTURING CO. INC.
P.O. Box 308
Webster, NY 14580
Phone: 716-265-1991
Fax: 716-265-2621
Email: grifhold@aol.com
Manufacturer of yardstick compass, pounce wheel, crafts knife sets.

ITW INDUSTRIAL FINISHING
Corporate Office
195 International Blvd.
Glendale Heights, IL 60134
Phone: 630-237-5000
Fax: 630-237-5011
Web Sites: www.devilbiss.com and www.binks.com
Manufacturer of DeVilbiss and Binks brand spray guns.

KLINGSPOR'S WOODWORKING SHOP
P.O. Box 3737
Hickory, NC 28603
Toll Free: 800-228-0000
Fax: 800-872-2005
Web Site: www.woodworkingshop.com
Manufacturer and distributor of coated abrasives, distributor of
woodworking supplies.

NATIONAL HARDWOOD LUMBER ASSOCIATION
6830 Faleigh LaGrange Road
Memphis, TN 38184-0518
Phone: 901-377-1818
Web Site: www.natlhardwood.org
A non-profit organization that formulates and publishes rules for the
grading and inspection of hardwood lumber.

NATIONAL INSTITUTE FOR OCCUPATIONAL SAFETY AND HEALTH (NIOSH)
Hubert H. Humphrey Bldg.
200 Independence Ave., SRoom 715H
Washington, DC 20201
Toll Free: 1-800-356-4674
Phone: 202-401-6997
Web Site: www.cdc.gov/niosh
NIOSH, part of the U.S. Department of Health and Human Services, is
an agency designed to help assure safe and healthful working conditions
by providing research, information, education, and training in the field of
occupational safety and health.

NATIONAL KITCHEN & BATH ASSOCIATION
687 Willow Grove Street
Hackettstown, NJ 07840
Toll Free: 877-652-2776
Fax: 908-852-1695
The National Kitchen & Bath Association is a non-profit trade association
that has educated and led the kitchen and bath industry for 40 years.

OLSON SAW COMPANY
16 Stony Hill Road
Bethel, CT 06801
Phone: 203-792-8622
Fax: 203-796-7861
Web Site: www.olsonsaw.com
Manufacturer and distributor of saw blades.

PAXTON WOODCRAFTERS' STORE
KANSAS CITY , MO
6311 St. John Ave.
Kansas City, MO 64123
Toll Free: 800-333-7298
Phone: 816-483-7000
Web Site: www.paxton-woodsource.com
Lumber and woodworking supplies available through retail stores and
online.

TAYLOR DESIGN GROUP
P.O. Box 810262
Dallas, TX 75381
Phone: 972-418-4811
Fax: 972-243-4277
Manufacturer of carpenter tools.

TOUCHUP DEPOT
5215 Sjolander Road
Baytown, TX 77521
Toll free: 866-883-3768
Phone: 281-421-0765
Fax: 281-421-2179
Web Site: www.touchupdepot.com

INDEX